Here is a unique and important work: the first book *by* teachers *about* teaching, and addressed to teachers—and everyone else who wants to share the fulfillments and frustrations of one of the world's most important professions. WILL IT GROW IN A CLASSROOM? is shop talk at its very best: Every article was written by a teacher and every one was written out of personal experience.

What happens if you try to be a pal to your students? If you let a class of young children talk about anything they like? If you act the part of "madman"? How do you bring science alive? Or persuade kids that reading is really worthwhile? And what happens if, as a parent, you give up on schools altogether and teach your children at home?

Wit, imagination, compassion, concern—these are the qualities that good teachers bring to their work, and all of them are amply in evidence in this

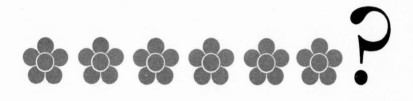

Will it grow in a classroom

EDITED BY
Beatrice & Ronald Gross

DELACORTE PRESS / NEW YORK

Manufactured in the United States of America
Designed by Jerry Tillett
First printing

LIBRARY OF CONGRESS CATALOGING IN PUBLICATION DATA

Gross, Beatrice, comp.
   Will it grow in a classroom?

1. Teaching.   2. Education—United States—
1965–   I. Gross, Ronald, joint comp.
II. Title.
LB1025.2.G77   371.1′02   73-20154
ISBN 0-440-08749-X

"Madman in the classroom" by Burt E. Schuman: Reprinted by permission of the author. First published in *The Teacher Paper*, February 1973, Vol. V, No. 3.

"Teacher evaluation (Socrates)" by John Gauss: Reprinted by permission from *Phi Delta Kappan*, January 1962. Reprinted by permission of the author.

"What's the capital of Upper Volta?" by Ross Burkhardt: Used by permission of the author.

Excerpt from *The Lives of Children* by George Dennison: From *The Lives of Children* by George Dennison. Copyright © 1969 by George

This book is dedicated
to the faculty of SUNY, Old Westbury
who are making a difference for the better
in the lives of their students,

and the students at Old Westbury
who will make a difference for the better
in the lives of children.

Preface

This book grew out of the work of The Free Learning Project.

The Project is a noninstitutionalized association of activists and researchers exploring new ways to empower individuals to take command of their educations, and thereby of their lives. Specifically, the Project takes seriously the proposition that education is an individual rather than an institutionalized process, that at its best it is lifelong and lifewide rather than concentrated in childhood and located in schools and colleges, and that radical changes both in people's attitudes and in the basic institutions of society are necessary to make true education possible.

One of the Project's particular interests is the revival of

the professions as individually fulfilling and socially constructive realms of learning and growth. Its findings on the status and prospects for free learning in the major professions were reported in an earlier volume, *The New Professionals.*

Subsequently, the Project has focused on the field of education, working with teachers in ways described in the final section of this book: toward individual, self-directed, non-institutionalized professional growth.

We wish to express our gratitude to those members of the Project's Advisory Committee whose own interest and major contributions to this field have inspired and aided this work. Their stimulation and guidance account largely for what is best in this book, though they bear no responsibility for it as a whole.

> William Birenbaum
> Robert Coles
> Elizabeth Drews
> Alvin Eurich
> Frank Jennings
> Nat Hentoff
> John Holt
> Cyril Houle
> Anne Long (Anna Banana)
> Charles Silberman
> Thomas Sobol
> Harold Taylor

We are also indebted, for invaluable guidance in the shaping of the final manuscript, to our editor, Nancy Gross.

A note on the sources

To maintain the informal tenor of this book, we have avoided footnotes indicating the sources of selections which have been published previously. All such sources are listed among the acknowledgments on the copyright page. A list of books by contributors, as well as of teachers' magazines from which material has been excerpted, will be found in the back of the book.

BG

RG

Contents

Contents

III ❦ Toward teaching—and beyond

It is in fact nothing short of a miracle
that the modern methods of instruction have not yet
entirely strangled the holy curiosity of inquiry;
for this delicate little plant, aside from stimulation,
stands mainly in need of freedom;
without this it goes to wrack and ruin
without fail.

ALBERT EINSTEIN

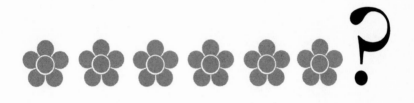

Introduction

Let us look to one another

Where shall we look for help in becoming the kinds of teachers we want and need to be? Our answer is: look to one another. That is the basis of this book.

If our profession is to undergo renewal in the seventies, then that big, drab, fearsome giant is going to have to burst into a thousand little flowers of joy, wit, and courage. We are going to have to learn together, joining with each other in genuine colleagueship and camaraderie and joining with our students in creativity and social awareness. If this sounds beamish, perhaps that reflects how far we have drifted from our true vocations.

To find the way back we need not merely more expertise, knowledge and understanding, technology and support.

1

We need, even more, mentors of our own—friends and colleagues who will share with us their lives, commitments, and insights. Even one such person may be more useful than a hundred ERIC centers, a thousand White House conferences, and God knows how many consultants' reports.

This book is our effort to introduce such people to each other. "I" is the word that appears most in these pages. Every piece is written by a practicing teacher from his or her own experience in a particular classroom on a particular day. Each teacher is writing mainly for his or her colleagues and friends, fellow teachers, with whom he or she wants to share what one of them, Jim Herndon, calls, "the foolishness and absurdity of our ways through the world and . . . the impact of the great, occasional and accidental joy which would be our only reward along those paths."

This is what the book is really about. But it takes the form of the best tricks we have seen or heard for turning kids on to learning and growing and doing.

If there is hope for the schools, it lies in the kind of work reported in these pages. Reform will come in American education only through American teachers. If teachers see proposed changes threatening their vital interests, they will oppose, resist, and ignore those changes. And in the end, they will defeat them. Even if the school boards and administrators mandate the reform, these changes will not come about in the classrooms except through the teachers, who are the inescapable conduits of change under the present setup. Moreover, with the increasing strength of teachers' unions, the decisive influence of the individual teacher in his or her classroom is augmented by the collective force of the profession.

Fortunately, there is reason to hope that teacher power of a fine sort can turn the schools around. "I am stunned,"

2

says Frank Riessman, professor of education at New York University and editor of *Social Policy* magazine, "by the successful experiments over the past ten years, that have shown how much schools can do for children." He cites a number of programs and projects that have demonstrably increased learning and scored other benefits for students.

The central role of the classroom teacher in educational change is stressed also by Seymour Lachman, vice president of the New York City Board of Education. "The radical reformers have continually and constantly criticized classroom teachers," he says. "Yet, it may be that the only possible reform that can become permanent is that which has the support, cooperation and commitment of those teachers. And teachers, the average as well as the gifted, will take reform seriously only when they are responsible for defining their own needs and receiving aid in a cooperative manner. . . . The cause of reform is hurt and not helped when [the teachers'] role is disparaged, their interests denigrated, their talents ignored, and they are blamed for the imperfect schools they inherit. Beset by bureaucratic regulations, they have become the devils of radical reformers who must find someone to blame for the defects in our larger society. In truth, the reformers have contempt for the hard-working, often effective and frequently harried teacher."

Of course, there are dangers in this line of argument. Teaching, like every profession, is a mixed bag. In each of the major professions, from medicine and law to the less conventional professions, such as business and writing, there is the same rough hierarchy: a vanguard of creative innovators; a small cadre of alert and dedicated practitioners who disseminate and adopt innovations; a large middle corps of routiners; and a straggling band of time-servers, incompetents, and real menaces. No profession likes to acknowledge the existence of this last group, and "professional ethics" is usually used to protect them against the interests of clients and the public.

All professions share this problem.* In medicine, for example, a good one-third of all doctors practice their professions in such a way as to make a financial killing, rather than serve their patients, according to Dr. John Knowles, head of the Rockefeller Foundation. The American Medical Association (AMA) insists that peer review is the only approach to putting a necessary floor under the quality of service. But it is a sociological truism that no profession or peer group has the will or the capacity to root out its inadequate members. No professional group can police itself.

So it is with teaching. There are clinkers in every school —mere warm bodies who bore kids to death, teachers who have been beaten down by the rules and regulations or demoralized by fellow teachers. And, occasionally, there are the verbal sadists who brutalize children's sensibilities. It does the best teachers no honor to pretend that all teachers are good. In fact, it ignores one of the most powerful obstacles to becoming and staying a good teacher: the indifference or hostility of one's run-of-the-mill "colleagues." So we must say up front: some teachers should be fired for the good of the children; many teachers need a vigorous kick to get moving. Yet even in disaster schools there are usually a few who are what we would like all teachers to be.

But *all* teachers have to be dealt with. Somehow they must be helped to grow. Somehow they must be enlisted in

* For a fuller analysis of the problems of corruption and the prospects of reform in the major professions, *see* Ronald Gross and Paul Osterman (eds.), *The New Professionals* (New York: Simon and Schuster, 1973).

4

their own professional advance. They are the decisive elements, for better or worse, in the schools as presently constituted. What is needed is the strongest possible affirmation of the *best* in the profession, its proclamation as widely as possible, and the provision of support and encouragement for teachers who want to associate themselves with it.

Currently, the reform movement in education,* like so much else in American radicalism, seems to have reached a watershed. Those waves of change that surged through our society and our lives in the sixties have broken and have begun to subside. Protest pauses; the Transformation has been postponed until tomorrow. In field after field we are waking to a sober awareness of the limits, liabilities and ironies of change.

In education it is a moment for distilling the wisdom we have won from the two major efforts of the late sixties and early seventies—open education and free schools. What are the lessons of these two bold attempts to teach better? Looking back at the initial five years of both will help us find a more solid basis for our reasonable hopes to make schools more decent.

Open education is, of course, that sensible impulse that reorders elementary education around the individual child, following his natural impulse to explore and create in a rich environment, under the guidance (but not the thumb) of a sensitive, thoughtful teacher. Charles Silberman's *Crisis in the Classroom*† endorsed and popularized the approach. And it became a shibboleth virtually overnight.

The best critical view of this phenomenon is by Roland Barth, an elementary school principal in Newton, Massa-

---

* For documentation of its development, *see* our *Radical School Reform* (New York: Simon and Schuster, 1969) .

† Random House, 1970; Vintage paperback, 1971.

5

chusetts. In 1968 Barth found himself involved in a typical late-sixties effort to radically reform two inner-city public schools. There was the typical foundation grant, the local university as *éminence grise,* the young groovy teachers (average age twenty-four, all white, great credentials from Amherst, Barnard, Wesleyan, and so on, but hardly any practical experience). Under Barth's supervision the teachers undertook to "open" their six classrooms. Within four months the project personnel were at each other's throats. "School didn't open," Barth dryly notes, "it exploded."

What went wrong? Barth analyzes his experiences and the whole theory of open education in his book *Open Education and the American School.** A basic problem, he concludes, was the delusion that massive amounts of money and massive numbers of people can improve a school, despite the lack of a real plan for effective teaching. "Almost any plan is better than no plan," he remarks. And one is reminded of Silberman's perception that the besetting flaw in our schools is "mindlessness."

The best summary and evaluation of the Free School movement is Allen Graubard's *Free the Children.*† Based on a national survey supported by the Office of Education, but informed by Graubard's "insider" view of the movement, his book examines the grass-roots impulse to create small, private, libertarian alternatives to the public schools. Graubard first reviews the literature by radical school reformers—John Holt, A. S. Neill, and so on—that sparked these enterprises. But the bulk of his book is an account of the scope and character of the free schools themselves: how

* New York: Agathon Press, 1973 (distributed by Schocken Books).
† New York: Pantheon, 1973.

the schools came to be, what they are like, and the problems they face.

The central section is the best single source of information about free schools. One knows in general what these schools are like: the rejection of the paraphernalia of public schooling (grades and grading, periods and bells, group instruction and tests, disciplines and punishment, standardized curriculum and textbooks) and the less focused positive thrusts: authentic personal relations, pupil-centered teaching, individualized programs, use of non-school people, places and materials. But Graubard gives us the stuff itself, from the rhetoric of the recruitment manifestoes to the enraged recriminations when colleagues fall out.

While there is nothing in *Free the Children* as fine as George Dennison's *The Lives of Children,** we do hear real voices speaking out of their lives and work. And there is much savvy counsel for people who are disposed to start schools themselves.

Graubard goes further than description. He discerns a fatal flaw in the theory and practice of free schools, and, in his later chapters, he tries to "peel off the rhetoric so that the problem can shine through clear and depressing." Briefly, the problem is that the radical reformers have not taken sufficient account of the wider context of their efforts. In a chapter titled "Teach Your Children Well," which echoes both a pop song and Jonathan Kozol's reaffirmation of the importance of teaching in free schools, Graubard accuses the free schoolers of "hiding behind a freedom ideology or the notion that anything anyone does is learning, and it is all cool."

Freedom, as John Dewey noted, only poses the problem

* Random House, 1969, Vintage paperback, 1970.

7

in education. The solution hangs on one's conception of the social, political, and personal challenges that face young people and on the ways adults can best help them learn what they need to know to meet them. Prince Kropotkin, in his "Letter to the Young," put it best: "Ask, What kind of world do you want to live in? What do you need to know? What are you good at and want to work at to build that world? Demand that your teachers teach you that."

Finally, Graubard considers the broader meaning of the free schools and of radical educational reform in general. His conclusion is that the schools inevitably reflect and embody the values of a society that has proved much more resistant to radical change than the sixties-style radicals envisaged. Moreover, the conditions that need transformation—inequities, racism, sexism, alienation—have neither their roots nor their cures in the schools. "My firm view is that attempts at truly humanizing the public schools must run up against the fundamental social realities—the sickness of American society," Graubard concludes. "The liberal dream of cure by means of education is misconceived."

Work in free schools can be an important contribution to shaping a better America, but it will be more effective when it becomes modest, unapocalyptic, and resilient. Graubard summons us not to a Big Rock Candy Mountain of joyous growth toward a counterculture, but to "serious, unglamorous, gritty, and long-term commitments to continue to organize, teach, start schools, work with public school reformers, criticize our own efforts, talk to people—all with modest expectations for the short term."

That gritty work aimed at better teaching is what this book is about. It is one contribution to the opening of communication and sharing between teachers and between teachers and others, particularly students and parents. This book

8

could not have come to be, if this process had not already started at the grass-roots level. For this reason, a few words on how this material was assembled is important to the book's message.

A couple of years ago we suddenly developed a big pile of clippings, manuscripts, and letters in the corner of our bedroom. There were writings by teachers that were sent to us or that we tore from the nascent teachers' underground presses, such as Boston's *The Red Pencil*, Portland's (Ore.) *The Teacher Paper*, Berkeley's *No More Teacher's Dirty Looks*, and New York's *The Worksheet*. Checking with some friends, we discovered that they too had collected materials. John Holt and Herbert Kohl, whose own writings proved so helpful to other teachers, received or collected similar materials, and they both generously opened their bedrooms, file cabinets, and so on, to us.

But, still we figured the writings that found their way to us were only a small part of the writings that must exist. We sent out a call, through both the straight and the alternative publications for teachers, for other such materials.

We asked for pieces by and for professionals, pieces that would say, in effect: "Here is something I have done, thought through, wondered about, got into trouble over, failed at, gained courage from . . . it might help you."

Among those who helped spread the word to teachers throughout the country, whom we might not have reached otherwise, were Ole Sand of the National Education Association (NEA), Robert Binswanger of the U.S. Office of Education, Steve Schrader of the Teachers and Writers Collaborative, and Hal Sobel of Queens College, New York City.

We got more than we bargained for. Contributions came from every part of the country. Everyone seemed turned on

9

by the idea. People wrote us from communes, from the inner cities, from the Mississippi delta, from jail, from inside the giant "Ed-Biz" think tanks.

To us the materials filled a conspicuous gap in the literature about education today. On one hand, there are the books of those prophets who awakened us in the sixties: Kozol, Holt, Paul Goodman, and Edgar Friedenberg. They show us the indecency, the mean-spiritedness, and the mind-murdering complicity of our schools.

On the other hand, there are the key counterculture prescriptions for "doing your own thing" in the *Big Rock Candy Mountain: Resources for Our Education* and comparable works. These are rather precious from the viewpoint of the teacher who turns up every day at 8:30 A.M. at an urban public school.

We believe the materials in this book plug that gap. *By* teachers, *for* teachers, *about* teaching, they seem to be what working teachers really need from each other. The pages glow with personal feelings, bravado and wit, intelligence and rage, anger and supportiveness. They represent the highest, brightest shoptalk we have ever heard, but, since the writings are about kids and "education," they have a larger resonance.

Almost every piece in this book describes something that a teacher can do in a classroom. However, we hope the book's real message is not the sum of these techniques. In fact, the real message does not have to do with techniques at all.

Techniques alone will not bring about the changes that are needed. Paulo Freire, the radical Brazilian adult educator, who has developed one of the most stunningly effective techniques in the history of modern education, says that his "technique," like all techniques, is "nothing," compared to the need for a deep commitment by the teacher to the real interests of the students he teaches.

10

So competence defined as technique is not enough. In none of the professions can competence alone be sufficient. The existential relationship of the professional to the person he is working with must be there. If it is not there competence does not mean a thing. We need an emphasis on competence undergirded by love and caring. We hope this work will spell this out, so that it is not mere sentiment. We need to identify very precise, observable phenomena that combine competence and love in our approach to teaching.

This implies what we call a "situational pedagogy," comparable to the "situational ethics" we have become used to in our moral lives. That is, rather than teaching according to fixed general principles, many teachers seem to be groping toward a style that is dependent on the particular situations in which one finds oneself. The uniqueness of a specific situation, the particularities of the human beings in it, their relationships to each other, and the environment—physical, social, even political—in which the situation occurs: from all these derives the right *praxis* for that time and place. Abstract rules or principles will not save us from the responsibility for continual existential choice. We cannot sink back into an ideology, a style, an approach, a technique. To teach truly means that every day, even minute, we must be ready to engage directly that specific situation before us, bringing to bear upon it everything we have learned and been. Of course, we will always fall short of this ideal of aliveness and conscientiousness, but it must remain our ideal.

We think this is where we are today in the school reform movement. Remember Whitehead's three stages of learning from *The Aims of Education*? He noted that the learner goes through a first stage of romance. In this stage a new field, a new problem, and a new horizon suddenly swim into view. "Learning is finding out that something is *pos-*

11

sible," said Fritz Perls. In the school reform movement, this was the period of the sixties, when suddenly we dreamt new dreams and realized some of them: Alternative schools *were* possible; a different kind of teaching and learning could go on in public school classrooms.

But there is a second stage, which Whitehead calls "precision." "In dreams begin responsibilities," Yeats wrote. There comes a time when we must translate our inchoate visions and our impulsive enterprises into more powerful and public instruments for social change. Here a concentration on technique is justifiable, indeed necessary, provided it does not become a fixation, undermining our grip on the basic purposes that technique must serve.

As this book goes to press, we are delighted to find signs of this impulse even in the most radical wing of the school reform movement. The *New Schools Exchange Newsletter,* the communications link among the free schools, carries an appeal from Len Solo, the dedicated and imaginative creator of the Teacher Drop-Out Center at Amherst, Massachusetts, for examples of good practice to share with readers of the newsletter. Citing Whitehead's paradigm, Solo notes that even the free schools are moving more and more into the stage of precision: "The concerns of these people are no longer with how do you start an alternative school but with how to grow new people, how to teach kids to read in a humane, individualized way, how to do science and math and social studies in human ways that also do not perpetuate the evils of the past (and present) —the racism, sexism, arbitrary authoritarianism, all the ways in which humans are diminished. The concerns are with curriculum, with materials (all old and dumb? Nay!), and with how people relate to each other around these materials, projects, curricula. I feel these concerns in the new school my own children attend and in most of the schools I've visited this past year."

12

The same conviction is emerging from the urban free school movement, best expressed by Kozol. In his eloquent *Free Schools,* he calls upon his colleagues in the nation's independent ghetto schools to become "teachers who are not afraid to teach." It is time, he argues, to reaffirm our commitment to empowering young people with the skills and understandings we know they need.

Teachers in all kinds of schools, at every level, with all sorts of kids, seem to be reaching for finer possibilities in their work. That, for us, is the beauty and the joy of these writings we have brought together to share with you. Through examples they show us what excellence looks and feels like in our profession. From them we can absorb, perhaps, a little wisdom, even greatness. In this profession that is so mired in mindlessness, unconcern, and passivity, we may begin to grow into our true vocations through learning to understand, care, and struggle.

To help us with this goal is the chief value of the new breed of teacher-writers who have emerged in the past five years. They share with us not only their ideas and experiences, but also their lives and spirits. This is all we ask. It is more than we deserve. Only through our responses will we reveal whether it is enough.

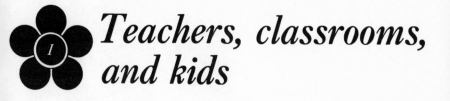

Teachers, classrooms, and kids

1 "I am the decisive element in the classroom"

New self-images of teachers

Teachers are beginning to talk in new ways about their work and themselves. Sometimes the tone is a high seriousness, a new professionalism that is miles above petty prerogatives and contract cavils. Other times it is a boisterous joyousness. And other times . . . well, read on.

Will it grow in a classroom?

"Madman in the classroom" was the novel
role Burt Schuman adopted in his first year of
teaching. But this does not mean that he
neglected to plan classroom activities. Burt
devoted enormous time and energy to
such plannings, as his account, which follows,
makes clear. The result worked well with his
fifth graders. With other materials, it
could work as well with older or younger
children.

BY BURT SCHUMAN

On a drizzly and bleak September morning, I stood confronted. Two months of training, rhetoric and ego-inflation now lay hopelessly behind me. All my lofty visions of master teacherdom had vanished in the presence of the tough and skeptical children who were filing ominously into the classroom, intent on having the substitute for lunch. In a desperate fit of panic, an idea was born—an idea which was to become my raison d'être in teaching. I was going to be mad—unremittingly, unabashedly, unreservedly mad; for if the children could be lunatics, so could the teacher.

A taste for madness must be cultivated, like the taste for a fine wine. With legions of second graders rushing headlong into the classroom at 8:40 [A.M.], telegraphing thousands of coded messages like ants at the sight of a picnic lunch, it's wise to do your cultivating early. A little craziness from the getgo is needed to set the proper mood and tone. Here is my favorite mood setter:

Mr. Schuman's Wake-Up Chant
Wake up!
Wake up!

We touch our faces and we say, "Good Morning!"
We touch our eyes and we say, "How do you do!"
Wake up!
Wake up!

If this didn't create the proper impression, there was always more elaborate fare. A friend of mine who had been teaching at the Rudolph Steiner School told me of an art form developed there called Eurythmy, in which movements are made to simulate sounds of speech. Not yet having seen Eurythmy, I was free to speculate as to what these movements might look like. My speculations were, of course, imposed upon the kids. My victims were summarily ordered to stand in a circle and move to the sounds of aaaaaaah, ooooooo, eeeeeeee, ooooooh, owwwww, and company. The entire panoply of human emotions was experienced in 540 degrees worth of movement. Several minutes of such exposure, and few children any longer doubted the score. The vast majority were quite content to sink numbly into their basal readers and work quietly for a spell.

Such devices helped to make six months of substituting bearable, if not always pleasurable. They could be used to warm up, tone down, or fill in while frantically trying to decipher the classroom teacher's lesson plans. Moreover, they served to leave an imprimatur upon the school, to identify you as a known quantity in the eyes of the children. I became known as a substitute upon whom the children could depend for several hours of clean, wholesome entertainment.

Beasts we have known and loved

In February of that school year, my craziness theory of education was to receive its supreme test. A rather beleaguered cluster teacher, who did as much screaming at her colleagues as she did at children, was "coaxed" into a substitute's position. Filling the void was to be none other than Schuman the Madman. I was to teach nine different classes, spanning three different grades, the arts of grammar, phonics, poetry, composition, literature, creative writing, and oral discourse. I spent the weekend prior to the assumption of my duties in a state that was typical for me in such situations—hysteria. Late that hysterical Sunday evening a miracle occurred—a veritable virgin birth of inspiration. Mr. Schuman had discovered unicorns.

Sitting benignly on the shelf was a copy of *A Cloisters Bestiary,* an anthology of medieval tales of beasts both mythical and real, compiled by the staff of the Metropolitan Museum of Art. The fanciful flavor of both fauna and fable proved pleasing to the mind's eye and tempting to the plan book. It was to inspire a new unit called *Beasts We Have Known and Loved.* The unit included tales and dramatizations about unicorns, griffins, harpies, manticores, centaurs, dragons, basilisks, and amphisbaenas. These were supplemented by a series of extension activities which included the following:

a. Acting out the story of the unicorn in pantomime.
b. Improvising a situation in which a unicorn walks into the classroom.
c. Initiating rumors of the unicorn's imminent death, and launching a campaign to save it.
d. Writing stories about the time when a griffin, harpy, manticore and centaur came to your house for dinner.
e. A television show called "Name that Beast," in which a griffin, dragon, basilisk, and amphisbaena try to stump our guest panel.
f. Writing love letters to a manticore.

The assignments were varied to meet the needs of seven of my nine different classes. The results were very exciting;

not only did the children produce some forceful and imaginative writing, but many developed a keen interest of their own in mythological beasts—such as the minotaur or the chimera.

My success with this unit inspired me to seek other sources of whimsy. One such source was the work of Lewis Carroll. Of particular interest was *Alice in Wonderland* and several of his collected poems. My favorite work of all was the "Mock Turtle's Song" from *Alice*. It appealed to me most because of spelling distortions like "beauoooooti-ful souooooooooop." I devised my own working tune and gave a maiden performance to my sixth grade class: it was an instant success. The performance was followed by an assignment to write a love letter to one's favorite food. Chicken and French fries received the greatest amount of fan mail.

I learned early in my substitute days about the magical powers of comic books. Children would constantly fantasize about being one comic strip hero or another, and allusions to Spider Man and the like consistently permeated their writing. What would happen if the kids saw themselves as comic heroes in their own right, performing feats of derring-do in the classroom or at home? The result was an assignment called "The Classroom Adventures of Super Me." It was curious indeed to see the meekest and most withdrawn of children inspired to paper acts of violence or valor. From then on, comic strip writing was to become a regular feature of room 304.

My final success of the season was due again to a museum anthology. Sitting unobtrusively on the rear shelves of the Museum of Modern Art Book Store was a collection of some of the juiciest and most blood-curdling stills in all horror-dom. They included scenes from classics such as "The Cabinet of Dr. Caligari," "Frankenstein," "Dracula," "Phantom of the Opera," "The Mummy," "King Kong,"

21

and "The Creature from the Black Lagoon." As I turned from the cash register and slinked through the museum's swinging doors, my entire face was stretched into a ghoulish leer. I couldn't sleep that night out of sheer anticipation. Finally morning came, and I was ready to spring my stills on an unsuspecting group of fourth graders. I challenged them to identify the various monsters in the stills, and drafted several to be monsters and to deliver monologues on how they felt about their roles. Written assignments were to come later in the week and included imaginary dialogues between King Kong and Fay Wray and essays by The Creature on water pollution. Later that year they were to be attached to task cards in my writing center. (Example: Describe the dance that the Bride of Frankenstein and her mate are working on.) After nearly three years of service, these stills remain an unending source of inspiration.

September 1970: The madman gets a class

In September of 1970, I returned from my whirlwind tour of Europe fully prepared to resume my language arts program. To my surprise, I discovered that I had been assigned a fifth grade class. Being low man on the seniority totem pole, I was given a choice selection of kids. They were behind two to three years in reading, had nothing that resembled work habits, and were generally reputed to be terrors. To put it mildly, they were not the most enthusiastic and motivated group of students. Even though the most disturbed children were subsequently removed, my task remained Herculean in nature.

My first priority was to get the children to concentrate on reading improvement, and like it. During my summer training period, I was exposed to a unique approach to reading, writing, and spelling called the Spalding or Unified Phonics Method. It appealed to me because it was

22

extremely logical and related the teaching of reading to the way American English is really pronounced. It had, however, two major drawbacks. One was that the method required memorization of several key spelling rules and the ability to apply them to a given word. The other was that the presentation of the method was hopelessly dull. I decided, therefore, to give unified phonics some hefty doses of pizzazz, razzmatazz, hotcha, and soft shoe—not to mention a love of the bright lights.

Our opening routine was a vowel cheer, in which each of the sounds of the five vowel sounds was chanted in cadence. Then came popular old numbers such as the Silent E Dance or Digraphs Personified. Examples of the latter are as follows: Ay, ai are the sounds Granny makes, oy and oi are said when it hoits, aw and au are what you say when the teacher is cheap, and ew and ui are what you say when little sister steps in something—ooo youuuuu. The phonic activity that proved to be the most fun, however, was that of developing dramatic improvisations to illustrate a given phonogram. One such assignment called for a sketch that would teach the sounds of ough—off, aw, ow, oh, oo, uf. One group dashed to the closets, and embalmed one of the cast in pillows and painting smocks; they produced a pregnancy sketch. Another group sought its inspiration in the Spanky movies of the thirties and produced a sketch about Baby Kwong smashing his thumbnail.

The popularity of these routines pushed us on to even dizzier heights—consonant blends. I took great pleasure in arriving early on Thursday mornings and improvising alliterative stories on the chalkboard, such as "Clarence and Cloe," "Brenda the Brat," and "Blind Blondie." The children had to recognize the given consonant blend, find words of their own, and write a story similar to the one on the chalkboard. Even more enjoyable were phonics contests, in which each table competed with the other to produce as

23

many words as possible beginning with a given blend. Quite naturally, I took great pleasure in running around the room and excitedly shouting out hints. Besides turning children on to phonics this exercise drove home some important values, such as the importance of teamwork and educated, as opposed to wild, guessing.

Dramatic improvisation in its own right has unlimited value in the classroom and is a wondrous tonic for shyness and insecurity. It's particularly effective in getting Non English Speaking (children who don't speak English) children to express themselves in front of the class. I found the best method for getting kids started on dramatic improvisations was to do a sample sketch with some volunteers, and then proceed to distribute sample situations for each table to act out and resolve. Here is a list of the dramatic situations that proved most effective:

a. A group of children bursts into the principal's office and informs him that there is a herd of elephants on the third floor.
b. A group of children visits the zoo and discovers their teacher trapped in the lion's cage.
c. A boy walks into the classroom without his head.
d. The "new arrival" in class turns out to be a praying mantis.
e. A drunken man is convinced that his living room furniture is trying to attack him.
f. A group of children is playing basketball, when a child walks over and eats the basketball.

These situations were only necessary as a starter. Dramatic improvisations became a regular feature of our class, and the skits the kids conceived of were far more surreal than those of the master.

Another subject area of high priority and low enthusiasm was math. In general, my efforts at teaching math were less successful than those at teaching reading; but I attribute this to lack of experience in teaching certain concepts, rather than a failure to motivate my class. In any event, I soon discovered that there could be lunacy in numbers.

Here the madman attacked on two fronts: whole class and individual. While struggling to develop a whole-class unit on set theory, I came across a rather quaint episode on "Sesame Street." In this sketch, Cookie Monster is presented with the challenge of grouping five musical instruments and a banana into two distinct sets; he proceeds to eat all the instruments and play the banana. Late that evening I made a fateful decision: I was going to play Cookie Monster. My educational assistant, Mrs. Evelyn Coulter, began the lesson by carefully eliciting the class's feelings as to how they would group five musical instruments and a banana. Then came my grand entrance. Using my raspiest monster voice and dressed in my shaggiest old turtle neck, I sauntered into the room and snatched the plastic violin at the edge of the table. "Every monster knows that you eat a violin," said I, and tucked the instrument under my turtle neck. "Every monster knows that a saxophone is even more delicious than a violin," said I, getting a bit raspy. Now came the punchline, the moment of glory for which I had spent all last evening rehearsing: "But every monster knows that you make beautiful music with a banana!" I could feel it in the roar of the children and the smell of the chalk dust. I had experienced a monumental moment of triumph, like Caesar crossing the Rubicon, or Woody Allen remembering a line from "Casablanca." Amid the swell of approbation and the thundrous cries for more, I realized that my children had grasped the concept of sets.

Nurds, quibbles, and orps
The individualized assignments were far less theatrical but no less surreal. An art consultant who worked in my class

suggested that children might learn a given unit of measure more readily if a nonsense name were attached to it. This suggestion led to the development of our system of nurds, quibbles, and orps. The nurd is a term used to describe the distance between your elbow and your wrist. It originated at the time when Prince Alfred decided that his entire body was a unit of measure, and leaped out his bedroom window to find the distance between his room and a bed of roses below. Upon seeing his son's arm in a cast, his father, King Hal exclaimed, "You nurd!"

The children were first given task cards listing various objects to measure in nurds. Then to show the glaring weakness of this unit of measure, I had each table select one person to have his body outlined on a sheet of poster paper. The outline was measured in nurds by each child in the group. The differences were compared, and we spent a lesson trying to arrive at a standard unit of measure. We agreed to use the long side of a 9" by 12" sheet of oak tag and call it a quibble. Our quibble rods were then subdivided into four equal parts called orps. After an experience lesson or two using this system, my class felt extremely comfortable in a world of inches, feet, and yards.

Topsoil Julienne and Gravel Surprise

The consummate act of madness revolved around a unit on liquid and dry measure. I recalled (in a brief return to toddlerdom) how much pleasure I had derived from making mud pies and soil burgers. Wouldn't it be a gas, mused I, for the entire class to mix disgusting imitation foods? I devoted a prep period to dreaming up recipes that would be revolting enough to be fun, yet simple enough to involve everyone in the class. Here is an example of one such recipe:

26

Wheatpaste Supreme
2 cups of wheatpaste
1 cup of angel food mix
1 cup of corn syrup
1 tablespoon of brown sugar
2 dozen golden raisins
2 dozen marshmallows

Mix the wheatpaste, corn syrup, and angel food mix thoroughly in a deep rectangular tray. Sprinkle cornflakes freely over the batter. Pour your pencil shavings carefully around the edge to form a border. Decorate to taste with your raisins and marshmallows.

Other dishes in our repertoire included Gerbil Chocolate, Macaroni a la Mud, Topsoil Julienne, and Gravel Surprise. The most pleasurable sounds of all were the blood-curdling screams emanating from colleagues when presented with samples of our Haute Cuisine. To say the least, our recipes had an impact.

Conclusion: lunacy and its effectiveness
It is difficult to determine, in the final analysis, whether the methods mentioned in this article have had any appreciable impact on the kids. It is equally difficult to determine whether my techniques constituted a serious pedagogical approach or just frivolous dilettantism of a rookie teacher. Any objective indices provide an inconclusive picture. Some children advanced into the higher exponent classes and did extremely well there; others were forced to repeat the sixth grade. One battery of reading tests shows an average gain of from one and one half to two years; another set shows very little gain indeed. Is there any way to measure, however, the amount a child grows in self-esteem, self-direction, enthusiasm, or intellectual curiosity during his stay in your

class? It is by these criteria that I wish most sorely to be judged.

I make no claim to having stumbled upon some divine logos of teaching. I make no pretense of having discovered a panacea, a new gestalt or some "groovy alternative to the system." I share with you the recollections of one teacher in one school struggling with the demands of first year teaching and striving to make his classroom more creative, more responsive, and more human.

BY HERBERT KOHL

Of course the teacher is a moral exemplar—an example of all the confusion, hypocrisy, and indecision, of all the mistakes, as well as the triumphs, of moral man. The children see all this, whatever they pretend to see. Therefore, to be more than an example, to be an educator—someone capable of helping lead the child through the labyrinth of life—the teacher must be honest to the children about his mistakes and weaknesses; he must be able to say that he is wrong or sorry, that he hadn't anticipated the results of his remarks and regretted them, or hadn't understood what a child meant. It is the teacher's struggle to be moral that excites his pupils; it is honesty, not rightness, that moves children.

ERRATUM
Page 29 of this book should read as follows:

Teachers, classrooms, and kids

Teacher evaluation

BY JOHN GAUSS

A. PERSONAL QUALIFICATIONS

Rating: 1 highest rating;
5 lowest rating

Personal appearance — *5 Dresses in an old sheet draped about his body*

Self-confidence — *5 Not sure of himself – always asking questions*

Use of English — *4 Speaks with a heavy Greek accent*

Adaptability — *5 Prone to suicide by poison when under duress*

B. CLASS MANAGEMENT

Organization — *5 Does not keep a seating chart*

Room appearance — *4 Does not have eye-catching bulletin boards*

Utilization of supplies — *1 Does not use supplies*

C. TEACHER-PUPIL RELATIONSHIPS

Tact and consideration — *5 Places students in embarrassing situations by asking questions*

Attitude of class — *2 Class is friendly*

D. TECHNIQUES OF TEACHING

Daily preparations — *2 Does not keep daily lesson plans*

Attention to course of study — *3 Quite flexible-allows students to wander to different topics*

Knowledge of subject matter — *5 Does not know material-has to question pupils to gain knowledge*

E. PROFESSIONAL ATTITUDE

Professional ethics — *5 Does not belong to professional organization or PTA*

In-service training — *5 Complete failure here-has not even bothered to attend college*

Parent relationships — *5 Needs to improve in this area-parents are trying to get rid of him*

EVALUEE: *Socrates*

Teacher evaluation

BY JOHN GAUSS

TEACHER:

A. PERSONAL QUALIFICATIONS RATING
                (high to low)   1   2   3   4   5

Personal appearance   — — — — —

Self-confidence   — — — — —

Use of English   — — — — —

Adaptability   — — — — —

B. CLASS MANAGEMENT

Organization   — — — — —

Room appearance   — — — — —

Utilization of supplies   — — — — —

C. TEACHER-PUPIL RELATIONSHIPS

Tact and consideration   — — — — —

Attitude of class   — — — — —

D. TECHNIQUES OF TEACHING

Daily preparations   — — — — —

Attention to course of study   — — — — —

Knowledge of subject matter   — — — — —

E. PROFESSIONAL ATTITUDE

Professional ethics   — — — — —

In-Service training   — — — — —

Parent relationships   — — — — —

Will it grow in a classroom?

"Can you learn, if you're naked?" asks
Ross Burkhardt on the first day of class.
Understanding the job of the learner and the
limitations of the teacher is as important for
six-year-olds as for the ninth graders Ross
teaches. But would you have thought you
could ask this question of mixed
fifteen-year-olds without having them
"break up"?
 Could you raise similar questions with
children of different ages?

BY ROSS BURKHARDT

SETTING: The first week of school. Taped music as background. Desks and chairs in a circle. Posters, pennants,
flags, and banners hanging from walls and ceiling. Say-
ings—"The purpose of education is to make comfortable
people uncomfortable," "Today is the first day of the rest of
your life," "I hear and I forget, I see and I remember, I do
and I understand"—individual letters cut out from multi-
colored construction paper and pinned to tie-dyed sheets
along the walls. A 9th grade classroom in African/Asian
Culture Studies. Twenty-five kids. One teacher.

"How do you learn?" I directed the question at the class as
soon as the last student seated himself in the circle. No
response. I repeated the question. One student hesitantly
volunteered.

"From the teacher. We read books, and he tells us things,
and we learn."

"Is that the only way you learn?"

A pause. Then a girl with long red hair raised her hand.
"We learn from watching, listening, from looking at things.

We learn in school. That's why we come."

"In other words," I asked, "if you didn't go to school, you wouldn't know anything?"

Groans and assorted noises. "No, no. We learn things out of school."

"Like what? And how?"

"Like TV. Well, I learned something last night on the news," continued the redhead. "There was something about a city somewhere being bombed, and I learned about it and the people were killed." Her earnestness pervaded the room.

"Anybody have another way of learning without school?"

"Everybody learns without school," said a voice from behind me. "We all learn things before we get here, and we all know a lot of things without school."

"Such as?"

"Well . . ."

"Anybody want to help out?"

Hands here and there. I nodded to one of the more frantic wavers. "I learned to talk long before I came to school. And we learn names and things like that. We learn about traffic rules and lots of other things. So we all do learn without school."

"Everybody agree?"

Vigorous assent. Unspoken dreams of freedom apparently about to be realized in the first week of high school.

"Then," I challenged, "why bother to come to school at all? Why come if you don't need school to learn?"

Another pause. Then from the other side of the room, a sullen boy whose voice revealed a latent hostility. "Because we are told to. I wouldn't come if I didn't have to. It's a prison."

"Everybody agree?"

Hands and muttering. I nodded to a nicely dressed girl to

my left. "I don't agree with him. I come to school because I like it. I get to see my friends, and there are some teachers here who are nice and . . ."

"Wait a minute," I interrupted, "you've been in high school two days and there are some 'nice teachers' here? Isn't that a little fast judgment on your part?"

"Well, what I mean is, I don't come here because I am forced to, but because I want to."

"Anyone else feel that way?" Nods and signs of assent from scattered regions of the room. "Well, then, I guess you don't really need me to learn, do you? I guess you can do all right without me. I guess I can go sit at my desk and read the paper and let you learn by yourself, can't I?"

"No, no." They felt there was something wrong, but they were having difficulty saying it.

"Wait a minute," said one of the boys, "we can learn without you, but it's easier with you, and, anyway, there are lots of things you know that we don't that you can teach us. That's why you're the teacher and we're the students. So we do need you to learn certain things, like about Africa and all those places."

"Okay," I said, "what's the capital of Upper Volta?"

Silence.

"What?"

"Where?"

"Upper Volta," I repeated. "Its capital."

"How should I know?"

"Where's that?"

"Who cares?"

"One hundred thousand Upper Voltans who call it home care," I observed.

"Well, what's the answer?"

"Anybody? . . ."

"Whereabouts again?"

"Upper Volta's capital?"

"Where is Upper Volta?" Laughter, murmuring, growing noise.

"All right, look at this." I went to the board and wrote in large capital letters, OUAGADOUGOU.

"Wha-who-wha-what?"

"Dog-dog, goo-goo?"

"What's that?"

"Huh?"

"Ouagadougou," I replied, giving it the French accent.

"Never heard of it."

"Now you have."

"So what?"

"So you needed me to teach you that. So you do need teachers to learn after all, right?"

"Right."

"All right, anything you say," grumbled someone.

"Everybody agree?"

More cautious now, they paused and thought about it. Then a couple of hands went up. I looked at a girl with a bright smile on her face. "We didn't need you for that. We could have looked it up ourselves. That's on a map somewhere, and we don't need teachers for things that are on maps."

"Yeah, yeah," from her friends. They were getting into it.

"Okay, how many of you knew that before I brought it to your attention?" No hands. "Then, okay, so now you can go home and tell mommy and daddy what you have learned in school today, and tell them how your teacher helped you learn it."

A hand slowly went up from a boy who had been watching me closely all period but as yet hadn't said anything. I nodded at him. "You didn't 'help us learn' that. You *told* us that. Telling isn't learning. It's . . . it's . . . it's just

33

telling." Laughter and smiles and a lot of good vibrations, heads turning to neighbors and the like.

"Okay, okay, then I go back to my question, how do you learn?"

Groans this time.

"What does this have to do with Africa and Asia?"

"We already did that one," said a girl who had been whispering to her girlfriend.

"Okay, then how do we learn?" I asked her directly.

"Well . . . by listening and by reading books, by going to school."

"For example, everybody learned something when . . ." and I pointed to the chalkboard where Ouagadougou still perplexed a few.

"Yeah, that's how we learned it. You told us and we learned it."

"I told you. Hmmmm. Then do you need sound in order to learn? Can you learn if there isn't any sound or noise?"

"We can read, and that doesn't make any noise, does it?"

"Suppose you don't have a book? Can you still learn things?"

"Yeah, we don't need books to learn things," said one of the boys.

"Then we can get rid of textbooks because we don't need them to learn with," I suggested. The cheering was somewhat uncertain this time. "Can you learn if you don't have any desks?" (I grabbed a desk away from the closest student and asked him again. He nodded that he could.)

"Can you learn if you don't have a chair?" Two girls got off their chairs and sat down on the floor, pushed aside their desks, and smiled broadly. Some of the kids looked startled. I asked the two girls if they felt they could learn from where they were and they said that they could. "Then it doesn't matter where you sit when you learn, does it?"

As if in answer, a couple more kids got down on the floor and some climbed up on the radiators.

"Do you have to be in this classroom to learn about Africa? Suppose we had class in another room? Could you still learn about Africa and Asia over there? Suppose we went downstairs to the cafeteria and I told you about Ouagadougou, known as Ouaga by the Upper Voltans. Could you learn it just as well down there?"

"Yes," they agreed.

"Then we don't need classrooms if it doesn't matter where you are for learning. Looks like we might save the taxpayers a lot of money. No books, no desks, no chairs, no classrooms. . . ."

"But we still need teachers."

"Hey, can you learn about Africa from another teacher besides me? I mean, suppose we grabbed another teacher and brought him in here and had him teach you about Africa. Could you still learn?"

"Sure we can."

"How about the way you are sitting now? Can you learn in a circle? Or is it better to sit in straight rows? Has anyone here learned anything?"

"Yeah, I've learned you're crazy." Laughter erupted around the room.

"And I learned about Ouaga in Upper Someplace."

"Hey, suppose we got another class in here, another group of ninth graders. Could you learn with them in the room?"

"Outrageous," offered one smiling boy.

"Why not?" asked another.

"How about the room the way it is? Can you learn with all this stuff hanging around?" Eyes turned to photographs from *Life,* album covers, old license plates, a W. C. Fields poster, *National Geographic* maps stuck to the ceiling, student montages from last year, and a 48-star flag.

"Yeah, and if we don't want to listen to you, we can look at the things hanging, and we can learn from that," said the redhead.

"Okay," I smiled, "can you learn with that music going on?"

"Aw, leave it on, please? It isn't bothering anyone."

"I'm not going to turn it off. What I said was, can you learn even though it's on in the background?"

"Yes," as "Woodstock" became half a million strong.

"Suppose that no teacher was talking, just music playing. Could you learn then?"

The girl with long blond hair and glasses raised her hand. "We could learn about rock music and what's happening. Rock music has a lot of messages in it," she said intensely.

"Suppose all I do is show some slides of Africa? Can you learn from just them?"

"You mean without you telling us what they were?"

"I mean just the slides, nothing else."

They circled slowly for a moment. One girl ventured, "I think I could learn from just the slides. I mean, I could see what Africa was all about, and that would tell me something."

"Slides, records, talking, not talking—you say you can learn from all of these things. Suppose, suppose you painted the windows? Could you learn anything by painting the windows?"

"Well, if it was a design that came from Asia, we would learn about Asia, I think, wouldn't we?" asked a long-haired boy.

"Okay, so you can learn a lot of things in a lot of ways. But what about me? Am I out of a job? Is there any place for a teacher in all this? What do you need me for, if anything?"

"Oh, we need you, or else we wouldn't get any homework."

"What do we need homework for?" shouted several boys.

"I was only kidding," the girl fired back.

"Say, can you learn if you don't get any homework?"

Vigorous assent.

"What if your teacher has a beard?" I asked, stroking a summer's growth. "Can you learn then?"

"Sure we can. What difference does a beard make?"

"I don't know. You tell me. Does a beard on a teacher make any difference?"

"No, not to me," said one of the girls. "In fact, I like it. It's cute."

"What about if your teacher doesn't have a tie on?" I asked, unknotting the four-in-hand speckled with Sagittarius designs.

"Why not? None of us has ties on," pointed out one of the kids.

"Then it doesn't matter how a person dresses whether he learns or not?"

"Nope."

"Can you learn if you don't have anything on at all?"

Gales of laughter, some red faces, turned away blushes from the girls, but not all the girls, and scattered applause.

"Don't answer that. What about if I'm on this side of the room? Can you all learn when I am over here?" I asked from the chalkboard.

"Yes, we can," they replied.

Walking over to the extreme opposite side of the room, I repeated the question. Again, assent from my charges. "In other words, then, it doesn't matter where I stand in the room for you to learn, does it?"

"No."

Leaping up on a desktop, I asked a startled boy, "What's

the capital of Upper Volta?" He looked at the board, laughed, and said something about "away-dog-away." I began walking around the room on the circle of desktops, waiting for students to grab their new binders and books from my path, casually talking to them and repeating the same question, "Can you learn when I'm up here?"

"Yes," from a dozen upturned faces.

"How about when I'm down here?" I asked, jumping down in one fluid motion to the floor and assuming the lotus position next to a couple of the girls who had sat on the floor earlier.

"Right on."

"Suppose I go out of the room? Can you learn even then?" I asked, as I closed the door behind me and went into another classroom to see what a colleague was up to. After a couple of minutes I returned to the room, none the worse for my absence, everyone still in the seat he had before I left, only a slightly higher decibel level present. The noise subsided and I asked, "Did anybody learn anything while I was gone?"

"I did, but I can't tell you," she said smilingly, and broke into giggling with her girlfriend who turned red and then turned away.

"I don't know what I learned, but I learned something," said another student. In the background, Arlo softly flew into Los Angeles.

There were only a couple of minutes left in the period. "For tomorrow, your assignment is to bring in an example of something you can't learn by yourself, that you need me to teach you. Lots of good things said today. Lots of good vibrations. I think this is going to be a good year. Bring in anything at all that you can't learn by yourself. Write it down. See you tomorrow."

I went over and turned up Sha-Na-Na and began to take random attendance to learn the kids' names.

BY HAIM GINOTT

I have come to a frightening conclusion.

I am the decisive element in the classroom.

It is my personal approach that creates the climate.

It is my daily mood that makes the weather.

As a teacher I possess tremendous power to make a child's life miserable or joyous.

I can humiliate or humor, hurt or heal.

In all situations it is my response that decides whether a crisis will be escalated or de-escalated, and a child humanized or dehumanized.

2 The lover's formula

Seeing kids singly, truly, and whole

The lover's formula, as Hugh Kenner points out, is "one at a time." So, too, should be the teacher's. The ultimate knack, the final "performance criterion" which transcends professional technique, is seeing an individual child singly and whole and responding to him truly. Before we move on to particular subject areas, let us look at kids through the eyes of teachers who have cultivated their visions of what is there and what it means. There is no need for any background introductions to these extraordinary vignettes. From the first page of each one, you will begin to know both a remarkable child and a remarkable grownup, and you will know them better than you know some of your real-life acquaintances.

Jack McGarvey, a New York City secondary
school director, tells why "the lover's
formula" is so important for teachers.

BY JACK MCGARVEY

"It takes discipline to keep me from failing the children
who are in my school. I think I know now just when that
moment of failure might come. It will come when I talk
about a social studies program rather than shy Charlie's
pride when he wrote and produced a play on Colonial
America. It will come when I talk about a math program
rather than the moment little Sharon triumphantly discovered, in her own time and way, the meaning of a
minute. It will come when I retreat to the safety of talking
about the generalizations of curriculum rather than talking
about the humor, pain, joy, and bewilderment of each child
as he goes about making sense of his world."

José
BY GEORGE DENNISON

José had failed in everything. After five years in the public
schools, he could not read, could not do sums, and had no
knowledge even of the most rudimentary history or geography. He was described to us as *having* "poor motivation,"
lacking "reading skills," and (again) *having* "a reading
problem."

Now what are these *entities* he possessed and lacked? Is
there any such thing as "a reading problem," or "motivation," or "reading skills"?

To say "reading problem" is to draw a little circle
around José and specify its contents: syllables, spelling,
grammar, etc.

41

Since we are talking about a real boy, we are talking about real books, too, and real teachers and real classrooms. And real boys, after all, do not read syllables but words; and words, even printed words, have the property of voice; and voices do not exist in a void, but in very clearly indicated social classes.

By what process did José and his schoolbook come together? Is this process part of his reading problem?

Who asks him to read the book? *Someone* asks him. In what sort of voice and for what purpose, and with what concern or lack of concern for the outcome?

And who wrote the book? For whom did they write it? Was it written for José? Can José actually partake of the life the book seems to offer?

And what of José's failure to read? We cannot stop at the fact that he draws a blank. How does he do it? What does he do? It is impossible, after all, for him to sit there *not listening*. He is sitting there doing something. Is he daydreaming? If so, of what? Aren't these particular daydreams part of José's reading problem? Did the teacher ask him what he was thinking of? Is his failure to ask part of José's reading problem?

Printed words are an extension of speech. To read is to move outward toward the world by means of speech. Reading is conversing. But what if this larger world is frightening and insulting? Should we, or should we not, include fear and insult in José's reading problem?

And is there a faculty in the mind devoted to the perception and recollection of *abc?* Or is there just one intelligence, modified by pleasure, pain, hope, etc. Obviously José has little skill in reading, but as I have just indicated, reading is no small matter of syllables and words. Then reading skills are no small matter either. They, too, include his typical relations with adults, with other children, and with himself; for he is fiercely divided within himself, and this conflict lies at the very heart of his reading problem.

José's reading problem is José. Or to put it another way, there is no such thing as a reading problem. José hates books, schools, and teachers, and among a hundred other insufficiencies—*all of a piece*—he cannot read. Is this a reading problem?

A reading problem, in short, is not a fact of life, but a fact of school administration. It does not describe José, but describes the action performed by the school, i.e., the action of ignoring everything about José except his response to printed letters.

Let us do the obvious thing for a change, and take a look at José. This little glimpse of his behavior is what a visitor might have seen during José's early months at the First Street School.

He is standing in the hallway talking to Vicente and Julio. I am sitting alone in the classroom, in one of the students' chairs. There is a piece of paper in front of me, and on it a sentence of five words. The words appear again below the sentence in three columns, so that each word is repeated a number of times. Now since José came to us with a reading problem, let us see what relation we can find between these one dozen syllables and the extraordinary behavior he exhibits.

He had been talking animatedly in the hall. Now as he comes to join me, his face contracts spasmodically and the large gestures of his arms are reduced to almost nothing. There is no one near him, and he is absolutely free to refuse the lesson, yet he begins to squirm from side to side as if someone were leading him by the arm. He hitches up his pants, thrusts out his lower lip, and fixes his eyes on the floor. His forehead is lumpy and wrinkled like that of a man suffering physical pain. His eyes have glazed over.

43

Suddenly he shakes himself, lifts his head, and squares his shoulders. But his eyes are still glassy. He yawns abruptly and throws himself into the chair beside me, sprawling on the tip of his spine. But now he turns to me and smiles his typical smile, an outrageous bluff, yet brave and attractive. "Okay, man—let's go." I point to the sentence and he
· rattles it off, for his memory is not bad and he recalls it clearly from the day before. When I ask him to read the same words in the columns below, however, he repeats the sentence angrily and jabs at the columns with his finger, for he had not read the sentence at all but had simply remembered it. He guffaws and blushes. Now he sits up alertly and crouches over the paper, scanning it for clues: smudges, random pencil marks, his own doodles from the day before. He throws me sagacious glances, trying to interpret the various expressions on my face. He is trying to reconstruct in his mind *the entire sequence* of yesterday's lesson, so that the written words will serve as clues to the spoken ones, and by repeating the spoken ones he will be able to seem to read. The intellectual energy—and the acumen—he puts into this enterprise would more than suffice for learning to read. It is worth mentioning here that whenever he comes upon the written word "I," he is thrown into confusion, though in conversation he experiences no such difficulty.

Now what are José's problems? One of them, certainly, is the fact that he cannot read. But this problem is obviously caused by other, more fundamental problems; indeed, his failure to read should not be described as a problem at all, but a symptom. We need only look at José to see what his problems are: shame, fear, resentment, rejection of others and of himself, anxiety, self-contempt, loneliness. None of these was caused by the difficulty of reading printed words —a fact all the more evident if I mention here that José, when he came to this country at the age of seven, had been able to read Spanish and had regularly read to his mother (who cannot read) the post cards they received from the literate father who had remained in Puerto Rico. For five years he had sat in the classrooms of the public schools literally growing stupider by the year. He had failed at everything (not just reading) and had been promoted from one grade to another in order to make room for the children who were more or less doomed to follow in his footsteps.

Obviously not all of José's problems originated in school. But given the intimacy and freedom of the environment at First Street, his school-induced behavior was easy to observe. He could not believe, for instance, that anything contained in books, or mentioned in classrooms, belonged by rights to himself, or even belonged to the world at large, as trees and lampposts belong quite simply to the world we all live in. He believed, on the contrary, that things dealt with in school belonged somehow to school, or were administered by some far-reaching bureaucratic arm. There had been no indication that he could share in them, but rather that he would be measured against them and be found wanting. Nor did he believe that he was entitled to personal consideration, but felt rather that if he wanted to speak, either to a classmate or to a teacher, or wanted to stand up and move his arms and legs, or even wanted to urinate, he must do it more or less in defiance of authority. During his first weeks at our school he was belligerent about the most innocuous things. Outside of school he had learned many games, as all children do, unaware that they are engaged in "the process of learning." Inside the school this ability deserted him. Nor had it ever occurred to him that one might deliberately go about the business of learning something, for he had never witnessed the whole forms of learning. What he had seen was reciting, copying, answering questions, taking tests—and these, alas, do not add up to learning. Nor could he see any connection between school and his life at home and in the streets. If he had heard our liberal educators confessing manfully, "We are not getting through to them," he would have winced with shame and anger at that little dichotomy "we/them," for he had been exposed to it in a hundred different forms.

One would not say that he had been schooled at all, but rather that for five years he had been indoctrinated in the contempt of persons, for contempt of persons had been the supreme fact demonstrated in the classrooms, and referred alike to teachers, parents, and children. For all practical purposes, José's inability to learn consisted precisely of his school-induced behavior.

It can be stated axiomatically that the schoolchild's chief expense of energy is self-defense against the environment. When this culminates in impairment of growth—and it almost always does—it is quite hopeless to reverse the trend by teaching phonics instead of Look-Say. The environment itself must be changed.

When I used to sit beside José and watch him struggling with printed words, I was always struck by the fact that he had such difficulty in even *seeing* them. I knew from medical reports that his eyes were all right. It was clear that his physical difficulties were the sign of a terrible conflict. On the one hand he did not *want* to see the words, did not want to focus his eyes on them, bend his head to them, and hold his head in place. On the other hand he wanted to learn to read again, and so he forced himself to perform these actions. But the conflict was visible. It was as if a barrier of smoked glass had been interposed between himself and the words: he moved his head here and there, squinted, widened his eyes, passed his hand across his forehead. The barrier, of course, consisted of the chronic emotions I have already mentioned: resentment, shame, self-contempt, etc. But how does one remove such a barrier? Obviously it cannot be done just in one little corner of a boy's life at school. It must be done throughout his life at school. Nor can these chronic emotions be removed as if they were cysts, tumors, or splinters. Resentment can only be made to yield by supporting the growth of trust and by multiplying incidents of satisfaction; shame, similarly, will not vanish except as self-respect takes its place. Nor will embarrassment go away simply by proving to the child that there is no need for embarrassment; it must be replaced by confidence and by a more generous regard for other persons. It need hardly be said that when these transformations take place, the child's ability to learn, like his ability to play and to relate positively to his peers and elders, will increase spectacularly. But what conditions in the life at school will support these so desirable changes? Obviously they cannot be taught. Nor will better methods of instruction lead to them, or better textbooks.

When, after ten minutes of a reading lesson, José said to me that he wanted to go to the gym, and I said, "Okay," a little revolution began in his soul. His teacher respected his wishes! This meant, did it not, that the teacher took him seriously as a person? It became easier for José to take himself seriously as a person. And when he cursed, bullied, fought with classmates, and the teachers responded only with their own emotions, not ever with formal punishment, demerits, detention, etc., did it not mean that they were encountering him precisely as he was, and that in order to face them he did not first have to suppress everything but his good behavior? He could stand on his own two feet; they could stand on theirs. His anxiety diminished, and his resentment—and his confusion.

The gradual changes in José's temperament proceeded from the whole of our life at school, not from minuscule special programs designed expressly for José's academic

47

problems. And not the least important feature of this life (it was quite possibly the most important) was the effect of the other children on him. I mean that when adults stand out of the way so children can develop among themselves the full riches of their natural relationships, their effect on one another is positively curative.

Renee

BY MAYZETTE E. STOVER

The bell rang, and my seven-year-olds flocked into the room with the usual morning ritual: "Guess what? Lemme tell you!" "I gotta . . ." "He pushed me!" "Kin I go to the lost and found?"

Close behind them came the principal, bearing the information that a new child would be arriving within the next half hour.

She handed me a folder marked "Confidential" and whispered, "You'd better read this before she gets here."

I hastily absorbed the key words: "Raped . . . beaten by mother . . . hospitalized . . . ward of the state . . . foster home."

Like most teachers, I had read newspaper accounts about battered children, but the victims never seemed real. They were cardboard characters in a flat world, particularly in our quiet suburban community. Our area is naturally and comfortably an ethnic catchall, and we have escaped both the explosiveness of the ghettos and the unrest of more affluent neighborhoods.

I slipped the report into my desk drawer and told the children that a girl named Renee was joining our class. All energy was immediately channeled into readying a welcome for the newcomer. Joanne, front teeth missing, yellow hair veiling bright blue eyes, wrote, "Be my friend!"

48

Victoria, brown skin almost iridescent, copied out the spelling words so that Renee could catch up.

With the authority of experience, Tony stated, "Everybody makes mistakes!" So saying, he bit his eraser in half and placed the damp offering on top of the empty desk.

There were footsteps in the hall. All faces turned—curious, smiling, excited.

Renee stood poised at the threshold of the room. She was slender, of a deep cinnamon color, pigtails askew.

Reflected in those dark eyes was her vision of us. We were her enemies. White faces! Black faces! Teacher face! One hand clutched at her stomach as if she were in pain.

"Hello, Renee! Come in! Your . . ."

My greeting was interrupted by garrulous Barbara. "Hey, she's Miss Jamison's latest from state welfare. She got nobody but ol' Miss Jamison, my mother say."

Renee turned to the voice. "Damn!" she screamed. "Damn! Damn!" I could almost see the knotted ball of hate and fear inside her.

Her delicate hand caught the vase of flowers on the bookcase. She hurled it to the floor and observed the wreckage. She'd smashed it. Water flowed in all directions. Glass with jagged points. The flowers crushed. She smiled, and the tension in her body eased.

All eyes now turned to me, waiting for my reaction. "Never mind, Renee. Come, sit down. We'll clean up later," I said as quietly and soothingly as I could.

With a quick movement, Renee leaned over and picked an aster from the debris. Tenderly she brushed off the broken glass. Still holding the flower, she walked to the indicated desk and sat down. Her hand clutched at her stomach again.

"Do you hurt?" I reached out tentatively, but she pulled away from me. I had never seen such an expression of hate and fear.

"When you want me, I'm here," I said. "Maybe I can help you." But she had turned to the flower. She touched it gently with a long, brown finger. I saw there was peace.

I rallied the class, shushed their comments, and we turned our attention to the day's plans. What tasks had priority and who was working on what projects? My mind wandered from the discussion. The meaning of those words in the confidential report suddenly hit home. The victim of a tabloid news item was real. Renee, this child, obsessed with pain and rage, occupied a place in my second grade. And somehow I was to help her, and I didn't know how.

During the next few weeks, Renee's behavior pattern became an established part of our school life. There would be sudden crises. Books would fly across the room. Her desk would crash noisily to the floor. She never hurt anyone nor did she try. She seemed for the most part unaware of our presence, even when we spoke to her directly. Her response was always the same: "Damn!"

We learned to work around her rage, getting lessons done between outbursts. While we worked, she stared out the window, smoldering, or she would pace back and forth across the room.

She never came to school on time but slipped in after everyone else was busy. In a way, this was fortunate, because it gave me an opportunity to help the other children accept her. I explained that she was very unhappy and needed our patience.

"Keep talking to her," I suggested.

"Kinda hard when all she says is 'damn,' " said Tony.

"When I hand out even the most fun kind of paper, she just tears it up," complained Barbara.

"Just pretend she wants them."

I invited Miss Agatha Jamison, Renee's foster parent, to a conference. Painfully she hobbled into the room. She was old, kindly, and overflowing with soft, warm flesh.

"Time," she soothed me. "It takes time when you been hurt real bad." I agreed.

"You ever had trouble?" She looked at me speculatively. I nodded. "But nothing as cruel as this."

"Well, then, maybe you know something about feelin's. We'll try, you and me, to help. Bes' we can! We got to be kind and firm!"

Our interview was finished. I had to give her both my hands to ease her to her feet.

"I'm too old, maybe. I wasn't supposed to take no more children. But this one needs me bad, the state lady say."

"Oh, I meant to ask you. What about the pain in her stomach?"

"The doctor say that is just her sorrow sort of boilin' inside her. Then there's them welts over her body. I keep puttin' on the ointment. What that man done make her feel ugly. The beatin's her mother gave her hurt lots. But worst was that people suppose to love her got no use for her. That's the pain she can't get out."

Then Miss Jamison left, leaving courage, insight, and direction behind her.

The first change I saw in Renee came about because of a doll clown named Pixie. Anyone in the class can write Pixie letters, and he obligingly answers all such mail—a Dear Abby of the second grade. I ghost his answers in hopes that I may give children some understanding of their problems—the new baby, the big brother tease; now and then, something more serious.

Renee had been restlessly pacing back and forth on this afternoon. She paused at Pixie's house and grabbed him. Doubling up one fist, holding him in the other hand, she beat him until her inner fire burned out. Some of the children were close to tears. Others protested loudly.

Then she hugged him gently and took him to her desk. "I'm sorry, Pixie. I didn't mean it."

51

I reassured the class. "Pixie is all right. See, she's sorry."

The incident proved to be the first breakthrough. The child had actually related to something, if only a doll. "Can't we get her to a psychologist?" I pleaded with the principal. "She needs so much more help than we can give her."

Everyone was sympathetic. And everyone was helpless: The appropriate state social-service agencies were booked a full year ahead.

"What about local agencies?" I asked. But we learned that if a child is a ward of the state, then she can receive only state aid. We were snarled in the red tape of understaffed and overloaded agencies.

Worse, the children were tired of Renee's tantrums, and I found myself near exhaustion. Yet each day, Renee took Pixie to her desk and played with him in little-girl fashion.

The second breakthrough came unexpectedly. Renee arrived early with a folded note in her hand and furtively crammed it into Pixie's mailbox.

I could hardly wait until noon. As soon as the children had left, I rushed for the letter.

Dear Pixie: You hate me. I ugly! I bad. Renee

I wrote and rewrote my answer and illustrated it with pictures of Pixie and Renee smiling at each other. I used few words. I wasn't sure how much she could read.

Dear Renee: You are my friend. You are not bad, just a little bit bad like I am. Write again. Love, Pixie

The next morning, Renee, far from being late, was at school before the other children.

"Good morning," I said cheerfully.

She ignored me, grabbed the note from Pixie and eagerly read it. When the class entered, Renee was busy writing another letter.

I shushed the other children.

52

At noon, I deciphered her note, full of misspellings and smudged erasures.

Dear Pixie: You think I a nut. I mean to you. I mean to the teacher. You be happy if I go. Your bes chil

" 'Your bes chil.' " I laughed aloud and at the same time was painfully sad. How much she must want to be a "bes' chil'."

Thereafter, the mailbox was filled with her letters, pouring out her feelings of self-revulsion and her pleas for acceptance. She never referred to her terrible experiences.

The tantrums continued. It was not easy to remain calm. One day, I lost my temper. Eyes flashing, face red, I bellowed at her to stop this ridiculous behavior.

The children were stunned. As for Renee, she clutched her stomach and looked so full of anguish that I hated myself.

At three o'clock I stormed into the principal's office and promptly burst into tears. "Probably she won't even come to school tomorrow," I sobbed. "I've ruined everything."

But the following morning, there she was, and she began to write immediately.

Dear Pixie: She two teachers. One laugh like little girl but not little girl. The other ugly, angry at me. You think she like me? Your bes chil

My answer took the entire lunch hour to compose.

Dear Renee: Sometimes the teacher gets angry. Sometimes she is sad. Mostly she is happy. But she always loves you. So do I. Love, Pixie

Renee read the note. Her black eyes twinkled. She then wrote:

Dear Pixie: You know I can read? The teacher don' know. I fool her. Your bes chil

Dear Renee: Why don't you find a book first thing tomorrow and let's surprise that teacher. Love, Pixie

53

The next morning, with Pixie tucked under one arm, Renee chose an easy reader. She approached my desk with a smug look. Words came slowly, but there was no doubt about it—she could read. I reached out to pat her approvingly. I knew better than to touch her, but in my elation, I forgot. She threw the book to the floor and became a whirlwind of rage. But later that day, there was another letter in the mailbox.

Dear Pixie: The teacher sad! I part bad! I part good! Why I be like this? Your bes chil

Dear Renee: The teacher is sad because she scared you. She didn't mean to. She's happy you can read. Everybody is part good and part bad. Love, Pixie

The next two weeks were filled with happy events. Renee read daily. She smiled at the children and said hi to me each morning.

Another breakthrough occurred when Joanne came to school one day looking pale and tired. "Are you all right?" I asked.

"My daddy's sick in the hospital," sobbed Joanne.

I did my best to soothe her. At recess time we headed for the playground. Joanne was red-eyed but under control.

"Git outta my way," said Renee roughly. She pushed herself ahead of several children. There was a brief scuffle, then Renee reached Joanne's side. She took her hand. "I'm your friend," she said.

After that the girls were inseparable. The volume of Pixie's mail decreased now that Renee had found Joanne. There were still periods of anger and despair. But now she disrupted the class with boisterous activity and mischief that was closer to normal behavior.

So we were progressing, and one morning, I sensed that this day was going to be wonderful. I knew it as soon as Renee whirled into the classroom.

"I'm gonna be bud of promise," she shouted. "I'll have a

white dress. Everybody will say, 'Renee is bud of promise.' "

"What is . . . ?" I began. She interrupted me.

"Me and Aunt Agatha, we go to church every Sunday. The minister, he say, 'Renee and some others going to be buds of promise.' "

"I got to be one last year," beamed Victoria.

"Hmmmm!" said Renee, with a little-girl toss of her head. "You're not so smart. How could I last year, when I wasn' even here?"

In my mind, I could see Aunt Agatha's slow, painful walk to church with Renee dancing beside her.

I had visited Miss Agatha Jamison at home during those months. Each visit gave me renewed courage. But I was worried about her health. How much longer could this elderly lady take care of Renee?

Then one terrible Friday, Renee came to school in a somber mood. She immediately began to write a letter. She handed it directly to me.

Dear Teacher: Aunt Agatha is very sick. Renee

For the rest of the morning she brooded silently. I tried to talk to her, but she would not answer. At lunchtime, I called Miss Jamison's house, but there was no answer. When Renee did not return to school in the afternoon, the secretary phoned a neighbor.

"Miss Jamison has been taken to the hospital in an ambulance. Something wrong with her insides," the neighbor reported.

Renee was staying with them until the state lady got there.

At three o'clock, I checked. Renee had been whisked away. The social worker had arrived, packed the few belongings and left with her charge.

I called the welfare office. "Don't worry," I was assured. "She will be placed with a family."

"May we write to her?" I asked.

55

"Oh, no. That only confuses the children."

"Of course, she will visit Aunt Agatha," I speculated hopefully, "or write her."

"No, that won't be allowed. We know what's best. All former contacts have to be cut off." She was courteous but firm.

On Monday when I returned to school, Renee's empty desk and a limp, lifeless Pixie confronted me. I felt a helpless sense of loss.

I knew that somewhere there was a slender child, of deep cinnamon color, pigtails askew, standing at the threshold of her new class, carrying within her a hard knot of pain, fear and sorrow.

As she scans the faces, please let her see one that looks something like Joanne's. And a boy as mischievous as Tony. Another little girl with a gentle smile like Victoria's. Let the teacher welcome her and have more wisdom than I.

But if she clutches her stomach, and can see only white faces, black faces, teacher face, menacing and hateful, then please let there be a flower to give her a moment of peace.

Luther

BY JAY NEUGEBOREN

Luther arrived at Booker T. Washington Junior High School (Columbus Avenue and 107th Street, Manhattan) in September of 1955, six months before I did. I met him at the end of February, the third week I taught there, when one of the assistant principals asked me to cover the cafeteria during fifth period for a teacher who had to be at a conference. "Good luck with the animals," I remember him saying.

I was on my guard when I entered the cafeteria; perhaps even a trifle scared. The stories I had been hearing in the teachers' lounge had prepared me to expect anything. During the winter months the students were not allowed to leave the lunchroom and the results of keeping them penned in—the fights, the food-throwing, the high-pitched incessant chattering in Spanish, the way the Negro and Puerto Rican boys and girls chased each other around the tables—such things did, I had to admit, give the room a zoo-like quality.

The day I was assigned, however, was a Catholic holy day and many of the students were absent. Those who remained filled a little less than half of the large room and though they were noisy, it was relatively easy to keep them in order. Luther sat at a table by himself, near the exit to the food-line. Occasionally, I noticed, a few boys would come and sit next to him. The third time I patrolled his area, however, his table was empty and he stopped me.

"Hey, man," he said, poking me in the arm to get my attention, "you new here?"

He had a stack of about ten cookies in his other hand and he put one into his mouth as he waited for an answer. When I told him that I was not new, he nodded and looked at me. "You have any trouble yet?"

"No," I said, as sternly as possible. Despite my feelings of sympathy for the students, I knew that if I ever hoped to get anywhere with them, I had to appear tough and confident. "No," I repeated, almost, I recall, as if I were challenging him. "I haven't."

Luther cocked his head to one side then and smiled slowly. "You will," he said, and went back to his cookies.

In the teachers' lounge, the first time I told the story, somebody asked if the boy who had stopped me was a little Negro kid, very black, with a slight hunchback. I said he was. The teachers laughed. "That's Luther," one of them said.

"He's batty," said another. "Just leave him be."

I repeated the story endlessly. It was the first anecdote of my teaching experience that excited admiration and some sort of reaction from those I told it to, and this was important to me then. I had no more direct encounters with Luther that term, though I did see him in the halls, between classes. I always smiled at him and he would smile back—or at least I thought he did. I could never be sure. This bothered me, especially the first time it happened. Through my retelling of the story, I realized, he had become so real to me, so much a part of my life that I think I took it for granted that our encounter had assumed equal significance in his life. The possibility that he had not even repeated the story to a single one of his friends disturbed me.

Once or twice during the term I spotted him wandering around the halls while classes were in session, slouching down the corridor, his body pressed against the tile walls. When I asked the other teachers if he was known for cutting classes, they told me again to just leave him be—that the guidance counselor had suggested that the teachers let him do what he wanted to. He was harmless, they said, *if* you left him alone. Those teachers who had him in their classes agreed with the guidance counselor. Left alone, he didn't annoy them. When he wanted to, he worked feverishly—and did competent work; but when he did not want to work he would either sit and stare, or just get up, walk out of the room, and wander around the building. He was, they concluded, a mental case.

I returned to Booker T. Washington Junior High School the following September, and Luther turned up in one of my English classes. He had changed. He was no longer small, having grown a good five inches over the summer, and he was no longer quiet. When classwork bored him now he would stand up, and instead of leaving the room, would begin telling stories. Just like that. He had favorite topics too—his cousin Henry who had epilepsy, Willie Mays, what was on sale at the supermarket, the football team he played on, the stories in the latest *Blackhawk* comic book. When he ran out of stories, he would pull *The National Enquirer* out of his back pocket and begin reading from it, always starting with an item in the "Personals" columns that had caught his eye. I never knew what to do. When I would yell at him to sit down and be quiet, he would wave his hand at me, impatiently, and continue. Moreover, no expression on his face, nothing he ever said, indicated that he thought he was doing anything wrong. An hour after disrupting a class, if I would see him in the corridor, he would give me a big smile and a hello. After a while, of course, I gave up even trying to interrupt him. I listened with the other students—laughing, fascinated, amazed.

I tried to remember some of his stories, but when I retold them they never seemed interesting, and so I purposely gave Luther's class a lot of composition work, trying to make the topics as imaginative as possible—with the hope, of course, that he would use one of them to let loose. But all of the topics, he declared, were "stupid" and he refused to write on any of them. Then, when I least expected it, when I assigned the class a "How To—" composition, he handed one in. It was typewritten on a piece of lined notebook paper, single-spaced, beginning at the very top of the page and ending just at the first ruled line. It was titled "How to Steal Some Fruits":

> *How To Steal Some Fruits, by Luther*
> Go to a fruit store and when the fruitman isn't looking take some fruits. Then run. When the fruitman yells "Hey you stop taking those fruits" run harder. That is how to steal some fruits.

The next day he sat quietly in class. When I looked at him, he looked down at his desk. When I called on him to answer a question, he shrugged and looked away. At three o'clock, however, no more than five seconds after I had returned from escorting my official class downstairs, he bounded into my room, full of life, and propped himself up on the edge of my desk.

"Hey man," he said. "How'd you like my composition? It was deep, wasn't it?"

"Deep?"

"Deep, swift, *cool*—you know."

"I liked it fine," I said, laughing.

"Ah, don't put me on, man—how *was* it?"

"I liked it," I repeated, my hands clasped in front of me. "I mean it."

His face lit up. "You mean it? I worked hard on it, Mister Carter. I swear to God I did." It was the first time, I remember, that he had ever addressed me by my name. He stopped and wiped his mouth. "How'd you like the typing? Pretty good, huh?"

"It was fine."

"Christ, man," he said, stepping down from my desk and moving to the blackboard. He picked up a piece of chalk and wrote his name, printing it in capital letters. "How come you so tight? Why don't you loosen up? I ain't gonna do nothing. I just want to know about my composition. That's all."

I felt I could reach him, talk to him. I wanted to—had wanted to for some time, uncomfortable, embarrassed. "Where'd you get a typewriter?" I offered.

He smiled. "Where I get fruits," he replied, then laughed and clapped his hands. I must have appeared shocked, for before I could say anything, he was shaking his head back and forth. "Oh, man," he said. "You are really deep. I

60

swear. You really are." He climbed onto my desk again. "You mind talking?"

"No," I said.

"Good. Let me ask you something—you married?"

"No," I said. "Do you think I should be married?"

"It beats stealing fruits," he said, and laughed again. His laugh was loud and harsh and at first it annoyed me, but then his body began rocking back and forth as if his comment had set off a chain of jokes that he was telling himself silently, and before I knew it I was laughing with him.

"I really liked the composition," I said. "In fact, I hope you don't mind, but I've already read it to some of the other teachers."

"No shit."

"They thought it was superb."

"It's superb," he said, shaking his head in agreement. "Oh, it's superb, man," he said, getting up again and walking away. His arms and legs moved in different directions and he seemed so loose that when he turned his back to me and I noticed the way his dirty flannel shirt was stretched tightly over his misshapen back, I was surprised—as if I'd noticed it for the first time. He walked around the room, muttering to himself, tapping on desks with his fingertips, and then he headed for the door. "I'm superb," he said. "So I be rolling on my superb way home—"

"Stay," I said.

He threw his arms apart. "You win!" he declared. "I'll stay." He came back to my desk, looked at me directly, then rolled his eyes and smiled. "People been telling stories to you about me?"

"No."

"None?" he questioned, coming closer.

"All right," I said. "Some—"

"That's all right," he said, shrugging it off. He played

61

with the binding of a book that was on my desk. Then he reached across and took my grade book. I snatched it away from him and he laughed again. "Oh, man," he exclaimed. "I am just so restless!—You know what I mean?"

He didn't wait for an answer, but started around the room again. The pockets of his pants were stuffed and bulging, the cuffs frayed. The corner of a red and white workman's handkerchief hung out of a back pocket. He stopped in the back of the room, gazed into the glass bookcase, and then turned to me and leaned back. "You said to stay—what you got to say?"

The question was in my mind, and impulsively I asked it: "Just curious—do you remember me from last year?"

"Sure," he said, and turned his back to me again. He looked in the bookcase, whirled around and walked to the side of the room, opening a window. He leaned out and just as I was about to say something to him about it, he closed it and came back to the front of the room. "Man," he exclaimed, sitting on my desk again. "Were you ever scared that day! If I'd set off a cherry bomb you'd have gone through the fan." He put his face closer to mine. "Man, you were scared green!"

"Was I scared of you, Luther?" I asked, looking straight into his eyes.

"Me? Nah. Nothing to be scared of." He hopped off the desk and wiped his name off the blackboard with the palm of his hand, then he started laughing to himself. He looked at me over his shoulder. "Bet I know what you're thinking now," he said.

"Go ahead—"

"You're thinking you'd like to *help* a boy like me. Right? You're getting this big speech ready in your head about—"

"No," I interrupted. "I wasn't."

He eyed me suspiciously. "You sure?"

62

"I'm sure."

"Not even with compositions? Oh man, if you'd help me with compositions, before we'd be through with me, I'd be typing like a whiz." He banged on a desk with his palms and then his fingers danced furiously on the wood as he made clicking noises inside his mouth. "Ding!" he said, swinging the carriage across. "Ain't it fun to type!"

"Okay," I said. "Okay. Maybe I was thinking that I would like to help you."

"I knew it, man," he said, to himself. "I just knew it."

"You have a good mind, Luther—much better than you let on."

"I do, I do," he muttered, chuckling. I stood up and went to the closet to get my coat. "Okay. What do I get if I work for you?" he asked.

I shrugged. "Nothing, maybe. I can't promise anything."

"I *like* that, man," he said.

"Could you call me Mister Carter?" I asked, somewhat irritably. "I don't call you, 'hey, you'—"

"Okay, Mister Carter," he said. He took my coat sleeve. "Let me help you on with your coat, Mister Carter."

We walked out of the room and I locked the door. "You ain't a *real* social worker like the others," he commented as we started down the stairs. He held the door open for me. "I do like that." I nodded.

"Playing it close to the vest again, huh? Tight-mouthed."

"Just thinking," I said.

When we were outside he asked me what he had to do.

"For what?" I asked.

"To get you to help me to be somebody, to educate myself—all that stuff."

"Do what you want to do," I said. "Though you might start by doing your homework. Then we'll see—"

"I know," he said, cocking his head to one side again. "If

63

I play ball with you you'll play ball with me. Right? Okay, okay. I know."

Then he was gone, running down the street, his arms spread wide as if he were an airplane, a loud siren-like noise rising and falling from him as he disappeared from view.

The next few months were without doubt the most satisfying to me of any during the eight years I've been a teacher. Luther worked like a fiend. He was bright, learned quickly, and was not really that far behind. He did his homework, he paid attention in class, he studied for tests, and he read books. That was most important. On every book he read I asked him to write a book report: setting, plot, theme, characters, and his opinion of the book—and once a week, on Thursday afternoons, we would get together in my room for a discussion. During the remainder of the term he must have gone through at least forty to fifty books. Most of them had to do with sports, airplanes, and insects. All the reports came to me typed, and on some he drew pictures—"illustrations" he called them, which, he claimed, would be a help to me in case I had not read the book.

When we would finish talking about books, I would help him with his other subjects, and his improvement was spectacular. I looked forward to my sessions with him, to his reports, to just seeing him—yet from day to day, from moment to moment, I always expected him to bolt from me, and this pleased me. Every time he came to me for a talk I was truly surprised.

When the term ended he asked if I would continue to help him. I said I would. He was not programmed for any of my English classes during the spring term, but we kept up our weekly discussions. As the weather improved, however, he read less and less; I didn't want him to feel as if he *had* to come see me every Thursday, and so, about a week before the opening of the baseball season, I told him that I thought he had reached the point where he could go it alone. "When you feel like talking, just come knocking—" I said. "We don't need a schedule." He seemed relieved, I thought, and I was proud that I had had the sense to release him from any obligation he might have felt.

Then, suddenly, I didn't see him anywhere for three weeks. I asked his home-room teacher about him and she said she hadn't seen him either; she had sent him a few postcards, but had received no reply. That very night—it was almost as if he had been there listening, I thought—he telephoned me at home.

"Is this Mister Carter? This is Luther here."

"Hi, Luther," I said.

"I looked you up in the telephone book. You mind me calling you at home?"

"No, no. I don't mind."

"Okay," he said, breathing hard. "I just wanted to let you know not to worry about me because I'm not in school. Okay?"

"Sure," I said. "Sure."

"I had some things to take care of—you know?"

"Sure," I said.

"Man, you *know* you're itching to ask me *what?*" He laughed. "You are deep. I'll be back Monday."

That was all. On Monday, as he had promised, he returned to school and came to visit me in my room at three o'clock. We talked for a while about the way the pennant race was going, and then he said, "Okay, let's cut the jazz, man. I got something to say to you." He seemed very intense about it and I told him that I was listening carefully. He pointed a finger at me. "Now, we stopped our sessions, right?"

"Right," I said.

"And the day after we stopped, I began to play the hook for three straight weeks, right?"

"Right."

"Okay. Now you can tell me it ain't so, but I'll bet you'll be thinking it was your fault. It ain't. If you want the truth, I ain't done a stick of work all term for *any* teacher—so don't go thinking that I stopped being a good student cause we stopped our meetings."

He let out a long breath. "I'm glad you told me," I said.

"Shit, man," he said, getting up and going to the door. "Don't *say* anything, huh? Why you got to *say* something all the time?" He came toward me. *"Why?"* He was almost screaming and I slid my chair back from the desk. He shook his head frantically. "Why, man?" he said. He reached into his side-pocket and I started to stand up. Abruptly, he broke into laughter. "Oh man, you are deep! You are just so deep!" He clapped his hands and laughed at me some more. "Ra-ta-tat-tat!" he said as he banged on a desk. "You're real sweet, man! Just so sweet! Ra-ta-tat-tat! Comin' down the street!" He sat down in one of the seats. "But don't worry none. I got seven liberry cards now and books growing out the ceiling. I got a liberry card for Luther King and one for Luther Queen and one for Luther Prince and one for Luther Jones and one for Luther Smith and one for Luther Mays and one for Luther B. Carter." He banged on the top of the desk with his fist, then drummed with his fingers again. "But don't you worry none—ra-ta-tat-tat—just don't you worry—"

"I'm not," I said.

"That's all," he said, and dashed out of the room.

He attended classes regularly for about two weeks and then disappeared again for a week. He returned for a few days, stayed away, returned. The pattern continued. In the halls when we saw each other he would always smile and ask if I was worrying and I would tell him I wasn't. Once or twice, when he was absent, he telephoned me at home and asked me what was new at school. He got a big charge out of this. Then another time, I remember, he came riding through the schoolyard on a bicycle during sixth period, when I was on patrol. "Don't report me, man!" he yelled and rode right back out, waving and shouting something in Spanish that made everybody laugh.

Near the end of May, the assistant principal in charge of the eighth grade called me into his office. He knew I was friendly with Luther, he said, and he thought that I might talk to the boy. For the past six or seven months, he told me, Luther had been in and out of juvenile court. "Petty thefts," the assistant principal explained. I wasn't surprised; Luther had hinted at this many times. I had never pressed him about it, however, not wanting to destroy our relationship by lecturing him. The assistant principal said he didn't care whether I said anything to Luther or not. In fact, he added, he would have been just as happy to get rid of him—but that before he was shipped off to a 600 school or put away somewhere else, he wanted to give me an opportunity to do what I could. More for me, he said, than for Luther.

About a week after this, on a Friday, Luther telephoned me.

"How've you been?" I asked.

"Superb, man," he said. "Hey listen—we ain't been seeing much of each other lately, have we?"

"No—"

"No. Okay. Listen—I got two tickets to see the Giants play tomorrow. You want to come?" I didn't answer immediately. "Come on—yes or no—tickets are going fast—"

67

"I'd like to," I said. "Yes. Only—only I was wondering where you got the money for the tickets?" I breathed out, glad I had said it.

Luther just laughed. "Oh man, you're not gonna be like that, are you? You been listening to too many stories again. That judge from the court must of been gassing with you. Tell you what—you come to the game and I'll tell you where I got the tickets. A deal?"

"A deal."

"Meet you in front of the school at 11 o'clock—I like to get there early to see Willie go through batting practice. Batting practice—that's more fun than the game, sometimes. You know?"

He was waiting for me when I got there a few minutes before 11 the following day. "Let's go," he said, flourishing the tickets. "But don't ask me now, man—let's enjoy the game first. Okay?"

I did enjoy the game. The Giants were playing the Cardinals and to Luther's delight, Willie Mays had one of his better days, going three-for-four at bat, and making several brilliant plays in the field. For most of the game, I was truly relaxed. Along about the eighth inning, however, I began to think about the question again—to wonder when would be the best time to ask it. Luther, it seemed, had forgotten all about it. The Giants were winning 5–2.

"Oh man," he said. "If only that Musial don't do something, we're home free. Look at Willie!" he exclaimed. "Ain't he the greatest that ever lived. He is just so graceful! You know? How you like to see a team of Willie Mayses out there? Wow!" Wes Westrum, the Giant catcher, grounded out, short to first, and the eighth inning was over. "One to go, one to go," Luther said. Then he jabbed me in the arm with his finger. "Hey listen—I been thinking. Instead of an All-Star game every year between the leagues, what they

68

ought to do one year is have the white guys against our guys. What you think?"

I shrugged. "I don't know," I said.

"Sure," he said. "Listen—we got Willie in center. Then we put Aaron in right and Doby in left. He's got the raw power. Some outfield, huh? Then we got Compy catching and Newcombe pitching. You can't beat that. That Newcombe—he's a mean son of a bitch, but he throws. Okay. I been thinking about this a long time—" He used his fingers to enumerate. He was excited, happy. "At first base we put Luke Easter, at second—Junior Gilliam, at short—Ernie Banks, and at third base we bring in old Jackie Robinson just to give the team a little class—you know what I mean? Man, what a line-up! Who could you match it with?"

When I said I didn't know, Luther eyed me suspiciously. "C'mon—Musial, Mantle, Williams, Spahn—you name 'em and I'll match 'em, man for man, your guys against ours." He stopped and cheered as a Cardinal popped out to Whitey Lockman at first. "What's the matter—don't you like the idea? Ha! Face it, man, we'd wipe up the field with you. Swish! Swish!" He laughed and slapped me on the knee. "Hey, I know what's bugging you, I bet—" He leaned toward me, cupping his hand over his mouth, and whispered in my ear. "Tell the truth now, would you have ever offered to help me if I wasn't colored?"

"Would I—?" I stopped. "Sure," I said. "Of course I would. Of course—"

Luther smiled; triumphantly, dubiously. "Look," I said. "As long as we're asking questions, let me ask you something."

"About the tickets, right?"

"No," I said. "Forget the tickets. No long lectures, either. Just a question. Just one: how come you steal?"

"Oh, man," he said, laughing. "That's an easy one!—Be-

69

cause I'm not getting what I want and when you don't get what you want, man, you got to take. Don't you know that?"

I stared at him, not sure I had heard right. He winked at me. "Enjoy the ballgame, man! Say hey, Willie!" he shouted, as Mays caught a fly ball, bread-basket style, for the second out. "Ain't he the sweetest!"

A minute later the game was over and the players were racing across the field toward the clubhouse in center field, trying to escape the fans who scrambled after them. "They won't get Willie," Luther said. "He's too swift, too swift."

When we were outside I thanked Luther and told him how much I had enjoyed the game. "How about a Coke or something?" I offered.

"Nah," he said. "I got things to do." He extended his hand quickly and I shook it, the first time we had ever done that. "Okay. You go get spiffed up and get a wife. Time you were married." He tossed his head back and laughed. "Ain't you married yet? No, no. *Smile,* man—how you gonna get a wife, never smiling." He started away, through the crowd. "Stay loose," he called back. "Don't steal no fruits."

I never questioned him again about stealing, but even if I had wanted to, I wouldn't have had much opportunity. He did not come to see me very often the rest of that year. When he returned to school in September of 1958 for his last year of junior high school, he had grown again. But not up. He never did go higher than the five-five or five-six he had reached by that time. He had taken up weightlifting over the summer, however, and his chest, his neck, his arms—they had all broadened incredibly. Instead of the dirty cotton and flannel shirts he had worn the two previous years, he now walked through the halls in laundry-white T-shirts, the sleeves rolled up to the shoulder, his powerful muscles exposed. There were always a half-dozen Negro boys following him around now also, and they all dressed the way he did—white T-shirts, black chino pants, leather wrist straps, and—hanging from their necks on pieces of string—miniature black skulls.

The guidance counselor for the ninth grade came to me one day early in the term and asked me if I could give him any evidence against Luther. He claimed that Luther and his gang were going around the school, beating and torturing those students who refused to "loan" them money. All of the students, he said, were afraid to name Luther. "The kid's a born sadist," he added. I told him I didn't know anything.

The term progressed and the stories and rumors increased. I was told that the police in Luther's neighborhood were convinced that he and his gang were responsible for a series of muggings that had occurred. I tried not to believe it, but Luther all but gave me conclusive proof one afternoon, right before Christmas. He came into my room at three o'clock, alone, and said he had something for me. He said he trusted me not to tell anybody about it or show it to anyone. I said I wouldn't.

"Okay, man—here it is—" His eyes leapt around the room, frenzied, delirious. He took a little card from his wallet. "You might need this sometime—but don't ask me no questions. Ha! And don't you worry none. I'm doing okay. Expanding all the time. Don't you worry." I took the card from him. "See you now, Mister Carter. See you, see you."

He left and I looked at the card. Across the top was printed: THE BLACK AVENGERS, and below it was written: "Don't touch this white man. He's okay." It was signed by Luther and under his name he had drawn a skull and crossbones. I put the card in my wallet.

In January, to no one's great surprise, Luther was sent away to reform school in upstate New York. I was never exactly clear about the precise event that had led to it—the policeman assigned to our school said it had to do with brutally beating an old man; Luther's friends said it had to do with getting caught in a gang war. They claimed the fight was clean but that the cops had framed Luther. There was nothing in the papers, Luther had not contacted me, and I did not find out about it all until he had already been shipped off.

I received a postcard from him that summer. It was brief.

> I hate it here. I can't say anymore or they'll beat shit out of me. I hate it. I'm reading some. I'll visit you when I get out and we'll have a session.

I answered the card with a letter. I told him I was sorry about where he was and that I'd be glad to talk to him whenever he wanted. I gave him some news of the school and included some current baseball clippings. I asked him if there was anything he needed and if there was anybody in his family he wanted me to get in touch with. I told him that in return for the time he'd taken me to the baseball game I had ordered a subscription to *Sport* magazine for him.

He replied with another postcard.

> Visiting day this summer is August 21. I'd like for you to come.

When I arrived, he seemed glad to see me, but I remember that he was more polite than he had ever been before, and more subdued. I wondered, at the time, if they were giving him tranquilizers. I was only allowed an hour with him and we spent most of that time just walking around the grounds—the school was a work-farm reformatory—not saying anything.

The visit, I could tell, was a disappointment to him. I don't know what he expected of me, but whatever it was, I didn't provide it. I wrote him a letter when I got home, telling him I had enjoyed seeing him and that I'd be glad to come again if he wanted me to. He didn't answer it, and I heard no more from him for a year and a half.

Then one day in the spring of 1961, just about the time of the Bay of Pigs invasion of Cuba, I remember, he popped into my room at school. He looked horrible. His face was unshaven, his clothes were filthy and ragged, his eyes were glazed. Underneath his clothes, his body had become flabby and he bent over noticeably when he walked. At first I didn't recognize him.

When I did, I was so glad to see him, I didn't know what to do. "Luther—for crying out loud!" I said, standing up and shaking his hand. "How the hell are you?"

He smiled at me. "I'm superb, man—can't you tell from looking at me?" He laughed then, and I laughed with him.

"You've gotten older," I said.

"Past sixteen," he said. "That means I don't got to go to school no more—"

He waited, but I didn't offer an opinion. "How about going down with me and having a cup of coffee? I'm finished here for the day—just getting through with midterms."

"Nah," he said, looking down and playing with his hands. "I gotta meet somebody. I'm late already. But I was in the neighborhood so I thought I'd come let you know I was still alive." He came to my desk and looked down. He shook his head as if something were wrong.

"What's the matter?" I asked.

"Don't see no wedding ring on your finger yet." He looked straight into my face. "Hey, man—you ain't a fag, are you?"

"No," I said, laughing. "Not that I know of—"

73

He laughed, his mouth opening wide. "Okay. That's all the gas for today. I'll see you, man."

During the next few months he visited me several times. Sometimes he looked good, sometimes bad—but I never could find out what he was doing with his days. He never gave a straight answer to my questions. More and more, I felt that he was asking me for some kind of help, but when I would touch on anything personal or even hint that I wanted to do something for him, with him, he would become defensive.

I didn't see him over the summer, but the following fall he came by periodically. He seemed to be getting a hold on himself, and sometimes he would talk about going to night school. Nothing came of the talk, though. In November he was arrested and sent to Riker's Island—to P.S. 616, the combination prison-school for boys between the ages of sixteen and twenty. His sentence was for eighteen months and during the first three months I visited him twice. Both times all he wanted to do was to talk about the English class we had had, and the stories and compositions he had made up. He said he was trying to remember some of them for the English teacher he had there, but couldn't do it all the time. He seemed to be in terrible shape, and I didn't have much hope for him.

So I was surprised when I began getting postcards from him again. "I am studying hard," the first one said. "There is a Negro who comes here to help me. I like him. I will be a new man when I come out. Yours sincerely, Luther." It was neatly and carefully written. The ones that followed were the same and they came at regular intervals of about five weeks. He told me about books he was reading, most of them having to do with Negro history, and about how he was changing. "Improving" was the word he used most.

I answered his cards as best I could, and offered to come see him again, but he never took up any of my offers. When

74

his eighteen months were up, I expected a visit from him. He never came. Sometimes I wondered what had become of him, but after the first few months passed and I didn't hear from him, I thought about him less and less. A year passed—two since we had last seen each other at Riker's Island—and then we met again.

I spotted him first. It was a beautiful summer night and I had gone up to Lewisohn Stadium for a concert. It had been good, I was relaxed and happy as I walked out of the stadium. Luther was standing at the corner of Amsterdam Avenue and 138th Street. He was wearing a dark blue suit, a white shirt and a tie. He was clean shaven, his hair was cut short, and he looked healthy and bright. He was stopping people and trying to sell them newspapers.

"How are you, Mister Carter?" he asked, when I walked up to him. His eyes were clear and he seemed very happy to see me. "Interested in buying a newspaper to help the colored people? Only a dime."

"No thanks," I said. The paper he was selling, as I had expected, was *Muhammad Speaks,* the newspaper of the Black Muslims. "You look fine," I added.

"Thanks—excuse me a second." He turned and sold a copy to somebody. People snubbed him but this didn't stop him from smiling or trying. I waited. When the crowd had gone, he asked me where I was going. "Home," I said. "Cup of coffee first?"

"No thanks," he said. "Thanks, but no thanks."

"When did all this start?" I asked, motioning to the newspapers.

"At Riker's Island," he said. He put up a hand, as if to stop my thoughts from becoming words. "I know what you're thinking, what you hear on TV and read in the newspapers about us—but don't believe everything. We're essentially a religious organization, as you may not know."

"I know," I said.

"And it's meant a lot to me—I couldn't have made it without their help. They—they taught me to *believe* in myself." His eyes glowed as he twisted his body toward me. "Can you understand that?" It seemed very important to him that I believe him. *"Can* you?" He relaxed momentarily and shrugged. "I don't believe everything they teach, of course, but I follow their precepts: I don't smoke, I don't drink, I don't curse. I don't go out with women who aren't Muslims—I feel good *inside,* Mister Carter. Things are straightening themselves out." He paused. "It hasn't been easy."

"I know," I said, and smiled.

He nodded, embarrassed, I thought. "I'm going back to school also—"

"I'm glad."

"Even my body feels good! I'm lifting weights again, too." he said. Then he laughed and the sound tore through the warm night. His eyes were flashing with delight. "Oh man—someday I'll be the head of a whole damned army! Me and my old hunchback." He laughed again, pleased with himself. Then his laughter subsided and he patted me on the shoulder. "Oh man, you are still so deep, so deep. Don't worry none, Mister Carter. I don't go around advocating no violence." He chuckled. "I've got to go," he said, extending a hand. "It's been good seeing you again. Sure you don't want to buy a copy?"

"I'm sure," I said, shaking his hand. "Good luck to you Luther. I'm glad to see you the way you are now—"

"Thanks." We looked at each other for a minute and he smiled warmly at me. Then I started toward the subway station. When I had crossed the street he called to me.

"Hey—Mister Carter—!"

I turned.

"Let me ask you something—do you still have that card I

76

gave you?" He howled at this remark. "Oh man, I'd save that card if I were you! I'd do that. You never know when you might need it. You never know—"

I started back across the street, toward him. He tossed his head back and roared with laughter. "You never know, you never know," he repeated, and hurried away from me, laughing wildly. I stared at him until he disappeared in the darkness. Then I just stood there, dazed, unable to move—I don't know for how long. Finally I made myself turn around, and as I walked slowly toward the lights of Broadway all I could feel was the presence of his muscular body, powerful, gleaming, waiting under his white shirt, his clean suit.

3

"Do you call *this* a classroom?"

Transforming structure and process

How should a good classroom in action look?

Today the fashion is the "open classroom." We think it offers a lot and is well worth your attention, if you have yet to see it work or to try it yourself. (Some of the selections that follow show how other teachers got into it.)

But neither squatting alongside children nor sitting cross-legged on a rug is equivalent to good teaching. A very casual style (the popularity of which may ultimately depend on the continued popularity of slacks) is merely the outer shell of that respectful, questioning, mind-freeing inner core of the real teacher.

A wise teacher may choose to "open" the structure for only one or two hours a day, perhaps in the one or two subjects that he or she is confident in handling. Other times one may decide to keep the group working together because the support of a group of children learning how to care about one another is more important than the individual discoveries a single child may make. This is the kind of decision that a professional teacher makes every day, matching her experience and capabilities with the experience and maturity of a given group of children.

The answer to "Do you call *this* a classroom?" is: A real classroom is simply an environment where a particular group of children can and does learn important things.

In a classroom in inner-city Boston, Kim Marshall reorganized and decentralized his sixth-grade class. The autonomy and success he had within his classroom led him to conclude that "with tact and a little luck, a good teacher can do a great deal with a group of kids, and the experiences which that teacher has with those kids are for keeps and can't be taken away."

Will it grow in a classroom?

BY KIM MARSHALL

I began my third year at the King School with much less trepidation than the second. I felt that the learning stations were bound to work if I was flexible enough and kept the standard of the material up, and I concentrated on improving the physical layout of the room. My class was 6-D, an expression of confidence from the administration since I had been entrusted with one of the "academic" sections. By November I had accumulated a class of twenty-six kids, and I was struck by how little difference there was between this class and 6-G the year before. Despite the tracking system, both were filled with bright, attractive kids; both had their share of problems.

Within the first month I got rid of all the desks in the room and replaced them with large plywood tables. This proved to be a very cheap way (at seven-and-a-half dollars a table) of creating large amounts of very flexible workspace and making the room seem bigger and quieter (the latter because we could do without all the clanking and banging of the old desks). The tables are eight feet long and four feet wide and five-eighths of an inch thick, and rest on three-foot-high cardboard cylinders which the International Paper factory in Framingham discards every day.

At first the kids had fun sanding down the edges and decorating the surfaces with a myriad of designs, names, and other thoughts. After a while the surfaces of the tables got cluttered with these inscriptions and began to get dirty, so the kids suggested painting them. Within a few weeks almost all the tables were painted as huge flags—most of them the black, red, and green of the black nationalist flag.

There were six tables, one of them for the three typewriters and a resource area with all the games and puzzles, and the other five for groups of kids. The tables lent much more cohesiveness to the groupings the kids had made for themselves, since no one could split apart or be rejected from a group and become isolated by moving an individual desk away from the group. The tables also gave people more room to work and allowed them to spread out and separate from each other while still sitting in a cozy clique.

Another major change was ripping out the closet doors in the back of the room and installing a four-level, twelve-foot-long bookcase. I went and bought some exciting paperbacks and raided my mother's house for other interesting books from Peanuts to picture books on nature and the First World War. I then put all the books on the shelves with their covers facing outward, so that the color and appeal of the paperback jackets was working with me to get the kids reading. (As it turned out, this was not enough, and in November I started a compulsory one-book-a-week program with a book report every Friday.)

After building the bookcase, I put the rug down in the corner next to it and put a magazine rack and filing cabinet on the other side of the rug as a kind of room divider. The typewriter, game table, and rug created a whole section of the room that was devoted to "fun" activities, while the rest of the room was filled with worktables. The division was appropriate and worked well, although the "play" area was perhaps still too noisy for enough reading to take place. At one point I considered buying acoustical tile for the ceiling to deaden the sound in the room somewhat, but decided it was too expensive and would spoil the kids, allowing them to talk louder than they would be able to in other classrooms.

I then bought games and puzzles—Monopoly, Stratego, Scrabble, Quizmo, Soma, Battleship, and many others—and built a lot of small cubbyholes in the middle of the typewriter table to accommodate all of them and other jigsaw puzzles, flash cards, and word games.

With the tables, the bookcase, books, games, and a few more posters, my expenses came to about two hundred dollars (I had spent around a hundred dollars my first year). A little under half of this was covered by a grant from the Educational Collaborative of Greater Boston; the rest came from my own pocket, and from my income from the two magazine articles I had written about my first two years. Some teachers feel that this is about what you should spend out of your own income each year (Steven Daniels suggests a policy of "Teaching on $2.00 a day" in his book, *How 2 Gerbils, 20 Goldfish, 200 Games, 2,000 Books and I Taught Them How to Read*). But clearly there are a lot of teachers with more commitments and less outside income than I had for whom this is grossly unfair. The Philadelphia public schools recently started giving every teacher in the system twenty-five dollars in cash at the beginning of each year to spend on their classrooms. This is not enough, but is a step in the right direction. Perhaps every principal should have discretion over a certain amount of money that could be dispensed to any teacher who submitted a reasonable proposal.

With Grade 6-D I started the learning stations on the second day of school, went through the stage of moving around from station to station, and settled the class into smoothly-functioning groups at five tables. Writing the station worksheets proved a much less arduous task the second year, although there were so many chances to introduce fresh material and improve old material that I found myself in no danger of becoming bored with writing them. I kept one copy of the first year's stations, and was able to improve on them and add to them when I felt creative and fall back on them when I didn't. In my third year my material was meatier and longer and I covered more topics more quickly, but I still tried to "tune" the work to the class day by day.

One change I made was that the Creative Writing was no longer on a sheet like the other station worksheets. Instead, I wrote the title suggestion for the day on one of the remaining patches of usable blackboard at the beginning of the day, and the kids wrote a page every other day in spiral notebooks. This way they could see their progress, and I could get into more of a written give-and-take with them when I read the books. They were not required to write on the topic, and they could copy out of a book if they didn't feel like writing something original. The theory of this comes from Daniel Fader (*Hooked on Books*)—that any writing is better than none and kids will eventually build up enough confidence to launch out on their own writing after they have copied for a while.

One innovation in the learning station sheets was that I numbered each one and had the kids file them in loose-leaf binders when the previous day's work was corrected. This not only gave them good experience in organizing themselves and a feeling of the cumulative work of the year, but also proved the only way to keep the tables neat, since with no desks there was no other place to put papers.

With the stations somewhat meatier and with all the other things there were to do in the classroom, the station time easily filled most of the day, overcoming in a stroke the amorphous residual time that sometimes bothered me the year before. Aside from the correcting at the end of the day, I addressed the whole class not more than five or ten minutes, usually in thirty-second bursts when something came up that I wanted to share with everyone. I continued to use the tape recorder and lyrics of songs in odd moments at the beginning and end of days.

83

The kids were in the room much more than was 6-G because of cutbacks in Art and Industrial Arts and Gym periods and because the Spanish teacher preferred to come to our room and work individually with the kids rather than fighting the whole group in her room. At any given moment in the day, most of the facilities of the room were being used. Walking into the room you would find perhaps half the class busy at work on the station worksheets, some alone, some with groups of friends, some at the tables, others sprawled on the rug; a few kids playing Monopoly and Stratego, one or two doing jigsaw puzzles, a few reading books, three pounding away on the typewriters, and a few talking with me or fooling around. I spent my time the same way I had the first year of stations—talking to individuals or small groups, helping people with their work, and prodding people who didn't look as though they were going to get through it before the end of the day. The atmosphere through most of the day was serene and friendly, with occasional altercations (usually about my "bugging" them about their work) and occasional noisy days when nobody seemed to be in a very good mood.

So basically the year saw the fleshing out of the potential of the learning stations. This process can go on for several more years; there is always something else that can be done in such a flexible setting. Some items on the agenda are: gerbils and fish in the room; curtains in the windows; flower boxes in the windows; more comfortable furniture in the reading area; and many more math and science games and projects. One exciting development was that in November two parents (the mother and aunt of a girl in the class) volunteered to help in the room on a full-time basis. They were initially attracted by the station worksheets the girl was bringing home (especially those dealing with current events such as the Attica State Prison rebellion). They visited the class after school, and then came in several times during school. They were so impressed by the atmosphere that they wanted to help; the idea was entirely their own, and I naturally embraced it. Their presence in the room was an enormous boon—it allowed us to pay much greater attention to kids with problems in certain areas, and brought new people with different experiences and viewpoints into the room.

Alas, this did not last. Both women became enmeshed in domestic problems (lead poisoning of young children at home, pressure from the Welfare Office to get a job) and had to leave after only a month. But they had made a sizable contribution and showed me the possibilities of using parents in the classroom.

Perhaps even more important than this development was the creeping impact of the learning stations on the rest of the school. At least five teachers in the building were strongly influenced by the system by seeing it in operation, talking to me, and reading my worksheets, and variations of the system appeared in their classrooms. Each teacher developed his or her own style of running the station idea; all slowly moved toward a more open and flexible setup. Even some classrooms without learning stations got typewriters, bookcases, and tables and allowed kids more freedom to use their time in such unstructured activities. Other teachers came into my room and were impressed by the atmosphere of freedom and intense involvement. There was virtually no criticism of the system, and the level of acceptance seemed to rise every day.

I also started circulating my station worksheets to all the sixth-grade teachers every day, and many of the other teachers quietly used the material or their own variations of it. Since I felt inadequate as an Art teacher and had very little idea how to use audio-visual aids, I got ideas from my colleagues in those areas in return for my worksheets.

I continued to take kids on field trips, and although it

85

seemed that they had been more places than the kids in 6-G (a reflection of favoritism in the tracking system?), these were still very successful.

Even experienced teachers can find themselves facing apathy, sarcasm, or hostility. Farnum Gray faced all of these. Now he offers a diagnosis of the way they happen, and some prescriptions for fast relief.

BY FARNUM GRAY

The change from formal to open teaching is intended to make schools places where children can learn in natural ways, with no need for the devious strategies they develop to cope with adults in coercive situations in school, home, and society. But the strategies are deep-rooted. In the transition from teacher-dominated to child-centered schools, students bring their institutional bad habits with them. Many will need adult help and understanding to reacquire natural ways of learning and being with people. When teachers fail to anticipate this problem, they often become so disillusioned by the children's continued use of inappropriate strategies that they enter a phase of thinking that the children can't handle—or are not worthy of—freedom.

In a coercive environment, a child's strategies enable him to preserve his feelings of safety, worth and capability. He might use strategies to get the authority off his back or to become a winner in the race.

"In the short run, the strategies seem to work," John

Holt writes. "They make it possible for many children to get through school even though they learn very little. But in the long run these strategies are self-limiting and self-defeating, and they destroy both character and intelligence. The children who use such strategies are prevented by them from growing into more than limited versions of the human beings they might have become. This is the real failure that takes place in school; hardly any children escape."

Strategies for coping vary widely from child to child, but four basic types are almost certain to challenge informal teachers working with students already adapted to formal classrooms. I call them The Good Kid, the Saboteur, Dr. No, and the Fun Consumer.

These strategies presented some typical transitional problems when an alternative school was started in Colorado. Although children happily transferred into the Aspen Community School because they and their parents favored its avowed respect for each child's individuality, they continued to behave in many of the ways they had learned in formal schools.

Trying to bring a typical problem into the open, a teacher started one day by saying to a group of ten- to thirteen-year-olds, "If you know how you feel, right now, raise your hand."

No hands.

"I mean, how does your body feel? Do you feel good? Or tired? Or full of energy? If you know, raise your hand."

Eyes searched the teacher's face, trying to get a clue to the right answer. How were they *supposed* to feel?

Two hands rose weakly.

"Is it possible for anyone else to know how you feel? Who else could know more about it than you?"

"*You* do!" they chorused.

Wanda, the teacher, broke into laughter, and the kids

giggled in embarrassment as they recognized for the first time their absurd dependence on psyching out teachers.

They were using the Good Kid strategy. The Good Kid determines what will please the teacher and then does it, or appears to do it. The Good Kid never risks an answer or opinion until he has figured out what the teacher expects. Obviously each kid knew the answer to Wanda's question better than she, but because none would risk committing himself, they denied their own knowledge.

In this new school, the Good Kid strategy was frustrating the teachers, who wanted the children to take greater responsibility for their own learning. The blandness of Good Kids was sapping their conversation, writing, art work, and involvement in learning.

Immediately following the how-do-you-feel incident, Wanda gamely tried again to elicit some honest answers.

"Let's think about three musical groups—the Jefferson Airplane, Lawrence Welk and his band, and the Supremes. We're going to go around the room, with each of you putting these three musical groups in order, from best to worst. We'll start with Carol."

"Um, the Jefferson Airplane, then the Supremes, then (giggle) Lawrence Welk."

So it went. A few ranked the Supremes first. Welk was a unanimous dead last. Until Wanda's turn. She ranked Welk first.

"Wan*da*!" came the outraged cries. "You're putting us on!"

"Lawrence Welk is the best," Wanda insisted coolly.

Pandemonium. "You can't believe that!" "He's so icky!" "How can you say that?"

Wanda firmly stated the facts. "He's been on TV longer than the others. He has sold more records."

"That doesn't mean anything!" "That's *we*ird!"

"You can't argue with the facts."

But they did argue—long and strong. The teacher's musical values were just too outrageous; adaptive strategies be damned. Without the teacher having to tell them, the students learned that they could state opinions without first figuring out what the RIGHT answer might be. Through the year, they continued to develop and express their own opinions and values.

The Aspen school had teachers with long experience in open teaching, but if the teacher is as new to child-centered styles as the students, problems are compounded. Strategists might bait him into returning to the formal teacher style he is trying to abandon. If he doesn't break up these strategies, a teacher might react by becoming authoritarian or try to avoid that reaction by going to a permissive extreme.

The Good Kid strategy is especially insidious because it is so easy to live with. Teachers might need to remind themselves that these students are not developing their full capability and might not even like school.

Haim Ginott quotes a high school student's description of the Good Kid strategy he developed early in his school life.

> It is easy to "snow" teachers. If you appear motivated and don't disturb them, they let you live. I became "school wise" early in the game. I figured out what makes teachers mad: violation of simple rules and "not trying." So, I come to school on time, I don't ask troublesome questions, and I am polite. And, of course, I am never caught "not trying."
>
> Our principal stopped me on the way home and asked an original question: "What did you do in school today?" I was tempted to tell him the truth:
>
> I apple-polished the English teacher.
> I faked interest in social studies.

89

I read comic books during arithmetic.
I cheated on a science test.
I did my homework during recess.
I wrote notes to my girlfriend during Spanish.
I replied, "It was a busy day." He smiled in satisfaction.

At least this student is aware of his adaptations to the institution of school. For the teacher trying to open up his class, a greater problem is presented by unconscious adaptations. Some students are quite sincere about their deceits. Conditioning starts early. When a small boy was transferred in the middle of a year to the Aspen Community School, his parents told me—the director—that they were disturbed by the effects on the boy of the competition and violence in the public school he had attended. The next day, a volunteer helped the child with reading. After their session, in which he was unable to read, the boy asked the volunteer to tell the head teacher (he was quick to psyche out the power structure) that he had read perfectly. When he wrote or drew, he asked if he could have an A or a gold star. He was seven years old.

The results of such schooling stay with people as they get older. I once asked a group of ten adults—a mixture of college and primary teachers—to say which was the longer of two lines I had drawn on a chalkboard. One woman laughingly said that line A was obviously longer, which it was. The other nine hedged about and said they were both the same, or line B was longer, or it was impossible to tell. After we had measured the lines, we talked about what had happened. Some said they assumed that if the line that *looked* longer *were* longer I would not have asked them in the first place. Some had immediately recalled specific incidents of being fooled in their early years in school and had been wary of committing themselves.

In rooting out the Good Kid strategy, abstract discussion is likely to be useless. A student could think: "Teacher wants us to be original and disagree with him. Okay, I'll give him what he wants." So all of the Good Kids become original together and compliantly disagree with the teacher. If feelings are involved, either through real experiences or convincing simulations, strategic defenses might drop—as in the dispute over Lawrence Welk.

Naturally, a Good Kid strategy works best for a child who can easily get on the good side of teachers. A youngster who tends to get classified as a loser might turn to a strategy—such as the Saboteur—that requires no teacher approval. Even students bright enough to be winners easily sometimes become Saboteurs. They might need the greater excitement of pitting their wits against the teacher, or their sense of integrity might require their using recognizably hostile strategies against people, including teachers, whom they have learned to associate with oppression.

In a teacher-dominated situation, where positive ways of asserting initiative and personal power are difficult, the Saboteur is hard to stop. Saboteurs often talk openly about what they can get away with, and other students, including some of the Good Kids, enjoy it.

But when a child sabotages a school situation that the students enjoy, his efforts are likely to annoy his peers. The strategy has become inappropriate because better channels of assertion are open. The disapproval of peers gives the good child-centered teacher an excellent chance of helping the Saboteur to break his habit.

Greta, a blue-eyed sprite of eight, was a precocious creator of chaos. Although her classmates were a frisky lot—anything but Good Kids—they found Greta's disruptiveness excessive and often loudly stated their opposition to her tactics.

In starting an improvisational drama elective, I invited Greta to participate. She was proud, and she loved the class, but she was going to sabotage it anyway because that was what she always did.

She came to our second meeting sucking loudly and wetly on *something* that bulged in her cheeks. The other students—ranging upwards in age to thirteen—were keenly annoyed.

Knowing Greta, I recognized a setup for verbal sabotage. If I asked her to get rid of the chewing gum, her slobbery reply would be, "Ik nok choongum." We could then run through some alternatives. Pistachio shells? Bubblegum? A prune being soaked for recess? By the time Greta had exacted her price and agreed to put her weapon in the wastebasket, the pace and spirit of the class would have sagged.

So I innovated. I grasped the back of her head firmly in my left hand. With my right index finger, I gouged an amorphous glob from her mouth and flipped it into the basket. No words exchanged. The class promptly regained momentum.

On two later occasions when Greta tried sabotage, our group gathered in a tight circle on the floor and talked about the effect she was having on the other students and the improvements they would like her to make. The students did the talking as I cuddled Greta on my lap. In that class, at least, Greta was soon an ex-Saboteur.

A problem presented by Saboteurs is, If the teacher reacts to sabotage by becoming oppressive, he loses; if he is easily duped or allows some students to interfere with the activities of others, he also loses.

One of the more devastating sabotages I have seen was generated on the first day of a school that was to be highly innovative. Here is the scene:

A bright young Ivy Leaguer—in his first teaching assignment—sits on the floor, surrounded by tough inner-city eighth-grade boys sitting in chairs.

"Hey, you guys, my name is Phil."

His disarming smile disarms no one. Looking down on him, the boys keep up a commentary on his line of patter.

"Phil. He say he Phil."

"Phil who?"

"Phil 'er up."

"Fill 'er up with my dick."

Phil continues as if everything is just fine. "I'm going to be your science facilitator. When you do science kinds of things, you'll be using me as your resource person.

"To start with, why don't you tell me what you'd like to know about science? We should be learning what *you* want to learn, so suppose you tell me what you'd like to learn about?"

"Don't you know? Why *we* have to tell *you*?"

"How are we s'posed to know what we should learn when we don't know science?"

After more urging by Phil, a large boy who is already developing into the class leader exclaims with satanic delight, "Fool's gold!"

Others: "Yeah, fool's gold!" "We wanna learn about fool's gold."

"Oh, uh, fool's gold," Phil's eyes glaze. "Yeah, fool's gold. Iron pyrites. Okay, and what else would you like to learn about?"

"Just fool's gold, man!" It is said threateningly by the large boy, who leans over Phil and stares down at him with a hard gleam in his eyes. "Yeah," says another boy. "Fool's gold is the onliest thing."

The rest of the day is all downhill.

Phil had prepared for nothing that first day but to chew the fat about What Do We Want to Do Here? (Anything else would be authoritarian.) The kids sabotaged that by uniting on a single rigid and wonderfully appropriate answer that ended discussion.

Although sabotage is maddeningly hard to deal with in a coercive situation, where it might be justifiable, it is one of the less difficult strategies to overcome in an open school. Basically, the teacher needs to keep his affection for the child and his sense of humor intact as he analyzes and breaks up each stratagem before it gets off the ground. He should see that all students have plenty of opportunity for open discussion of their concerns, and help the ex-Saboteur find genuine involvement in alternative ways of expressing himself.

Many Saboteurs—even hard-shell cases—respond dramatically when given opportunities to teach younger children. The experience gives them a constructive sense of power and responsibility and some empathy for the plight of the teacher.

In the transition to openness, the Saboteur is far less likely to blow the teacher's mind than the Dr. No strategist. Kids using the Dr. No approach implicitly insist, You have to try to make me do something so I can refuse to do it.

James Herndon writes of how he and his teaching partner were victims of this strategy:

> We were bothered and confused and upset because the kids who never would do anything we suggested they might do were always the very kids who kept complaining to us that they were bored, that there was Nothing to Do In Here (and Out There), that We Never Do Anything In This Class and We Don't Learn Anything In Here. When we heard that complaint, we'd haul out some idea (figuring we had the kid this time!) and say *Then why don't you do* this or that? Then the complaining kid would say triumphantly, *Naw, I don't want to! Well, what about doing* this or that other

thing, we'd say, and the kid would say *Uh-uh,* and then we'd say *O.K., what about* . . . and the kid got to say *No Good* and then cut out and go to the bathroom and arrive back later saying *There's Nothing Going On.*

This drove us out of our minds, and it drove us out of our minds every day. . . . they could steadfastly refuse to do everything and then complain that there was nothing do do.

These juvenile Dr. No's are inevitable in newly founded open school programs. Having learned the satisfactions of resisting commands, Dr. No strategists push against authority as they would push against a closed door. When the door flies open, they fall. Without adult coercion to rebel against they are lost. So in an open classroom, they may find it necessary to try to provoke coercion.

These contradictory kids seem to be prompted by two conflicting fears. First, uncomfortable with freedom, they are afraid to make their own choices. Second, they fear that if they carry out a teacher's assignments or suggestions, their performance will be found inadequate.

One way the teacher can help, as Herndon learned, is to make firm decisions about what the Dr. No should do to get started, being careful that the decisions are based on the real needs of the student and not on the neatness of their fit with the teacher's plans. Unlimited choice is frightening to some children, and the teacher can ease anxiety by offering such a child only two or three activities and telling him he may choose the one he is going to do.

To a greater extent than the Good Kid, the Saboteur and Dr. No, the Fun Consumer strategy lends itself to use by whole groups of students.

Everyone has known an entertainer-teacher. He keeps the attention of students by putting on a good show, though such attention should not be mistaken for active involvement and initiative. Nonetheless, if he has talent and keeps his material fresh, he might be a hit.

A child-centered teacher does not set out to be an entertainer. But he is always in danger of falling victim to Fun Consumers, who play on the ham in a teacher by getting him to entertain—day . . . after day . . . after day.

While they manage to avoid active learning, Fun Consumers usually are not entirely passive. As they lure the starstruck teacher ever deeper into showbiz, they gradually become entertainment critics, which gives them the same sense of power other critics enjoy. (This ploy seems particularly effective with male teachers. They being hammier, perhaps.) After a period of applauding the teacher's efforts, the Fun Consumers know the hook is set. Then comes the switch: "This isn't *fun!*" "We had more fun last week." "Why don't we do fun things like the time we made the red bubbly stuff and got it all over everything?" "Mr Berle's class last year was more interesting. He was always fun."

One hears actors complain that drama critics are not creative and get their rewards by ripping at the bowels of those who are. A teacher who blunders onto the entertainer track might at first be stung by sudden criticism. The real hurt, though, comes when he realizes that the kids are making him entertain them, when that was not what he wanted to happen. He wanted *them* to be creative, not an audience for his creativity. I knew a strong man of 30-plus to howl anguished curses on the day he finally recognized that for months he had been the infatuated dupe of a class of nine-year-old Fun Consumers. His awareness of what was happening in his class had been far too dim, and he was coming to realize that teaching better requires more than providing neater things to entertain students.

To help children get free of these strategies, a teacher must eliminate the institutional demands that nurture devious ways of coping. He must root out of himself the tendency to judge, sort, and classify students. Rather than dispensing his own knowledge in his own way, he must help students find their own ways to their own insights. He must provide enough stimulation that students don't need to scheme to escape numbing boredom.

Of course, there will be regressions on the part of both students and teachers. Once a person has learned a way of coping, he is likely to use it again sometime.

Teachers can gauge progress in getting free of strategies by the quality of students' experience and work. When stereotypical work and dullness prevail, chances are energy is being siphoned into strategies for coping. Vitality, freshness, and creative attempts to deal with real problems indicate that students' energies are finding authentic outlets.

One of the most significant changes possible in the classroom is to put the emphasis on students asking questions—not questions of the teacher, but of themselves, of each other, and of the world around them. Lee Swenson explores ways to work toward this climate. Her report is from a high school, but teachers of younger children know it is even easier to get them to question creatively and to answer without feeling self-conscious.

BY LEE SWENSON

Questions are the engines of intellect, the cerebral machines which convert energy to motion, and curiosity to controlled in-

quiry. There can be no thinking without questioning—no purposeful study of the past, nor any serious planning for the future.
David Hackett Fischer

As today's students face tomorrow's world, the art of asking excellent questions may be their most necessary skill. A curious mind possessing this skill has a great advantage when facing a problem, whether it be small and personal, or complex and universal. Yet most teachers rarely think about the type of questions their students are asking and the power inherent in them. We must begin to nurture curiosity and to teach the skill of questioning to our students, that they may benefit from its penetrating strength.

Because questioning is an integral part of inquiry, it has received some attention from educational reformers during the last few years. But this attention has been scant and insufficient. Often it is either lip service or a passing comment. Two notable exceptions to this are Chapter Four in *Teaching as a Subversive Activity,* which talks about the importance of relevant questions, and a book by Norris M. Sanders, *Classroom Questions.*

The central question in Sanders' book is this: What questions should teachers ask if they want to stimulate all appropriate types of intellectual activity without overemphasizing some and neglecting others? Sanders' goal is admirable. Knowing that most teachers are fixated at the intellectual stage of recall, he is trying to help them exercise their students' minds in higher intellectual realms. Sanders places questions into the following categories: Memory, Translation, Interpretation, Application, Analysis, Synthesis, and Evaluation. Unfortunately, his book, like almost all articles written on questioning in education journals, has two weaknesses: first, the stress on *teacher's* questions will not help students learn how to ask their own questions, and second, little is said about stimulating the ultimate source of the inquiring attitude, curiosity toward life in general.

Most students show little curiosity in the classroom, as visitors to high schools are well aware. For a few students, this lack of curiosity extends to the world outside the classroom. How can this be explained? Is curiosity something we inherit, something we learn, or is it a combination of these?

To discover if curiosity is an inherited drive, psychologists have studied primates and young children. Robert Butler found that monkeys work tirelessly solving problems where the reward consisted of a quick glance outside of their cages. One monkey performed this task at thirty second intervals for nineteen hours! Young children behave in a similar fashion, as all mothers well know. Babies often have an insatiable curiosity urging them to taste and touch everything, much to their parents' dismay.

So the deficiency of curiosity found in many students is apparently not inherited, but learned. "Don't be curious" is the message they get from nearly all adults: from their parents whenever curiosity leads to embarrassment or inconvenience, from their culture which teaches them habits and patterns they soon take for granted, and from their teachers, who know that spontaneous curiosity is the mortal enemy of a well-organized lesson plan. But what is learned can usually be unlearned, and there is still hope. What specific things can teachers do to rekindle a sense of curiosity and wonder in their students?

A magician has much to teach us about one way of stimulating curiosity. When he saws the beautiful lady in half, and later presents her walking and talking, he is using a method that is central to learning. Our urge to investigate is strengthened when a familiar law is broken. This may happen to a young child when his first helium-filled balloon never returns. It may happen in a classroom when an egg rises in one liquid and sinks in another or when, in a particular congressional vote, a firm conservative suddenly finds himself on the side of ultraliberals. Unfortunately, these intellectual stimulants do not always work. First, the student must be fully aware of the principle that is being violated. Second, he must care about it.

On another level, curiosity is stimulated when one's care and involvement embraces a personal goal. For example, I am very interested in my digestive system and its rejection of certain foods that I am sensitive to. I want to find a better diet that will lead to improved health. Yet I am not curious about something else my body is rejecting, the hair on my dome. Given the fact that I do not cherish being bald, why the absence of curiosity? Perhaps it is because I feel I have no control over this part of my destiny. If this explanation is valid, it has ramifications for the classroom. Somehow we must encourage our students to feel that they have control over much of their future, and with this might come more curiosity, at least about the particular goals they set for themselves, such as becoming a better mechanic or being accepted by the top social group in the school.

The curiosity that can often be generated by observing dissonant events is quickly dissipated, and the curiosity generated by striving for personal goals is likely to be rigidly narrow in scope. A deeper, broader source of curiosity lies within us all, but it is scabbed over with years of inactivity, and this crust prevents a total immersion in life that is experienced by creative men like John Keats:

> I leaped headlong into the sea, and thereby have become [better] acquainted with the sounds, the quicksands, and the rocks, than if I had stayed upon the green shore and piped a silly pipe, and took tea and comfortable advice.

We sit piping our pipes and asking advice, unaware that this passivity and our straitjacket of habitual action dams up our curiosity and breaks our contact with the environment.

Powerful drives to question and to learn are released when we are able to make direct relationships with our deeper selves and with our surrounding environment. Great strides are being made in this area by the Gestalt School of psychotherapy.

A primary concern of the Gestalt therapist is to help people contact the environment in the "here and now." As children grow up, barriers are formed that deaden their senses and stifle their imagination. These barriers must be broken down. Gestalt psychologists have developed several creative activities that can be used in any classroom to "sharpen your appreciation of the difference between staring and looking, between dulling trance and alive participation." One example follows:

> Concentrate on your eating without reading or "thinking" . . .
>
> Do you taste the first few bites and then fall into a trance? . . . As you eat with awareness, do you experience greed? Impatience? Disgust? . . . Do you experience a "symphony" of flavors and textures in your food . . . ?
>
> When it is not a matter of physical but of "mental" food, how does the matter stand?

Many other exercises are found in two excellent books: *Gestalt Therapy* by Frederick Perls, Ralph Hefferline, and Paul Goodman (from which the above example was taken), and *Human Values for Human Learning* by George Brown. I believe we must move in the direction suggested by these authors if we are to stimulate that most basic source of questioning, raw curiosity, which is nothing else than an extended sense of relevance and involvement.

Given the power of inquisitiveness, how can we teach the students in our classes to apply it skillfully with excellent questioning? First, barriers that can prevent the transformation of this inner curiosity into the form of a stated question must be broken down. One obstacle described by Richard Jones (*Fantasy and Feeling in Education*) is our desire only to share questions with those we love. "After all, there is little risk in giving an answer; it is either right or wrong and that is usually the end of it. But to share a question is often to invite inspection of one's tenderer parts. Like other loving acts, this is not something we do with strangers." If we want students asking questions in our classroom, then they must feel the trust that comes with intimacy.

As students start to feel secure, they might begin to develop their questioning skills by participating in "warm-up" activities. After a spring and summer away from the stadium, a football player must spend many hours exercising his unused muscles before he can expect polished and precise results. It is wise to begin questioning in a similar fashion. I have found two warm-up exercises helpful in my classes. In one, I simply asked students to write down four or five interesting questions, and then with a friend, to think of three or four subquestions about each major one. Tina, a quiet girl who rarely asked questions, turned in these:

1. Why don't people talk through their noses?
   a. Are mouths that important?
   b. Why do people kiss with their mouths?
   c. Why don't nice things come out of people's mouths if they have to talk with them?
2. Why am I lonely?
   a. Why did I move in the first place?

   b. Why can't I make friends easily?
   c. Will it last forever?
3. Why are we asking questions?
   a. What are we going to learn from them?
   b. Are questions important?
   c. Will we get answers from questions?

A second method is to give students a quote and have them ask as many questions as possible about it. To introduce a unit on technology, I use the statement "It is important to know that technology brings progress," which stimulated responses like, What is technology? How does one go about controlling the evils of technology yet have free enterprise? Is technology good for spiritual progress? How does it relate to me?

After sufficient warm-up exercises, the brain should be limber and ready to sharpen its skills of inquiry. Almost all students are fully aware of the importance of wording—not from their classroom experience, but from facing the interrogation squad on the home front after a late party. Father: "Did you drink any beer?" Son: "No, Dad, of course not." (Under his breath to himself: "But I sure guzzled a lot, heh, heh.") It's a tragedy such linguistic care and logical skill are not displayed in each homework assignment.

There are several ways we can help students learn to use more precise words in their questions. One way is to discuss some of the questions that have been generated in the previous warm-up exercises, trying to replace ambiguous words with more exact ones. Another way is to play "Who wrote which story?" Everyone is asked to write a five-sentence story about a young boy and his first gun. Three students are selected, and their stories are read anonymously. Through questioning each of these authors, the class attempts to discover who wrote each story. After a few weak questions, the class can discuss how they might im-

103

prove them to get better results. For example, "Are you violent?" could become more productive when stated as "What situations have made you angry and aggressive in the past?" Exercises like this should help each student realize the importance of a precisely worded question.

Along with precise wording, strategy is also important. Let me illustrate with a puzzle:

> How can you cut a circular cake into eight pieces with only three straight cuts of a knife?

These two questions should make the solution easier if you are having trouble:

    a. Is the knife a long one?
    b. What are the different ways you can cut more than one piece of something with only one slice of a knife?*

These questions fall into two categories, and when combined, their problem-solving advantages are more than doubled. The first is a *convergent* question. It focuses down, defines terms, asks for specifics. The second question is *divergent,* which means it rises above the problem to offer a broader perspective. It reaches out for larger generalizations; the convergent question concentrates on the details. As a simple rule, problems are more easily solved when both types of questions work together.

Try your skill on another puzzle:

> There are three coins lying on the table like this:
>
>   *quarter   nickel   quarter*
>
> How can you get the right-hand quarter into the middle position without moving the nickel or touching the left-hand quarter?

* First, with a horizontal slice, cut the cake into two layers. Leaving the top layer on the bottom one, use two vertical slices to cut the cake into quarter sections. There should be eight separate pieces after your last cut.

There are at least two solutions to this puzzle, and perhaps effective questioning will reveal others.*

The foundation of inquiry is a series of precisely worded, convergent and divergent questions. The emphasis here is on the word *series,* for too often we try to teach this skill by asking or examining a single question without placing it in the context of an investigative progression. Like an old bronze hero high on his pedestal, a question alone is hard to evaluate; it must be judged in the company of its contemporaries. The best way I know to illustrate this in the classroom is to play Twenty Questions. From the beginning of the game, the novice is a wild-eyed gambler, blurting out such inquiries as "Is it Natalie's left earlobe?" and "Is it that ugly belt you're wearing, Mr. Swenson?" These students firmly believe that you only learn something when you can elicit a "yes" and anything associated with a "no" is quickly forgotten. They do not solidly and patiently build on preceding results.

Any student of Twenty Questions knows that the focus of a question is greatly determined by its predecessor, whether the answer was yes or no. The secret is to limit the range of remaining possibilities by one half with each inquiry, and thus a "no" is as informative as a "yes." Thrusts that impatiently leap out of this gradual progression into the realm of wild guesses are invariably wasted and add as little new information as a poorly worded question like "Is it soft?" "Soft" is a fuzzy word not clearly defined. It leads to multiple meanings and misleading answers, which places the entire future investigation on an unstable foundation. This classroom activity can teach much about questioning, but it certainly does not comprehensively cover all types of in-

* Place one finger on the nickel to keep it from moving. Slide the right hand quarter firmly into the nickel. This should push the left quarter far enough to allow you to place the right quarter between the left quarter and the nickel.

vestigation. Other valuable methods of problem solving may not be as systematic as this and often require imaginative leaps.

There is insight in the old phrase "The more you know, the more you know you don't know." Slightly modified, another version might read, "The more knowledgeable you are in any area, the better your questions will be." To test the truth of this, pose the following problem to two of your students—a girl getting "A's" in your subject who knows little about cars, and an auto shop freak who doesn't know the difference between a verb and a noun. The problem: "Make a list of five questions you would ask to discover the quality of a used car. Do not refer to an outside expert." Have the class evaluate their responses, discussing the strengths and weaknesses of each question. Is there any doubt about who would have the better list?

Like the auto shop expert, the professionals in any discipline have much to teach us about valuable questions in their field of knowledge. These people know the most important issues and variables that they should direct their attention toward, and phrase their questions accordingly. For example, here is a list of questions historians tend to ask to help them understand causation based on a similar list in Carl Gustavson's *A Preface to History:*

a. What were the immediate causes for the event?
b. What kinds of significant agitation can be found previous to these immediate causes?
c. What individual people were involved on either side whose strengths or weaknesses may have helped to determine the outcome of the struggle?
d. What potent ideas stimulated the loyalty of a considerable number of people?
e. How did the economic groups line up on the issue?

f. What religious forces were active?

g. Which new technological developments influenced the situation?

h. How do weakened or strengthened institutions help to explain the event that occurred?

i. How was the physical environment a factor in the situation?

Any student interested in history should have a working knowledge of this list. If students are interested in other areas, have them make their own lists. Encourage a student interested in film criticism to read several film reviews, discover what important issues are dealt with, and finally, create his own set of the ten most important questions a film reviewer should ask.

A thorough mastery of all the skills discussed here—precise wording, convergent and divergent questions, a sound strategy, and an understanding of a discipline's key questions—will probably still leave us short of solutions to the difficult problems. One cause is the most basic fact of our existence: we are social animals. Much like each individual discipline, a culture rests on a cluster of widely accepted questions and assumptions. For a society to cohere, its members must share a world view about the nature of reality and the proper way to investigate it. This inner rule book tells us immediately which problems and answers are acceptable, and which are blatantly nonsensical. Einstein's idea that matter shrinks as its velocity approaches the speed of light is still nonsense to the majority. It is as if there were a territorial border, or high wall, restraining us.

Our questions are thus confined by the tether of our world view; when our inquiries reach a certain depth, we suddenly feel the sharp jerk of our culture-bound perspective pulling us back to familiar, unthreatening terrain. To

107

gain the new perspective that is often a prerequisite for solving a difficult problem, this tether must be severed. The great thinker is always on the periphery, playing irreverently with his liberated imagination.

As we move from "E equals mc^2" to more weighty matters like finding the rattle in our '66 Ford, the same holds true. A creative vision helps to solve a troublesome problem by generating exciting questions and new points of view. Foreigners and children find this escape from our visual straitjacket quite easy. A South Sea Islander once described a three masted steamer with two funnels as: "three pieces bamboo, two pieces puff-puff, walk along inside, no can see." It is precisely this unusual way of seeing our everyday reality that we must nurture. William Gordon calls it making the familiar strange. It is impossible to guarantee creativity in three easy steps, but he has found several methods that encourage the creative vision. Gordon identifies four metaphorical mechanisms that help make the familiar strange: Personal Analogy, Direct Analogy, Symbolic Analogy, and Fantasy Analogy. An example of a personal analogy would be a technician thinking ". . . himself to be a dancing molecule, . . . throwing himself into the activity of the elements involved. He becomes one of the molecules." To understand each type of analogy fully, his book *Synectics* should be read. The main point, however, is to twist reality around so that we can see old things in new ways.

With luck, making the familiar strange will inspire more creative questioning, which is 90 percent of any solution. Unfortunately, the ramifications of this approach extend far beyond any problem's answer. Questions can be very painful, both to the self and to others. Whenever basic assumptions are cast into doubt, anxiety reigns. Frustration and ambiguity quickly become heavy burdens, and we cast out all those among us who see in strange and imaginative ways.

Documents from all ages tell us this same old story, as is found in the *Ratio Studiorum* of 1599:

> Even in matters where there is no risk to faith and devotion, no one shall introduce new questions in matters of great moment, or any opinion which does not have suitable authority, without first consulting his superiors . . .

We must destroy this lingering curse and bring questions back into our students' lives.

In the present climate of American education, classroom reform sometimes seems like a flower too fragile to survive. The demands on the schools today are harsh and sometimes narrow. For examples, many black parents understandably demand measurable reading achievement and other test scores to assure that their children are no longer being given short shrift. At the same time, white parents are often concerned that the schools continue to give their children an advantage in status over someone else's children.

In such a climate, open education seems precariously based on a kind of trust little evident in education today. Teachers must

109

trust children's imaginations, feelings, curiosities, and natural desires to explore and understand their worlds. They also must learn to trust themselves—to be willing to gamble that they can retain the children's interest and respect once they relinquish the external means of control: testing, threats, demerits, petty rules, and rituals. School administrators, in turn, must trust teachers enough to permit them to run a classroom that is not rigidly organized and controlled. They must allow classrooms that are bustling, messy, flexible, and impulsive. Parents must trust schools to do well by their children, without the assurance provided by a classroom atmosphere recognizable from their own childhoods and validated, however emptily, by standardized tests.

Much recent experience suggests that the basis for such trust may not exist in American education at present. But perhaps the burgeoning of classrooms where learning based on such trust is taking place will itself create the beginnings of a new climate.

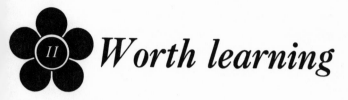

II Worth learning

4 Getting the words back to the kids

Joy and power in using language

Every child comes to school for the first time with a mastery of language that boggles the mind. But from the moment he steps in the door, the school all too often begins to chip away at this power, asserting that *it* is the only legitimate source and use for his further growth in reading and writing. (No wonder two black educators have written *Damn Reading!*, an attack on the teaching of reading as the last refuge of teachers bent on maintaining control of their students' minds.) Yet despite these abuses, kids and their parents still want and expect the school to help them take firmer, more creative command of their native tongue and its lovely literature. But how?

Will it grow in a classroom?

In his book of that title, Steve Daniels
describes "how 2 gerbils, 20 goldfish, 200
games, 2000 books, and I taught them how to
read." Here's how.

BY STEVE DANIELS

The other afternoon, while browsing through children's
books in a Philadelphia store, I overheard a salesman
asking a twelve-year-old customer what he wanted. The
youngster said that he'd "like a good, exciting mystery
book." "How about Alfred Hitchcock's *Stories for Late at
Night?*" he was asked. "Naw," said the boy, "I've already
read that one. What else've you got?"

The most mundane, ordinary type of conversation—except to me. I'm surprised that any child can read Hitchcock.
Certainly the fourteen-year-olds that I teach cannot. Of the
150 eighth graders I have this year, which includes the sixty
students in the "academically advanced" sections, *only
three* can read at an eighth-grade level. Over fifty of the
other 147 cannot read a book written at above a third-grade
level (as measured by the Stanford Reading Achievement
Test).

The increasingly publicized gap between national
"norms" and the reading test results of ghetto children is
much more than just numbers. A student with a fourth-
grade reading ability can comfortably handle this:

> Let's go up to the hillside today,
> To play, to play,
> To play,
> Up to the hill where the daisies grow,
> Like snow, like snow,
> Like snow.

114

Worth learning

(From *Round the Corner,* a basal text in The Bank Street Readers [New York: Macmillan, 1966]. In my opinion the best basal reading series now available.)

An eighth-grade student reading at his proper level, though, has no difficulty at all with this passage from *The Autobiography of Malcolm X:*

> All through the war the Harlem racial picture never was too bright. Tension built to a pretty high pitch. Old-timers told me that Harlem had never been the same since the 1935 riot.

If the world had gone completely McLuhan by now, this gap would make no difference, and we'd all be "watching" Malcolm X instead of reading his book. But, because nonlinear communication has yet to replace the printed word, the ability to read must—repeat twice and underline—must transcend every other learnable skill. Until ghetto students learn to read, the teaching of any other academic discipline in a slum school is an unsupportable delusion.

A math teacher cannot expect his students to figure out whether Train A will pass Train B three hours out of the station at X miles per hour if his students can't read the problem. A science teacher cannot expect her students to extract oxygen from the atmosphere if they can't read the procedures for setting up the experiment. It's true that if the science teacher could find a different way to do the experiment, her students might be able to work a little chemistry. But it's equally true that that knowledge wouldn't help them figure out at what point Train A will pass Train B. Reading, though, allows a student to do both, and more. Essentially, it gives him the opportunity to learn what he wants to learn. Without it, despite his desire, there is little that he can learn.

115

This emphasis on reading is not a novel concept, yet the fact remains that a twelve-year-old suburban child can read books that are too difficult for most urban high school graduates. Why is this the case, when the process of learning to read, be it in Scarsdale or in Watts, is identical for both children?

Reading, to begin with, is the ability to decode and translate symbols into sounds. It is nothing more than that. It is *not* comprehension, interpretation, extrapolation, or any of the myriad of other skills that teachers tend to confuse it with. Being able to draw conclusions and inferences from presented material, for example, are skills in themselves. They apply to any situation or subject, and shouldn't be considered the domain of reading teachers. (For a penetrating analysis of this argument, see James Moffett's *A Student-centered Language Arts Curriculum,* Houghton Mifflin Company, 1968.)

In other words, if you can say, "Lirute en quartine regmire wiselbang," you can read.

Having decoded, you are ready for the second step, which is understanding. "Lirute . . . wiselbang," in our particular code, means "The batter hit the pitched ball." If you even remotely know the game of baseball, you've had sufficient life experience to comprehend what you've read. But if you've never seen, heard of, nor in any other way participated in the sport, to you it remains "wiselbang." (This life experience is one of the antecedents to learning those thinking skills so often confused with reading ability.)

Decoding and having life experience mean little, of course, if you don't care to read about baseball. The third and last step is desire.

Suburban children learn to decode in the early grades, either through the sight method—learning whole words

116

and recognizing them through constant repetition in pictured contexts—or through the phonic method—pronouncing the sounds of different combinations of letters—or through some mixture of the two. (The effectiveness of each technique is definitively reviewed in Jeanne Chall's *Learning to Read: The Great Debate*, McGraw-Hill Book Company, 1967.)

Suburban students have life experience. They've been to camp, on a subway, to a bowling alley, they know what a lawn looks like, know how to hold a tennis racquet. In addition, suburban parents verbally pass on their own experiences to their children.

Finally, middle-class youngsters have a generally healthy attitude toward books. They were read to when young and grow up realizing that books can be one of life's pleasures.

As a group, suburban students can read. (Some, of course, can't, but for reasons completely unrelated to those which affect the slum student. Many suburban children react to incessant pressure to read at an increasingly younger age by not reading at all. But this is an emotional, not a reading, problem.)

In contrast there are the children I teach. At least 25 percent of them cannot decode. Their elementary teachers didn't properly instruct them. Having thirty-five children say phonetic sounds in unison or using independent small-group instruction would only have encouraged discipline problems. Instead, these teachers had their pupils silently color in pictures of animals, filling in the blank between the *B* and the *T*, a poor substitute.

Seventy-five percent of my students can decode, but most of them have meager life experience. Read all the phrases that hide the blemish but don't make the necessary dietetic changes, "underprivileged," "deprived," etc. Too many of my children have never been outside the square-mile area

117

between home and school. Last year, for instance, I took a group of boys to watch the Philadelphia '76ers play basketball against the Los Angeles Lakers. The Spectrum sports arena was about an hour away from our meeting place. After what seemed an interminable ride on the subway, the boys and I transferred to a bus. As we alighted, eleven stops later, one of the young men looked around and in all seriousness asked me, "Are we in Canada yet?"

Some of my students, perhaps as many as fifty out of 150, can read. They just don't want to. Where have they ever seen a good book? Not at home, where there are few, if any, and not in school, where most textbooks are about as exciting as seeing Andy Warhol's film *Sleep* for the third time.

The urban teacher, then, is faced with this three-part combination: students who cannot decode, those who can but who lack the experience necessary to understand what they've read, and those who are convinced that a good book doesn't exist. What should he do?

During my first year I fell into the pit called Compensatory Reading. Compensatory Reading means you get federal funds to buy dull fourth-grade textbooks for illiterate eighth graders, instead of dull eighth-grade texts. Being a social studies teacher, I substituted the advanced history book with an elementary one. The obvious occurred. I lost every student who couldn't read fourth-grade words, lost the few students who found the book too easy, and lost everyone else because it was, to understate the quality of the text, a little dry.

During the summer between my first and second years I made an important decision—that to try to teach social studies to children who couldn't read was a waste of my effort and their time. I decided, with the help of a sympathetic principal, to teach reading instead. I began by trying to analyze the reading problem beyond the "compensatory" stage. It appeared to me (and still does) that people read for one of a combination of two reasons, either for enjoyment and entertainment, be it Harold Robbins or Søren Kierkegaard, or to obtain information needed to solve a problem. But I've yet to meet the business executive who goes to his office and for no reason at all reads pages 12 to 23 and answers the questions at the bottom of page 24.

Children, too, will read for pleasure and/or information, but both approaches require certain prerequisites.

First, the reading matter must be at the child's level. This is so obvious that mentioning it once is redundant, but most teachers find something embarrassing about issuing second-grade books to fourteen-year-olds. A while ago, I had the opportunity of addressing reading teachers on this question. Instead of opening the discussion with the hackneyed "Let's talk about reading," I gave each the following classroom assignment from Jean-Paul Sartre's *Being and Nothingness:*

> DIRECTIONS: Read the following passage, and answer the questions at the bottom of the page.
>
> The future is the determining being which the For-Itself has to be beyond being. There is a future because the For-Itself has to be it's being instead of simply being it. This being which the For-Itself has to be cannot be in the mode of the co-present in-itselfs; for in that case it would be without being made to be; we could not then imagine it is a completely designed state to which presence alone would be lacking, as Kant says that existence adds nothing more to the object of the concept.
>
> 1. How does Kant feel about objects?
> 2. Why do you think so?
> 3. What is the "For-Itself"? (*In your own words!*)

119

Second, slum children must be rewarded for their reading efforts in the immediate present. Middle-class students know that a Mustang, split-level home, and social acceptance await the end of the road, and this provides them enough motivation to sit through much of what passes for education in the suburbs. Ghetto students have no such incentives, so some substitute must be used.

Third, the children must be free to talk—absolutely an essential for those students who must check their decoding against reality.

Finally, for black students, the content of the books must be closely scrutinized. Many old books have racially condescending material—"There were even three Negroes there"—and much of the tremendous volume of hurriedly prepared new material presents only Stepin Fetchit stereotypes.

Keeping these prerequisites in mind, I elected to try the Reading for Pleasure/Reward method during my second year.

The initial step was to convince all the children that books were enjoyable and a satisfying experience. If they weren't, then students who couldn't decode wouldn't try to, and students who could read but didn't want to, wouldn't.

To accomplish this, I literally stuffed the room full of exciting, new books, from the simplest squeeze-me-and-I-make-a-noise cloth ones to *Manchild in the Promised Land*. Colorful, exciting volumes on gangs, race, sports, sex, fairy tales, the gamut of the Dewey Decimal System. I made sure that I (*a*) excluded anything that might be construed as a text and (*b*) included all those controversial titles that the vice-principal warned me to keep out. Then I told the kids to "walk around the room. Pick out any book that looks exciting to you. Read it, either by yourself or with a friend. If it turns out that it's a crummy book, return it and get another. There will be no tests, reports, or questions of any kind about anything you have read."

The children reacted cautiously. Was I sure that there would be no tests? Positively no book reports? You didn't have to know the author, publisher, and copyright date? Even reassured, the kids were hesitant. Why should my room be different from their other teachers'? All the students proceeded to select the hardest books they could find. They would prove to me that they didn't need "baby books like *Dr. Seuss.*" So they sat through the first two or three days professionally thumbing through incomprehensible pages. Nor did I exhort any child who could only read *Little Red Riding Hood* to put his copy of *Invisible Man* back on the shelf. The student knew he couldn't read, and he didn't need the ego deflation of being reminded of it.

As the weeks wore on, my students became more trusting. There hadn't been a test, had there? By the end of the month, the squeeze-me books were squeaking.

During this initial period, a teacher from down the hall kept popping into my room. On her third "pop" she asked me to justify letting the kids read such childish books as *Bambi.* How could they learn anything? I bet her the quarter I'd recently won on the geography puzzle experiment that any student she chose couldn't read three straight lines of *Bambi* without a significant error. She picked a student who fumbled on "regarded," and I was up to fifty cents.

At the beginning of the second month, I divided each of my classes into five or six homogeneous groups, from non-decoders to Malcolm Xers. Knowing that I couldn't simultaneously teach six groups, I appointed students to act as teachers (initially those children who had challenged my authority at the start of the year, a constructive outlet for their desire to lead). After the first month, these teachers were rotated so that everyone got a chance. Each student-teacher was to lead his group in the study of the basal reader that I had assigned for their particular level.

Grouping is a device that more teachers would use if they were sure that it wouldn't increase their discipline troubles, for nobody can have both eyes in four different corners of the room at the same time. Circumventing this problem isn't too difficult, but it requires that the teacher relinquish direct control of his class, something that most teachers are too insecure to try. Many teachers ask students to lead groups, but the breakdown occurs when classmates mistreat the student-teacher. The reason they can do this is that the teacher gives his student-teacher responsibility, but no authority with which to fulfill it. In my class, since he was completely responsible for the group's progress, the student-teacher had total authority over the group. Whether they read their text aloud or silently, front to back or back to front, or in rotation, was up to the student-teacher. He decided who could be excused to go to the bathroom, who had permission to get a drink of water, and who would be suspended from school for misconduct.

The student-teacher's power, however, was not arbitrary. It had a natural base, for the teacher of a third grade level group, for example, would himself be a fourth-grade reader. Self-protection ensured that the student-teacher would not abuse his power. He still had to walk out of the building with any student he suspended.

A typical "reading day" went like this. The kids "drove" their chairs, in bumper-car fashion, to their respective corners. At the same time the student-teacher got the texts, and the Word-Looker-Upper of each group (appointed by the student-teacher) got the group's notebook. As the group read, the Looker-Upper wrote down the definitions of words they didn't understand. At the end of half an hour,

122

the books were returned and the chairs were bruised back into their original positions.

The classroom atmosphere on a reading day was one of laxity and freedom. Just the simple action of moving chairs around provided a physical release, and since the kids were responsible to a student-teacher instead of a teacher-teacher, there was little mental pressure.

During the reading period I would spend half my time with the nondecoders and the other half testing groups who had completed their text. These tests were oral, and were composed of recall questions on the stories and word definitions from the group's notebook. If a group passed, they progressed to the next higher reader in the series, and they moved up on the Reading Progress Board.

The Reading Progress Board was one of the external motivational devices that I used to encourage the children's reading. One wall of the room was covered with dark Portuguese cork. Each student had his name affixed along the bottom, with a colored map-flag pinned over it. As his group finished a book and passed the test, his flag advanced two of the twelve total spaces on the board. If he reached the top by the end of the school year, he was appropriately rewarded—a giant Sugar Daddy candy sucker.

Another incentive that was very effective was the "Group of the Week." The best group each week (a subjective decision, as are most decisions) had its picture taken in full color. The photograph was posted on the wall, and each child got a Hershey bar. A well-read classroom marches on its stomach!

In addition to the board and photos, I recorded the children's reading. Hearing their own voices was a real thrill. A tape recorder, by the way, is much more than a motivational technique, as I discovered in the case of Henry Harris. Henry had the widest lisp outside of the Castilian

123

coast of Spain. The school's visiting speech therapist told me that he refused to come to her for assistance. Instead of forcing him to go, and causing him to become even more defensive, I recorded his group every couple of weeks. By the eighth or ninth session, Henry admitted to his lisp and asked for help. Today, two years later, he still adds a slight "s" to every word, but his speech is far more coherent.

The readers were good, the motivations excellent, and the entire approach worked out well. Statistically, the 150 children gained about 60 percent more in reading ability than what their "naturally expected gain" would have been. This increase, though impressive, didn't seem high enough to me. Another summer analysis gave me new answers as to why.

Although I had realized that all thirty students wouldn't want to read the same book, I hadn't carried this line of thought to its logical conclusion. There probably weren't more than two or three students in each group who liked their assigned text.

Also, I had dishonestly tricked my kids into using texts by urging them to read nontexts before the program started. (How many teachers use a half grain of motivation to open a student's mouth, then force-feed him a quart of castor oil?)

Then (a holdover from my own school days) I had made the dictionary definition of words mandatory. Until reading John Holt's *The Underachieving School* (Pitman Publishing Corporation, 1969), I wasn't aware that I, like most adults, don't look up words I don't know. I figure them out from context. If I had to stop every time I found a new word, I'm sure I'd never get through a book.

Worse than anything else, though, I had tested the kids on their knowledge of the definition, and I had tested them on the material itself. Had the reading been interest-

124

ing enough, I wouldn't have found this kind of "checking" necessary. In effect, I had forced their recall of information that they didn't want, and would undoubtedly forget as soon as the test was over. Impossibility Number One is trying to teach something to somebody who doesn't want to learn it!

During my third year (and thereafter), I set up a completely individualized program. I obtained two copies of each of close to three hundred different books and divided them into six levels of difficulty. All the children who read at any one level form that level group. The difference in approach is that a student reads only what he wants to read, not what I have imposed on him. On a reading day, he goes over to his level's bookcase, selects any book and then, either alone or with someone else in his group, reads it.

During a typical class period, students are reading widely divergent material. In Group One (a reading level between 0.1 and about 1.5), he might be looking at *Green Eggs and Ham* or *One Fish Two Fish Red Fish Blue Fish,* both Dr. Seuss books. In Group Two (1.3 to 3.0), any part of the Babar series, or perhaps *The Travels of Dr. Dolittle.* In Group Three (2.6 to 4.5), *My Brother Stevie,* the story of a young girl who has to take care of her baby brother while her mother is away, a typical situation for many of my students, or *Martin Luther King: Courageous Warrior.* In Group Four (4.0 to 5.5), a student may be reading *Lilies of the Field* or *The Soul Brothers and Sister Lou,* one of the most popular books in the room, about a young girl whose friends drop out of school, start a gang, get in trouble with the police, but who, *deus ex machina,* end up forming a successful singing group. In Group Five (5.5 and up), *Anything for a Friend,* the story of a young middle-class white girl's efforts to integrate the senior prom by having one of her suitors take the small New England town's only black

125

girl, or *More Stories from The Twilight Zone.* In Group Six (7.0 and up), a student could choose to read *Malcolm X Speaks,* or, if she's a girl, she might enjoy *Escape from Nowhere,* the tale of a teen-ager on drugs. Whatever the book, there isn't one that is less motivating and relevant than *Our American Story,* or some similarly titled eighth-grade history book.

If on a given day a student chooses not to read, he doesn't. Instead of getting his book, he goes over to my desk, which since my second year has been tucked in a far corner of the room, and he sits and does nothing. The students have nicknamed this part of the room the "Do Nothing Corner." The corner is not a retreat for students who never want to read (which rarely happens if they're given an almost unlimited choice of books), but for any child who on a particular day "just don't feel like it."

It's true that I could "force" the child to read—rather to look like he was reading. I can make him sit still, and I can make him put the open book before his open eyes, but I cannot make him move his eyes over the page. Further, this kind of "force" will only antagonize the child. If I continue to compel what won't come naturally, I am as much as sending out an engraved invitation for a discipline problem. Everybody has his off days. Most adults call in sick. Children should have the same opportunity.

When a student finishes a book, he goes over to the room's file box and writes on his card the name of the book and the date he completed it. Then he goes back to his level's bookcase and picks out another book, which he starts to read. To progress from one level group to another, a student must read a specified number of books, 20 out of 40 in the most elementary level, 5 out of 45 in the highest. If a student can't find any book that appeals to him, I take him to the public library after school.

I continue to use student-teachers, but their role is now limited to assisting with word definitions. If a student has trouble with a word, he asks his student-teacher for help. If neither of them knows the word, they ask me. And if the three of us can't define it, we go to the dictionary. Otherwise, I spend my time with the group of nondecoders.

I still use the Reading Progress Board and the payoff of a giant Sugar Daddy at the end of the year for students who reach the top, but I've dropped taking and posting pictures. The content of the books more than compensates for them.

Since my students read only books that they like, testing is superfluous. Statistically, the results of this program are astounding.

In September, 1969, I gave my students a standardized reading test. The average score was 4.5, which means that my eighth graders were collectively reading at a level equivalent to that of a student halfway through the fourth grade. On the basis of past performance I could reasonably expect that by the end of the year my students would be reading at exactly a fifth-grade level. In other words, over their past seven years in school, this group had a tendency to gain about six months for every ten months of school. If nothing changed, then, they would improve from 4.5 to 5.0 at the end of their first nine months with me. Instead, post-testing in May, 1970, showed that the average had increased to 5.7. This means that the 127 tested students had improved 130 percent more than could have been reasonably expected. This was more than twice as much progress as the year-earlier "grouped reading" had produced. On top of that, this gain beat the national average for growth in reading ability by 30 percent, which includes all schools, suburban as well as ghetto. Quite a remarkable performance!

The Pleasure/Reward approach to reading, as excellent as I have found it, is not perfect. Nondecoders can be helped by a teacher who now has free time, and students who have the ability to read now have the desire. But children who have insufficient life experience—even if they read books that reflect that experience—don't significantly enlarge it. Their background can be broadened, though, by the second approach to reading, Problem-Solving.

Solving a problem in real life requires reading. As John R. Seeley, in his article "Remaking the Urban Scene" (*Daedalus,* Vol. 97, No. 4, Fall, 1968), points out: "Whatever corresponds to skills will appear as natural emergents from activities and experiences creditable and valuable in their own general terms. . . . Put another way, the way of life will engender the skills that enhance it."

The problems that a teacher and his class attempt to solve must be significant ones to the students. If they become the same old "I wonder how a bill passes Congress," the students will react with their same old disinterest and misbehavior. But if the group decides to produce and give out to the community a handbook of phone numbers to call to complain about poor housing, rats, and discrimination in public places, there will be real interest. This project, by the way, was successfully undertaken in Harlem.

Another real-life problem is the favorite of a friend of mine, Gary Richardson. He signs his junior high school class out of school "on a trip," and loads his kids into a chartered bus. Each child is given two transportation tokens, ten cents, and a map of the city. Then they are blindfolded. The bus takes them to the outskirts of the city, dropping one in a dead end here, another in the middle of a park there, and so on until all of them have been left off. The first student to reach City Hall (in the center of Philadelphia) wins. A great game, and the signs and maps are real reading. Furthermore, going to the outskirts of the city is a longer trip from home than many of his students have ever taken. Parenthetically, his answer to the inevitable question is "No." He's "brought them all back alive" and happy.

Both approaches to reading can be combined. Classroom Reading for Pleasure can be enlivened with many special projects and activities. Problem-Solving can take place in the classroom—reading through the city charter, for example, to find out which office is responsible for the buses running late or why ghetto streets are always so filthy.

Having students write stories on consequential subjects, not their four hundredth "What I Want to Be When I Grow Up," but "What's Wrong (or Right) with the Housing Project I Live In" integrates both methods.

Sophisticated poet Kenneth Koch's experiences in a New York City fourth-grade classroom are a model of the creative fusion of "fine" arts, feeling, and fun. Try it with children "too young" to understand poetry.

BY KENNETH KOCH

Some things about teaching children to write poetry I knew in advance, instinctively or from having taught adults, and others I found out in the classroom. Most important, I believe, is taking children seriously as poets. Children have a natural talent for writing poetry and anyone who teaches them should know that. Teaching really is not the right word for what takes place: it is more like permitting the

129

children to discover something they already have. I helped them to do this by removing obstacles, such as the need to rhyme, and by encouraging them in various ways to get tuned in to their own strong feelings, to their spontaneity, their sensitivity, and their carefree inventiveness. At first I was amazed at how well the children wrote, because there was obviously not enough in what I had told them even to begin to account for it. I remember that after I had seen the fourth-grade Wish Poems, I invited their teacher, Mrs. Wiener, to lunch in order to discover her "secret." I thought she must have told her students certain special things to make them write such good poems. But she had done no more than what I had suggested she do: tell the children to begin every line with "I wish," not to use rhyme, and to make the wishes real or crazy. There was one other thing: she had been happy and excited about their doing it and she had expected them to enjoy it too.

I was, as I said, amazed, because I hadn't expected any grade-school children, much less fourth graders, to write so well so soon. I thought I might have some success with sixth graders, but even there I felt it would be best to begin with a small group who volunteered for a poetry workshop. After the fourth-grade Wish Poems, however, and after the Wish and Comparison Poems from the other grades, I realized my mistake. The children in all the grades, primary through sixth, wrote poems which they enjoyed and I enjoyed. Treating them like poets was not a case of humorous but effective diplomacy, as I had first thought; it was the right way to treat them because it corresponded to the truth. A little humor, of course, I left in. Poetry was serious, but we joked and laughed a good deal; it was serious because it was such a pleasure to write. Treating them as poets enabled me to encourage them and egg them on in a non-teacherish way—as an admirer and fellow worker rather than as a boss. It shouldn't be difficult for a teacher to share this attitude once it is plain how happily and naturally the students take to writing.

There are other barriers besides rhyme and meter that can keep children from writing freely and enjoying it. One is feeling they have to spell everything correctly. Stopping to worry about spelling a word can cut off a fine flow of ideas. So can having to avoid words one can't spell. Punctuation can also be an interference, as can neatness. Good poetic ideas often come as fast as one can write; in the rush to get them down there may be no time for commas or for respecting a margin. All these matters can be attended to after the poem is written.

Another barrier is a child's believing that poetry is difficult and remote. Poetry should be talked about in as simple a way as possible and certainly without such bewildering rhetorical terms as *alliteration, simile,* and *onomatopoeia.* There are easy, colloquial ways to say all these: words beginning with the same sound, comparisons using *like* or *as,* words that sound like what they mean. Poetry is a mystery, but it is a mystery children can participate in and master, and they shouldn't be kept away from it by hard words.

Again on the subject of language, the various poetry ideas should be presented in words children actually use. I don't think the Wish Poems would have been so successful if I had asked my students to start every line with "I desire." Nor would "My seeming self" and "My true self" have worked well in place of "I Seem to be/But Really I Am." One should be on the lookout, too, for words and phrases which tell the child what to say and take him away from important parts of his experience: I think "make-believe" and "imaginary" are such words. When I told a teacher at another school about the "I wish" assignment, she said that she had done almost the same thing but it

131

hadn't turned out as well. She had had her students write poems in which every line began with "Love is." I never heard a child say "love is" in my life, and so I wasn't surprised that they hadn't responded wholeheartedly.

One bar to free feeling and writing is the fear of writing a bad poem and of being criticized or ridiculed for it. There is also the oppression of being known as not one of the "best." I didn't single out any poems as being best or worst. When I read poems aloud I didn't say whose they were, and I made sure that everyone's work was read every so often. If I praised a line or an image I put the stress on the kind of line or image it was and how exciting it might be for others to try something like that too. That way, I felt, the talent in the room was being used for the benefit of everyone.

The teacher shouldn't correct a child's poems either. If a word or line is unclear, it is fine to ask the child what he meant, but not to change it in order to make it meet one's own standards. The child's poem should be all his own. And of course one shouldn't use a child's poetry to analyze his personal problems. Aside from the scientific folly of so doing, it is sure to make children inhibited about what they write.

A surprising discovery I made at P.S. 61 was that children enjoyed writing poems at school more than at home. I had assumed that like grownup writers they would prefer to be comfortable, quiet, and alone when they wrote, but I was wrong. Once it had to be done away from school, poetry was part of the detestable category "homework," which cuts one off from the true pleasures of life; whereas in school it was a welcome relief from math, spelling, and other required subjects. Closing their heavy books to hear about a new idea for a poem made the children happy and buoyant. There was also the fact of their all being there in the room, writing together. No time for self-consciousness or self-doubts; there was too much activity: everyone was writing and talking and jumping around. And it was competitive in a mild and exhilarating way: it was what everyone was doing and everyone could do it.

The children wrote a few lines, showed them to each other, copied, teased, called to me for help or admiration, and then went back to their writing. Out of this lovely chaos, after fifteen minutes or so, finished poems would begin to appear, handed to me written in pencil on sheets of notebook paper, that would make me gasp. That is how almost all these poems were composed. The classroom was so drab-looking and so noisy, with the students talking, the PA system going BOOP BOOP and the trash can going BOOM (during many a writing session it was rolled in and out of the room), that I couldn't imagine sitting there and writing a poem. The children, however, seemed not to be distracted at all.

I let the children make a good deal of noise. Children do when they are excited, and writing poetry is exciting. I let them change papers and read each other's poems too. Sometimes in that maelstrom of creation one student's idea would seem so irresistible that another would use it. But not many lines were stolen, and the poetry thief always went on to something of his own.

One important advantage to writing in class was that I was there: before the children wrote, to explain and to inspire; and while they were writing, to act as reader, admirer, and furnisher of additional ideas. It is true that I could have explained an assignment and let the children carry it out at home. What I couldn't have done was keep the new idea and their excitement about it fresh in their minds from noon till seven-thirty, or whenever they would

133

sit down to write. For each poem I did certain things and gave certain examples to help make the idea clear and to put the children in the mood for writing. In giving the Color Poem, for instance, I asked them to close their eyes; then clapped my hands and asked them what color that was. Almost everyone raised his hand: "Red!" "Green!" "White!" I asked them what color Paris was; London; Rome; Los Angeles. I told them to close their eyes again and I said certain words and certain numbers, asking them what color those were. The point was to get them to associating colors freely with all kinds of things before writing the poem. Almost always a part of my preparation was reading other children's poems aloud, and the effect of these was most vivid when the class wrote immediately after hearing them.

I could also be helpful to the children while they were actually writing. Often students got the feeling when they were about to start writing that they didn't really understand the assignment, so they would call me over to make it clearer. Sometimes a student would be stuck, unable to start his poem. I would give him a few ideas, while trying not to give him actual lines or words—"Well, how do musical instruments sound? Why don't you write about those?" or "What do you hear when you're on a boat?" Sometimes students would get stuck in the middle of a poem, and I would do the same sort of thing. Sometimes I would be called over to approve what had been written so far, to see if it was OK. I often made such comments as "That's good, but write some more," or "Yes, the first three lines in particular are terrific—what about some more like that?" or "That's not exactly what I meant. Turn it over; let's start again," or "I think maybe it's finished. What about another poem on the other side?"

So I was useful in the classroom for getting the children in a good mood to write and then for keeping them going.

134

And they were useful to each other in creating a humming and buzzing creative ambiance. They helped and inspired each other as well by the poetry they wrote, which afterwards everyone could read or hear. I have already mentioned my practice of reading aloud to one class the poems of another. Once I had discovered the various good effects of doing this, it became an important part of my teaching.

At first Karl Liikson responded to the pedestrian prose of his seventh-grade writing class in typical teacher fashion—he circled errors in spelling and sentence construction in red pencil. Uncomfortable doing this, he tried to find and to emphasize the occasional spots of beauty and clarity in the children's work. Then the children began to write for real. His praise worked, but it also led to an even more profound lesson: The teacher may fall into the trap of *using* praise and supportive comments to control his students. "Keep your goddam praise," a student screamed. Then Karl realized what was really involved in "getting the words back to the kids."

BY KARL LIIKSON

I came to Jack's story again. This was the second time I had seen it. It was now three pages long and already it had a history in my mind. I had seen him with two atlases intent in tracing his trip. It seemed as if he was trying to bolster his otherwise so-so account with massive research.

135

I have usually found that once the kids have started to listen to their own stories they are pleasantly surprised and then catch the "might-be" feeling—i.e., that there might be something worthwhile on their pages (but they are not sure!). So to tip the balance slightly they usually adorn the work with scrolls and frames and things. My job, in this instance, was to kindle that "might-be" feeling.

On Jack's paper, I remembered the detailed enumerations of the things to eat of the menus in the restaurants he visited on the trip. As a reminder to myself I had written at the top of the page:

> A long trip from Province to Province with an interesting side trip to a relative who has a farm. The best writing is still at the beginning where the account is more detailed and compact.

But I couldn't return to the first part again since I had already dealt with it during an earlier session and I was in the middle of explaining this to the group when Jack interjected by boasting, "Yes, and three places marked by the teacher!" (By that he meant that I had circled three, instead of the usual one place as being worthy of note.)

The exact words of the second part that I selected to read out were:

> So we got there at 2 o'clock on the button there it was 50 acres of land and I seen what my mother told. . . . Yes, there are horses, pig, cow, chicken and a dog and a car and I said wow that a lot of animal I said.

I read these sentences out loud without the obvious grammatical errors and happened to glance at Jack. He was sitting on the edge of his seat like a hockey player being told to take to the ice and score. For good measure I repeated the first lines over a couple of times so that his intentions as a writer were perfectly clear:

> So we got there at 2 o'clock on the button. There it
> was!—50 acres of land! I saw what my mother had told
> me.

The words had a masterful ring even to me and I fancied I
heard the voice shouting inside Jack.

For years kids put letter beside letter to make words and
then words beside words to make what usually amounts to
some kind of thought. They rarely sense the echo that these
thoughts make on the thoughts of others. For the most part
their words sink like stones without a ripple. One can't help
but to wonder why we don't read back at least some little
part of what they have written. By the time we do so for
those who most need it, they have become so convinced of
their own inadequacy that they don't want to listen. They
are afraid of ridicule, of losing face with their peers. Naturally they will give any teacher, who embarks on the
hazardous course of exposing them, a really hard time.
Many could be prevented from ever reaching this stage if
we did not have fixed ideas about what we want or believe
that we have to correct every kid's writing at every stage of
his development.

Secondly, it's a matter of resources at the crucial turning
point when the teacher wants to launch on a program of
positive feedback. Usually it's not too difficult to find one or
two sentences in children's compositions that "read well,"
provided you can muster up from within you the energy to
feel positive—to see beyond the pencil marks on the paper.
For that to happen you need a breathing spell during
which the everyday struggle cannot erode your will to do
the job properly.

Verna's composition ended with a line that the group—at
one point so reluctant to listen at all—visibly enjoyed:

That night when I went to bed I slept till 9 o'clock. Then I helped pack the car and started for the long trip home.

The prospect of reading back David's story caused me considerable apprehension. He had an unsettling effect on any group, and in this case I didn't expect him to remain silent or still. At the very least I was sure he would mimic me so effectively that I would stop or become confused. His usual encounter with teachers seemed to cry out, "Be firm and decisive with me. . . . Life's too slippery!" But as soon as anyone tried, he cried foul and caused more trouble than the whole thing seemed worth. Little digs, big distortions of fact and hints at appeals to higher authority in or outside school were all part of the game. The energy, inventiveness and persistence with which he attracted attention and then fought it off once he got it were too much for an ordinary person. . . . The school, trying to steer away from absolute authority, gave him the benefit of doubt and that caused him to be even more upset and upsetting. Except for being a rather clumsy way of reaching him, what earthly good was written English to this boy? "Leave," "said," "tomorrow," "know," "any," "caught," "took," "leaving," "next," I penciled in as inconspicuously as possible. They were words that David had probably meant and with their help I hoped to be able to read fluently his story. By luck the following introduction went off well and David listened without interruption to his own words:

Introduction:
When the writer is threatened with having to move away from home, he runs away. He has the usual brush with the law and is brought back home to discover that his mother has changed her mind about moving away. This, then, is David's story:

138

Worth learning

Story:
One Friday afternoon, I returned from school to find my mother packing the car. She said we were leaving the city. I said I don't want to leave the city, but mother said We have to leave, so get ready to leave tomorrow. So that night I ran away. I didn't know where I was going, but I didn't want to go back home any more so I just kept on going. Then I saw a cop. It was coming at me I ran as fast as I could go but he caught me and took me home. Then my mother said we are not leaving the city until next year. Then I was happy.

David's story could be interpreted as a sad parallel to his own life and what happens to him from day to day. Digging for hidden meanings has nothing to do with feedback, however. Still, it is important to be sensitive to writing that derives directly from life itself. To encourage such writing is not easy.

As in most first meetings, what the kids had written was generally hum-drum. I had hopes that somebody would write about a concrete situation as opposed to the usual "story." Annallee did. However, I hesitated. I did not know the group well enough; we had not progressed far enough; maybe we should wait. . . . I don't know exactly what the factors are that interfere, but I do know that if something that is close to the lives of the kids is not received correctly, if the group is not ready, a long time will lapse before anyone will venture along this path again. Instead, the kids will stick to what they think the teacher wants. This part of Wendy's "story" was a good example:

> Then my mother yelled out, There it is! There's our pretty house! . . . well, do you like your new house, Wendy?
> Yes, Mom, I thought it would be out in the country.

No. No, I wanted to surprise you. We live near your best friend, Colleen.

Oh, Mom, thanks! Now I am really glad I moved.

Not only was the content safe, but the language verged on the beautiful style of the primer. It wasn't lack of vocabulary on Wendy's part. Only two minutes before she had committed the above passage to paper, she had told, in a vivid phrase or two, a tall boy to keep his bony fingers to himself. I puzzled over Wendy's composition. Its bland quality made me decide that now was the time to present the most concrete part of Annallee's composition.

> Wouldn't you prefer to live in a house than this pile of garbage, we get all (our) are things stolen from our (lockers) lokes, boys sniff, smoke and drink in halls, people open up our mail, so what, do you want me to do, stay here and get all our stuff stolen, you stay but I'm not.

As I read I hoped that the words would ring true to life but that no fuss would be made about them. There was an unnatural stillness while I was reading and it remained for a moment longer than usual. The kids had listened.

At that point Angie recognized his story and told me privately (since he sat beside me) : "For Christ's sake it's the last one!"

His account had the elements of a good yarn—character, plot, action. It was committed to paper in a first class scribble which had taken me a while to decipher.

> *Angie's Story:*
> On Friday afternoon, I returned from school to find my mother packing the car. She said we were leaving the city.
>
> "Leaving the city!" I said "What for?" She said, "We are going to our farm."

Worth learning

I started jumping and cheering and the whole thing. She said to be quiet. It was a surprise for my younger brother on his birthday.

I was even happier because there was snow up north and I could get even with my brother for what he did to me last winter. I spent half the night trying to think of a plan to get even with him. I finally got a plan. It was a dilly.

When we got there I took my brother to the top of a hill and said, "Happy Birthday!" Then [I] pushed him over, but it backfired. He pulled me over the side with him. Half-way down I grabbed a branch and he kept on going. We finally found him and we went home. What an experience! I finally out-smarted him.

The group of kids leaned into the circle and totally missed a burst of laughter from four teachers who were off in the far corner of the staffroom. They were doing their thing and we did ours and the one did not distract the other. But these two groups of people were symbolically united. The time the kids willingly became involved was when they were playing the game of "dodge school"—which was most of the time. One of the few times the teachers were rejoicing was when they came to the staffroom for a rest from having to play the game.

When the kids and I returned to the classroom I became part of the dynamics of another force that blocks the success of positive feedback. Its dimensions are more subtle than restless kids or the correcting habit. As soon as we stepped inside the classroom, the kids who had been in a quiet, contemplative mood, went wild. (Jubilance, or something.) Annallee rushed to Linda and started whispering, loudly. David pretended he was lighting a cigarette and blowing smoke. Pat started protesting. Angie made a bullhorn of his paper and called out drill orders to everyone in the room.

141

In all this, Mr. S. and the rest of the class tried to conduct a study of maps. I felt responsible and started shushing the newcomers.

> Just because your story was pretty good, I pointed out to Angie, that doesn't mean you can shout all over the place.

He turned sharply and even while making his quick, alert repartee, I realized what in essence he was going to say:

> Don't use your encouragement to control me. I am going to resist responding to any effort on your part to make me feel good about my school work if it means that this will give you power over me. Keep your goddam praise.

Had he in fact caught me trying to take a shortcut in our relationship? Was this such a common shortcut in school that Angie was ever on the lookout for it? Do we pair positive comments with control? I think we do. Obviously Angie regarded the whole area of feeling good about what you have done in school as booby trapped—dangerous.

Feeling good about something is a form of surrender. If you depend on someone else to produce the feeling, then you are at least partially in his power. Better not to feel at all. What Angie was touching upon was elemental. I have seen kids sit poker-faced for hours, not wanting to give themselves away. They have an air of studied casualness, but their eyes tell a different story.

By the time the unsure learner has reached Grade 7, he sees school as a series of dangers either to be laughed off, fought off, or quickly suffered. Praise is among them: keep a sharp lookout for it and never allow yourself to be trapped into the feeling that there might be something good in what you are doing. Much of the apparent apathy I suspect derives from thinking in this fashion.

The fact that kids go to all this trouble to guard themselves has its good points. For the teacher who cares, the alertness helps to preserve the purity in the relationship between him and the learner: Good work should not be a means of control. Working class kids, who are not used to the usual "conditional love" handed out for good behavior, are most likely to resist the improper use of praise. The issue of control demands a basic trust in a teacher's integrity and judgment. In schools where this has *not* been resolved, it is understandable that the teacher might resort to using praise for the purpose of control. All too often nowadays, this issue has not been resolved.

Other obstacles make the inception of positive feedback difficult. One of these emanates from the mind of the hard-working, cautious teacher. He is afraid of praising school work because he believes that pointing out mistakes is a quicker way to teach than pointing out strengths. He also fears that telling somebody their good points is the same as the lowering of standards. So he steadfastly keeps up the pressure. Once the kids feel that they are getting somewhere, it makes good sense to point out weaknesses. Often they themselves ask for this kind of criticism and the cycle of raising standards can begin. Of course, the kids will go out of their way to test the teacher's sincerity. They have a habit of doing this as soon as they sense that the learning is going to really matter, i.e., alter their lives in a significant way.

Where the teachers have a chance, where their old correcting habit and a basic distrust of praise are not going to get in the way, positive feedback will pay huge dividends. In such a place and with such teachers, Angie's words "I got hurt in school today," may rarely be uttered. But those places are going to be difficult to come by; good teachers are going to have to fight hard to get them.

Will it grow in a classroom?

What is "correct" English? Is there such a thing? And, if there is, do you want to learn to use it, or do you choose to assert your individuality and freedom by continuing to speak as you now do?

We did not know whether to put "Stokely's Speech Class," recorded by Jane Stembridge, in the section on language or in the one on social change, so we chose to put it in-between the two. We had a similar problem of "proper" placement with many of the selections in this book, which is why we liked them in the first place.

BY JANE STEMBRIDGE

Stokely put eight sentences on the blackboard, with a line between, like this:

I digs wine.	I enjoy drinking cocktails.
The peoples wants freedom.	The people want freedom.
Whereinsoever the policemens goes they causes troubles.	Anywhere the officers of the law go, they cause trouble.
I wants to reddish to vote.	I want to register to vote.

STOKELY: What do you think about these sentences? Such as, "The peoples wants freedom"?

ZELMA: It doesn't sound right.

STOKELY: What do you mean?

ZELMA: "Peoples" isn't right.

STOKELY: Does it mean anything?

MILTON: "People" means everybody. "Peoples" means everybody in the world.

144

Worth learning

ALMA: Both sentences are right as long as you understand them.

HENRY: They're both okay, but in a speech class you have to use correct English.

(Stokely writes "correct English" in corner of blackboard.)

ZELMA: I was taught at least to use the sentences on the right side.

STOKELY: Does anybody you know use the sentences on the left?

CLASS: Yes.

STOKELY: Are they wrong?

ZELMA: In terms of English, they are wrong.

STOKELY: Who decides what is correct English and what is incorrect English?

MILTON: People made rules. People in England, I guess.

STOKELY: You all say some people speak like on the left side of the board. Could they go anywhere and speak that way? Could they go to Harvard?

CLASS: Yes. No. (Disagreement.)

STOKELY: Does Mr. Turnbow* speak like on the left side?

CLASS: Yes.

STOKELY: Could Mr. Turnbow go to Harvard and speak like that? "I wants to reddish to vote."

CLASS: Yes.

STOKELY: Would he be embarrassed?

CLASS: Yes! No!

ZELMA: He wouldn't be, but I would. It doesn't sound right.

* Hartman Turnbow, a black farmer from Mileston, Mississippi, the first black man to attempt to register to vote in the Holmes County registration campaign of that decade. A popular indigenous leader of extraordinary poise, charm, and courage, he used the common "reddish" for "register."

145

Will it grow in a classroom?

STOKELY: Suppose someone from Harvard came to Holmes County and said, "I want to register to vote." Would they be embarrassed?

ZELMA: No.

STOKELY: Is it embarrassing at Harvard but not in Holmes County? The way you speak?

MILTON: It's inherited. It's depending on where you come from. The people at Harvard would understand.

STOKELY: Do you think the people at Harvard should forgive you?

MILTON: The people at Harvard should help teach us correct English.

ALMA: Why should we change if we understand what we mean?

SHIRLEY: It is embarrassing.

STOKELY: Which way do most people talk?

CLASS: Like on the left.

(He asks each student. All but two say "left." One says that southerners speak like on the left, northerners on the right. Another said that southerners speak like on the left, but the majority of people speak like on the right.)

STOKELY: Which way do television and radio people speak?

CLASS: Left.

(There was a distinction by the class between northern commentators and local programs. Most programs were local and spoke like on the left, they said.)

STOKELY: Which way do teachers speak?

CLASS: On the left, except in class.

STOKELY: If most people speak on the left, why are they trying to change these people?

GLADYS: If you don't talk right, society rejects you. It embarrasses other people if you don't talk right.

HANK: But Mississippi society, ours, isn't embarrassed by it.

SHIRLEY: But the middle class wouldn't class us with them.

HANK: They won't accept "reddish." What is "reddish"? It's Negro dialect and it's something you eat.

STOKELY: Will society reject you if you don't speak like on the right side of the board? Gladys said society would reject you.

GLADYS: You might as well face it, man! What we gotta do is go out and become middle class. If you can't speak good English, you don't have a car, a job, or anything.

STOKELY: If society rejects you because you don't speak good English, should you learn to speak good English?

CLASS: No!

ALMA: I'm tired of doing what society say. Let society say "reddish" for a while. People ought to just accept each other.

ZELMA: I think we should be speaking just like we always have.

ALMA: If I change for society, I wouldn't be free anyway.

ERNESTINE: I'd like to learn correct English for my own sake.

SHIRLEY: I would too.

ALMA: If the majority speaks on the left, then a minority must rule society. Why do we have to change to be accepted by the minority group?

(Lunchtime.)

STOKELY: Let's think about two questions for next time: What is society? Who makes the rules for society?

147

5

Learning for a change

Studying the society that will be theirs

What is the "real" social studies curriculum in our schools? Is it "covering countries," memorizing the presidents, and learning about interest rates?

The way students learn about living together, about social organization, about becoming mature citizens is by seeing how their school and their society actually operate. The average school purports to teach democracy, respect for others, the rule of law; yet it imposes on students an autocratic authority, regiments them much of the time, and denies their basic rights.

Good teachers, however, are breaking this bondage. They, along with their students, are looking at the compelling issues facing us as citizens today. They are making history real by making it relevant. They are using their own classes as laboratories to explore both how individuals come into conflict and how they achieve harmony.

Social studies are taught best by offering students an opportunity to make a small society, a little history, themselves.

It is a balmy April morning. Yesterday Martin Luther King was murdered. What will you do today for "social studies"?

Ralph Berens knew that a social studies teacher in such a situation could not avoid teaching a moral lesson: To ignore what happened is itself a powerful lesson in uncaring. Most of us would ask, "But what can *I* do?" The answer is the lesson for today.

BY RALPH BERENS

It was the kind of early April day when all you wanted to do was to touch the tops of the trees, to breathe the sunwashed air, to smell the fragrance of the not-yet-ripe blossoms. It was the kind of day to take the kids outside and work with them there.

On this morning, however, I wasn't thinking about taking the kids anywhere. My eyes were closed, my nose dull to smells, my whole being insensitive to happiness. I didn't

149

want to touch anything or anybody. I felt out of contact with people. Martin Luther King was dead. My thoughts were focused around how I could help students understand the magnitude of the loss which all of us had suffered.

With the weight of numbness, I went to the cafeteria, where the teachers always gathered before school. It was not a place I often frequented because I always became frustrated with their intolerance for ideas which differed from their own. Discussions centered around sports, politics, and particularly students. (The phrase used with the latter was, "those kids," meaning students who were either rebellious or smarter than the teachers.) In spite of my reluctance to visit the cafeteria in the early morning, I felt the need on this day to make contact with people. There were the usual comments about sports. Baseball was just starting then and the talk centered around the school team and its products. I paid little attention to the details, except that somewhere inside me a gnawing uneasiness was growing. Why were they talking about baseball on this day? In time, however, they came around to politics. "What do you think of this Martin Luther King thing?" "I think it's terrible." "A nice guy, Martin Luther King, but the trouble was that he minded everyone else's business." For the first time that day, I was shaken out of my lethargy as I angrily replied, "That's exactly it. He cared enough to think there was a connection between other people's affairs and his own." Silence. Why couldn't the few who felt the same as I did speak up? I began to understand what kind of day it was going to be—a day of frustration and futility. I was going to be alone again and I didn't like being isolated. I left the cafeteria with a mixture of mute rage and consternation and went to my first period class.

That class was a nice group of kids, grouped together as "slow learners," less academic than others, but nicer and perhaps more sensitive to other people. I approached that group with some excitement, thinking that since we had been working with the issues of slavery and civil rights there might be some sympathetic reaction to what had happened. In any case, it couldn't be any worse than what I had heard in the cafeteria. "Isn't that the guy we were talking about the other day?" Students started taking sides. "I liked him. He was a good man." Another said, "Nah! He was a trouble-maker." Still another, "My father says he's a communist." My God, I thought, they're going to make a mockery out of this whole thing. They want to have a debate! Futility began to overwhelm me. A whole series of thoughts poured through my mind, most of them about what a poor job I had done.

If these kids were sensitive, I hadn't been able to get them to use their sensitivity. I could sense no particular feeling concerning Martin Luther King's death. I read a few passages from the Declaration of Independence and other things which I don't today remember. I do recall kids choking up when I choked up. So what had I accomplished? An allegiance to me—nothing concerning the larger issue of his death and its meaning. In one flash I could see the kids becoming like the teachers in the cafeteria.

The next period was a planning session for a humanities course. The three of us involved realized that planning was fruitless that morning. None of us could concentrate. I walked outside and looked up at the flag thinking about the general futility of the day and the meaninglessness of teaching.

Oh for God's sake, the flag isn't lowered. . . . I was sick. I ran into the principal's office. But I caught myself, saying, be effective, don't emote. So I walked into his office and gently asked him why the flag wasn't lowered. His answer so floored me that I bit my lip to keep from laughing. "It's not lowered, Ralph, because I haven't received a directive from the superintendent." Quickly I tried to think of strategy, but I was feeling so helpless that my mind went blank. So I said, "Please call the superintendent and ask him whether the flag can be lowered."

I was teaching a class around noon time when the principal came in and told me that I could lower the flag if I wanted to. Then he walked out. While the class sat there, I began to think about when I should lower the flag. Now, in the middle of class? And what were the students supposed to do when I was out front lowering the flag? So, I thought, I'll lower it after class. Then I realized that I didn't know how to lower the flag. (Several years ago, in a boys' camp, I had lowered the flag but that was no help now.) All of these thoughts were too confusing for me. So I told the class to hold on for a minute, and I simply stepped outside and did what I had to do. I don't remember how I did it or whether I lowered the flag to the correct position. I only remember the feelings I had. I was alone and embarrassed and I felt naked; and I was ashamed of the school for not having done this before.

When I walked back into class, kids rushed to their seats from the window where they had been straining to watch me. I saw a sea of faces staring at me, comprehending what I had done. For a moment I was overcome with emotion, realizing that lowering the flag was the most important thing I had done that day. No readings from the Declaration or from anything else could match it. We still had a few minutes until the end of class, and if I could have dismissed the students, I would have done so. I didn't know what to do with the class. But nothing needed to be done. Nor did anything have to be accomplished. No one said anything. There was nothing to say—only things to feel.

Worth learning

Is history a series of presidents, statutes,
battles, and inventions? Or is it someone's
attempt to tell us how we got where we are
today and what we must know about the uses
and abuses of power? Whose history are
we studying—the winners' or the losers'?
Linda Zaretsky raises the kinds of questions
that should be raised about historical
and literary portrayals of all minority
groups.

BY LINDA ZARETSKY

The following lesson plan, "A Native American Speaks,"
was used in a lower track American history class. All of the
students were white.

I chose the selection reprinted below because:

1. It deals with a subject which the students already had
   some opinions on; that is, they had a conception of the
   frontier Indian which they could compare with the one
   presented in the selection.
2. It deals with the question of genocide in a more complicated way than just a reversal on the cowboys and
   Indians theme. That is, the students can see that the
   threat to the Indian was not just that the white man
   was taking his land and killing his buffalo, but that he
   was threatening his culture.
3. It shows that the Indians were neither savages nor
   naive victims, but were aware of the threat they were
   facing and at times articulated that awareness.
4. It could help to raise the question of why selections
   like these are not included in standard high school
   history texts.

153

5. It is written simply enough for the students to be comfortable with it.

I began the lesson by asking students what image of the frontier Indian they had. They eagerly recounted some of the cowboy and Indian movies and TV shows they had seen with the usual stereotypes of the savage Indians scalping the innocent white settlers. Some of the students had seen more recent films in which Indians were treated more sympathetically. We talked briefly about why there was beginning to be a change in the way Indians were presented.

I then asked the students to look for passages in their own textbooks to see how Indians are presented there. While their books were not as blatantly discriminating as the films they had seen, it was obvious that the text treatment of Indians is one-sided, particularly when it comes to describing the "valiant" efforts that were made to "civilize" the Indian after the West was won.

We then read the selection together in class. I asked the students the following questions:

1. Why doesn't the Indian chief trust the white man?

We listed the reasons on the board. While this might appear to be a tedious exercise for students who have problems with the usual materials given to them, it was a positive experience to be able to extract answers from the text and support those answers with quotes.

2. The missionary does not appear to be there to take the Indians' land, yet the chief won't let him come into the territory. How would you explain this?

In response to this question, students were able to see that the Indian chief was struggling to preserve the customs and ways of his people.

154

3. What kind of image of the Indian does this selection express? Compare that image with the way in which Indians are presented in most movies and in your textbook.

The question of the Indian image provoked some good discussion. Students pointed out that in contrast to the films they had seen, the Indian in the selection we read wished the white man a safe return to his people, and far from scalping him showed him a remarkable tolerance. The discussion raised some other important questions, including: Why did the Indians take Alcatraz? Were they right in doing so? Students thought that they were, but then one student asked, "Shouldn't we then give them back the whole country?"

The lesson plan was effective in that it enabled the students to view at least this segment of American history from a minority group's point of view. It also provided insight into contemporary minority movements, movements to which these students are often hostile. A few days before we did this lesson, I had overheard one of my students tell another how that man Chavez was ruining the Chicanos, so that they were becoming as bad as the Blacks.

One problem with the lesson plan and with the discussion that followed is that it became very moralistic. Students were sympathetic to the Indians' plight to the point of wanting to undo American history rather than figuring out how America should treat its minorities now. Another problem was that students all too easily identified themselves as the villains in the story; that is, they talked in terms of what *we* did to the Indians and what *we* should do now, as though *they* had deprived the Indians of their land and culture and were continuing to perpetrate that wrong. This kind of thinking points to the great need for materials and approaches which not only show how minorities have been persecuted in this country but are at the same time very clear about who was doing the persecuting and what interests were being served. Perhaps then white students, particularly those in lower track classes, can begin to see the oppressive nature of their own situation, and in that way begin to identify with the groups which they now despise or at best feel sorry for.

"A Native American Speaks"*

Brother, listen to what we say.

There was a time when our forefathers owned this great island. Their seats extended from the rising to the setting sun. The Great Spirit made it for the use of Indians.

But an evil day came upon us. Your forefathers crossed the great water and landed on this island. Their numbers were small. They found friends and not enemies. They told us that they had fled from their own country for fear of wicked men and had come here to enjoy their religion. We took pity on them, granted their request, and they sat down among us. We gave them corn and meat; they gave us poison [liquor] in return.

The white people had now found our country. Tidings were carried back, and more came amongst us. Yet, we did not fear them. We took them to be friends. They called us brothers. We believed them. At length their numbers had greatly increased. They wanted more land. They wanted our country. Our eyes were opened and our minds became

---

* Excerpted from a piece with the same title as published in P. Jacobs, S. Landau, and E. Pell (eds.), *To Serve the Devil*, Vol. 1 (New York: Vintage, 1971). This selection was originally from *The American Spirit—United States History As Seen by Contemporaries.* Thomas A. Bailey (ed.) (Lexington, Mass.: D. C. Heath & Company).

uneasy. Wars took place. Indians were hired to fight against Indians and many of our people were destroyed. They also brought strong liquor among us. It was strong and powerful and has slain thousands.

Brothers, our lands were once large and yours were small. You have now become a great people, and we have scarcely a place to spread our blankets. You have got our country, but are not satisfied. You want to force your religion upon us.

You say that you are sent to instruct us how to worship the Great Spirit, and if we do not take hold of the religion which you white people teach us, we shall be unhappy hereafter. You say that you are right and we are lost. How do we know this to be true? We understand that your religion is written in a book. If it was intended for us as well as you, why has not the Great Spirit given to us, and not only to us, but why did he not give to our forefathers, the knowledge of that book? We only know what you tell us about it. How shall we know when to believe, being so often deceived by the white people?

Brother, we do not understand these things. We are told that your religion was given to your forefathers, and has been handed down from father to son. We also have a religion which was given to our forefathers, and has been handed down to us, their children. We worship in that way. We never quarrel about religion.

Brother, the Great Spirit has made us all, but he has made a great difference between his white and red children. He has given us different complexions and different customs. Since he has made so great a difference in other things, why may we not conclude that he has given us a different religion according to our understanding. The Great Spirit does right. He knows what is best for his children. We are satisfied.

157

Brother, we do not wish to destroy your religion or take it from you. We only want to enjoy our own.

Brother, you say that you have not come to get our land or our money, but to enlighten our minds. I will tell you that I have been at your meetings and saw you collect money from the meeting. I cannot tell you what this money was intended for, but suppose that it was for your minister; and if we should conform to your way of thinking, perhaps you may want some from us.

Brother, we know that you have been preaching to some white people who are our neighbors. We are acquainted with them. We will wait a while to see what effect your preaching has upon them. If we find it does them good, makes them honest and less disposed to cheat Indians, we will then consider again of what you have said.

Brother, you have now heard our answer to your talk, and this is all we have to say at present. As we are going to part, we will come and take you by the hand, and hope the Great Spirit will protect you on your journey and return you safe to your friends.

Cam Smith tried "covering countries," which was what she was supposed to be doing with this seventh-grade class. But the group really started learning when it "became a 'Social Studies' class, where 'social' was getting lived. People really discovered that there are others around and it is rather important how you act toward them."

Worth learning

BY CAM SMITH

This was the class where the most happened. It was a 7th grade, which seems 3 years younger than 8th grade. The difference in bodies between 7th grade children and 8th grade adults is pretty startling. The way they act is just as different as the way they look.

We met during the last wild period of the day. The class was a group of "slower" students, who have to have things very real and aren't civilized, and will throw things in a minute if they are bored. I have respect for them.

We started out the first week as a group in a new school, together and quiet and wondering what was going to be what. We defined "social" (human beings in their relationships with each other) and acted out people doing things together. We put on short plays of all the things the class could think of that were "social." We demonstrated "social action" with the whole class by moving chairs and tables around and seeing how quickly and quietly we could change the pattern to something else and then back again. We demonstrated communication as part of social action and did things giving each other non-verbal directions. Kids loved it and the class seemed like a fresh wonderful joy.

Our official subject was South America and Africa, so after grooving in on "social" for a week I started out trying to teach "South America." First we did maps. Since I remembered only total confusion about learning the subject on flat maps, I decided if we were going to learn about Meridians, etc., we had better do it on globes. We took a class period to make globes by covering toy balls with papier mâché. That day was pretty much of a disaster. Students went home with wet flour all over their clothes and it took a week of sending the "good" students out to scrub the

159

blacktop where we had worked, and the restrooms, besides having the upset janitor working on it, to get the flour-cement off. We did get some sloppy little globes out of it.

When we started on our textbooks things got even worse. I found out many students could barely read and couldn't relate at all to printed words. Any other class would have had quiet students in rows doing the work, whether they could read well or not, but this was already the "Social Action Class." "Pow . . . SOCK! Hey, man, solid communication!" That was real anyway, and they wondered, "How come we can't do 'social' anymore?"

Finally I told them to get themselves a group to work with and find some classroom space of their own (large tables), and a name and a president for their group. Somehow with much disorder they did it and were suddenly eager again . . . and surprisingly orderly. Some presidents of their groups were elected, one president got his job by saying he was the President, and one group asked everyone in the class, except members of their own group, to vote for their president. This looked like the class where action could happen. We got: "The Flaming Eagles," "The Communicators," "The Workers," "The Intelligent Kids," "The Social Brothers Five," "The Hell's Angels," and "Soul Sisters Number One." They tested out their new groups by doing a map project together and we had some big construction things; maps, flour, and paint handled in class surprisingly well. We sent students down the hall for mops and sponges often enough, but cleaning projects were fun too.

I passed out textbooks and showed them what a demonstration of information was. I had students demonstrate information with pictures and label each part of the picture. They had to read a section of text and (1) pick out what *they* thought was important information and (2) *show* it with drawings and labels. Intelligence involves the ability to evaluate importances. I didn't feel bad about leaving them on their own to practice that. And students who actually demonstrate information with drawings will gain a real understanding of it, even though it might look like "just drawing pictures" to an outsider. I felt very good about the way they picked up demonstrating information. There was nothing copied from the book, but parts of the text were understood and then shown. They got very sharp about statements like Brazil having more oil than any other South American country. You couldn't *show* that without showing Brazil, oil in Brazil, other countries, and oil in other countries. By the time they had figured out how to draw something like that, they had gotten some mental exercise and knew the information besides. It was a lot of fun.

This was something that everyone could succeed at. The most clever kids in the class did subtle and involved drawings with a lot of information communicated. The "slower" ones did simple things but they understood what they were doing, and they grew more clever. I knew something valuable was happening because the folder projects were really keeping people busy and interested. There was a large stiff folder for each group and each member contributed pages. Things which I never mentioned, like beans and coffee, arrived in pockets and were glued down on the pages. I could find out that they understood what they were doing by quickly going through their folders myself and learning a lot about South America from their drawing-demonstrations.

We did lots of folders. The class began to know when it was time to move to the next country and start a new folder. Messages which I didn't write began to appear on the board before class. "Finish your Chile folder today."

"Let's have good social action," "Social Action is Soul Power." A class who had started at Kindergarten crayon-grabbing level began doing pretty well, staying in their own groups, working hard, and learning.

A lot of confusion had blown off and people were happy and taking care of themselves in class. Confusion could be easily tripped back in and often was, but it could get handled and groups took care of their own problems. I put pressure on the group president if there was trouble in a particular group . . . and magically it would get handled. If a group was having internal communication problems, that was thought of as being pretty bad. Fights with other groups were still considered understandable.

One fight had an effect on the whole class. A girl in one group became so angry in an argument over a crayon, with some boys in another group, that she grabbed the other group's prized papier maché globe and hurled it across the room . . . where it shattered against the wall. There was sudden dead silence (startling in itself) while the class viewed the tragedy. I had them notice how wars start. It really did feel like someone had been shot just then. Both groups got busy making peace and pasting the pieces back together, and a whole semester later I heard students mention the episode of "the globe."

Communicating with other groups to borrow markers and glue was difficult, but we acted out again some of the bad social actions that happened and got people to look at themselves. If I heard two students arguing I'd make them say the exact words again to each other . . . and usually they would both laugh. People learned to cross a whole class and borrow a crayon politely without hitting anyone on the way, and make it back home, and I thought that was pretty good!

We had become a "Social Studies" class where "social"

was getting lived. People really discovered that there *are* others around, and it is rather important how you act toward them. It doesn't matter that they *should* have learned that in Kindergarten or first or second grade. A lot of order had been imposed on them all along in school and they knew how to "behave" very well if they had to, but obviously they hadn't had much experience as a group in creating their own order before.

Arlene Pincus turned her seventh-grade class-room into a living laboratory for an experiment in sexism. She found that the girls had been "socialized" so thoroughly that they could not see overt discrimination as anything but the "natural order of things."

BY ARLENE PINCUS

To my seventh-grade students, America is indeed a free country. Although almost all of them believe that some-where beyond the confines of their Rockland community— in Harlem and Nyack, the places where they wouldn't dare to walk alone—discrimination may sometimes exist, they all denied that they had ever been stereotyped or discrimi-nated against. Not as Jews nor as Catholics, not as girls nor as boys nor as children.

Talking it over, George, a fellow team teacher, and I concluded that of course these twelve year olds had experi-enced discrimination but they either justified it or weren't conscious of it. We set out, therefore, to create an experience where some of them were discriminated against before their very eyes.

We decided against the famous blue eyes–brown eyes experiment largely because George felt that in this predominantly Irish and Italian community such a division of the children would fall into ethnic groups rather than random groups, thereby seemingly justifying some preexisting prejudices the children were familiar with. I suggested we have a spelling bee, boys against girls, and discriminate against the girls. George agreed; since he doesn't see girls as particularly discriminated against, he saw this as random. I had different motives; I thought that this contrived experience would encourage the girls to recognize and discuss other times they had been discriminated against. In short, I saw it as quickie consciousness-raising.

When we announced the activity to the class, we explained that since there were fewer girls than boys, George would be the caller, and I would be on the girls' team. George started the game unfairly, by telling each team to line up and proceeding to scold some of the girls who weren't fast enough. Then he commenced the game with a word for the boys. *Horse.* When the boy answered correctly, George responded by praising him elaborately and giving the boys a point. Then he gave the first girl a much harder word. *Recommend.* When she spelled it correctly, he scowled at her, muttered, "I guess that's right," and had to be reminded to score the girls' column.

By the end of the third round there could have been little doubt that the game was stacked in favor of the boys. The boys had been asked to spell "West Virginia" and George had given the team a point even though the boy had forgotten to say "Capital V." The girls had been asked to spell "countenance," "disturbance," and "electrocute" while the boys had gotten "postcard" and "house." The

164

first protest from a girl—"The boys are getting easier words!"—was met with a lost point for their team. The boys cheered loudly and were smiled at. The girls, who were constantly reminded to straighten up their line, began to appeal to me. "He's giving them easier words—do something." But I pointed out that I was expected to play on their side and I couldn't call out. I also missed my word.

George continued the game, scowling at the girls, smiling at the boys, and occasionally calling a boy's misspelled word correct and a girl's correctly spelled word wrong. The girls began to mutter "I'm not playing" and "The teacher is a cheater!" but they kept playing. They even seemed to be trying harder.

The boys, who had long ago abandoned their line, managed to keep the poor spellers from ever having a turn. In addition, the fact that they were sitting in a group rather than in a line allowed them to conceal a dictionary among them. They had resorted to cheating, even though they had no need. Their words were getting easier.

Quite arbitrarily, George seemed to abandon the penalty for calling out, and the grumblings among the girls increased. All their comments centered around one idea— their teacher had turned out to be a cheater. Since the calling-out rules were no longer in force, each spelling of a word was accompanied by screams and/or cheering. One girl, who had often made it clear that she loathed George, announced that she was going to get the principal and show him what a cheater George was. She assured everyone, but no one in particular, that teachers weren't allowed to act that way.

During the whole episode, the boys seemed to become happier and more self-confident. Even their mistakes were easy to bear; not only was their score far greater than the girls', but George soothed each error with a comment like,

"I'm sorry, that's not quite right," or "I'm sure you'll do better next time." He also neglected to chastise one boy (a very poor speller), who kept coming up to an imaginary line down the center of the room, leaning forward, and calling, "The girls are stupids!"

When George and I finally ended the game by telling the class that George had favored the boys on purpose, we invited the students to tell us how they felt during the game. There were many comments—the boys were smart, the girls were stupid, so-and-so had spelled his word wrong but it had been called right—but the only fact all the girls seemed to be able to focus on was that George had cheated and I had let him. Yes, we said, but how did you *feel?* Angry, because the teacher cheated, was the response.

Our questions generated new anger among the girls because although we obviously expected them to have noticed more about their emotions than they had, they honestly could not see past this one point. The game had not made the girls feel any emotions about themselves and their competencies, nor was any of their anger directed at the boys, who had allowed the game to be weighted in their favor.

The boys were in a buoyant, undisciplined mood. When questioned by us as to why they had allowed such a game to go on, the boys either insisted that it had been a fair game or denied that it was their responsibility to see to it that it was fair. That was the teachers' job. Only one boy, a person who had allowed his sense of fair play to alienate him from his friends on other occasions, admitted that the girls had been discriminated against. He was shouted down by the boy who was rather pleased with the phrase he had latched onto: "The girls are stupids!"

The only people whose consciousnesses were raised by this experience were the teachers. We learned something we

166

had resisted believing—that our students found it impossible to recognize and discuss discrimination and prejudice. Furthermore, our students found it hard to imagine themselves as part of groups that either discriminated or were discriminated against. Part of this seems to be because twelve year olds of both sexes find it hard to imagine themselves as grown-ups whose actions matter and who have to choose their occupations, but it seems equally important that they consider sexual divisions of labor to be a matter of the natural order of things rather than a matter of discrimination. Sure, boys grew up and earned the livings, and girls grew up and cleaned the houses, but they assured us that this wasn't because women are discriminated against, but because this is the way people want it.

When the girls were given a chance to discuss this without the boys, they still voiced these opinions. They happily discussed and put down the standards of beauty set by *Seventeen* magazine. The girls who couldn't hope to meet these standards were especially relieved to find their female teacher unimpressed with the models in the magazine. All were astonished to find they expect principals, doctors, lawyers, judges, cabdrivers, and garbage collectors to be men, and teachers, nurses, secretaries, and typists to be women, but somehow they failed to connect these expectations with their own lives. Some girls were angry at a law that said girls couldn't have paper routes but others explained that it was for a good reason: girls, after all, shouldn't be out after dark. In similar ways, example after example of how females in this society are treated were explained away. One thing was because women are delicate and need to be protected, and another was because kids need their mothers to be home with them, and another was because women want it that way. Twelve-year-old females that I know just do not see themselves as part of an

167

exploited group. They are all going to be what they want to be when they grow up, and yes, they do all expect to marry and have kids except the ones who can't even imagine their faces on the pages of an inferior version of *Seventeen,* and what did they have to play that dumb spelling bee for, anyway?

How did the girls get into the frame of mind that Arlene Pincus describes in the preceding piece? All girls are exposed continually to "materials" on sexism. June Namias, a teacher in Newton (Mass.) high school, suggests ways to use what you find around to combat sexism.

BY JUNE NAMIAS

You don't have to look hard in this society to find "materials" dealing with sexism. Turn on the TV, open your daily papers, visit a toy store, listen to your favorite rock station, examine your local newsstand for "male" and "female" culture. Compare "girls'" comics like *Betty, Lois Lane, Love Comics, Lulu,* and *Archie* with "boys'": *Bat Man, Army, Mysterious Ugly,* etc., or in an older age set: *True Romances, Redbook, House Beautiful, Cosmopolitan,* and *Seventeen* to *Playboy, Male, Sports Illustrated,* and *Forbes.* Note the ads in each. Note the values. Ask kids to bring in pop records (or bring in yours) . . . "My boyfriend's back and there's gonna be trouble" . . . "Oh girl . . . sigh . . . oh girl," "I will follow him," "Under my thumb . . ." You can then talk about "love," heterosexuality, roles, etc. You can tape music off the radio. I did this with music about families (like "Me and Mrs. Jones," "Mother's Little Helper," "Papa was a Rolling Stone"). Kids can also relate to stuff about families by watching TV family programs like *All in the Family, The Flintstones, Brady Bunch,* etc. The Saturday morning cartoons are interesting (some horrid) in terms of family roles and sex roles. The ads are always one boy's toy like a racer and then one girl's toy, you guessed it, Barbie dolls. Note of caution: it's easy to attack what some kids see as their "culture." I'd say become aware of what your kids watch and read and how they spend their time and take off from there. How do they see what they're seeing and doing?

Here is a range of activities from the *Teacher Works* that, if expanded, provides social studies lesson plans for all the secular and religious holidays of the year and many national holidays as well. It is not hard to substitute Thanksgiving or Easter for Christmas, changing the details of the questions a bit. Need some help? Well, to translate gifts for Christmas (question 3) to the Thanksgiving celebration—"Make a list of everything you have to be thankful for. Now total up the cost of the elements—car, new bike, clean air, room of your own." Try your hand with it.

What age child? Any child from age four to sixteen can learn from many of these activities.

Pick one of the following projects—or make up your own.

1. What does Christmas mean? State it *nonverbally.*
2. From a personality box or a description of a person, figure out an appropriate gift for that person and *make* it for little or no money.
3. Make a list of things *you* want for Christmas, price the items at two different stores at least, and then figure out how many hours you'd have to work to be able to buy them with an income of $1.65 an hour.
4. How is Christmas celebrated in various neighborhoods? Are the numbers and kinds of decorations different in the West Hills, Albina, Lents, Irvington, etc.?
5. Price Christmas trees in three different lots in three different neighborhoods. How much difference in price did you find? Why do you think the price differs? How much *profit* is made per tree? (Try to find out the cost of getting to the tree, cutting it, bringing it to Portland, and selling it.)
6. How is Christmas celebrated in various places often forgotten at this time—hospitals (Shriners', Veterans', Dammasch, etc.), the police department, on 3rd and Burnside, in jails and prisons, etc.?
7. Contrast Christmas with anything—Christmas and war, Christmas and school, Christmas and Easter, etc., etc.
8. Make a list of gifts that you want that nobody could get for you.
9. Do a parody of Christmas traditions—for example, a hip "Night Before Christmas."
10. Look at Christmas advertising and see if any special techniques are used.
11. Interview a store manager to find out his store's strategies for selling at Christmas—when do they order, how many extra employees do they hire, when do they put up decorations, etc.?

12. Take three different stores (also try to get three different *kinds* of stores) and find out how much of the year's profit is made between Thanksgiving and Christmas.

13. Investigate loan companies' and banks' Christmas Clubs and their eagerness to loan people money during the holidays. Are their interest rates any higher?

14. Set up a Gift Suggestion Bureau for the class.

15. Investigate a day in the life of a sidewalk or department store Santa.

16. What is the average income paid to part-time workers hired for the Christmas season in the post office? department stores? a small gift or flower shop?

17. Find out about Christmas in another culture—including cultural groups in the United States, such as Indians, Chicanos, etc.

18. Put down guidelines for an ecologically sound Christmas.

19. Interview people about their feelings about presents —how do they feel about getting none, getting lots, about getting a more/less expensive present than they gave?

20. Christmas is . . .

21. How could you celebrate Christmas on a welfare budget?

22. Find out about war (and other violent or sadistic) toys—are there lots on the market, what argument do certain groups (like Mothers for Peace) have with the toys, what do the manufacturers think, etc.?

23. What can you do to make Christmas good for yourself and the people around you?

24. Investigate Christmas card sending. Is there status seeking involved? Who buys what kinds of cards? Are there special cards for special groups—like Indians, blacks, Chicanos, etc.?

25. What is the Jewish Festival of Lights, or Hanukkah, which is celebrated just before Christmas? What are its traditions?

Traditionally, social studies for young children meant they would get to know more about their neighborhoods and would start to read maps. But these young children barely manage to handle their bodies without falling and tripping over objects; and they can hardly understand the area maps they are asked to read. Here is a map-making activity in second grade, described by Nancy Schaffer, a teacher-advisor in P.S. 75, Manhattan, in which the teacher and the children are taught the relative importance of the children's immediate turf.

BY NANCY SCHAFFER

The bilingual second-grade class has been together now for two years. The thread that runs through the two years with greatest consistency has been a deep involvement with block building among the boys in the class. At first the teacher kept trying to rescue the Cuisenaire rods and the pattern blocks for math activities. The boys, left to their own devices, were incorporating everything that resembled blocks into their buildings. Later, as the teacher and I saw how intense this interest and involvement was, we began to gather as many miniature blocks, toy vehicles and tracks as

172

we could collect for them, and we set aside, at least for a time, plans to introduce wooden units for concrete math experiences. These children, it was becoming clear, realized their world best by recreating it in block constructions.

At one point, in an effort to extend the quality of the children's block building, the teacher and I prepared a large oil cloth map, on which we taped appropriate road-ways and subway lines. We hoped the children would build on the map, label appropriate streets, and position buildings they knew, thereby reconstructing the neighborhood immediately surrounding the school. The map was politely used for a brief period. The scale was wrong for the children, however. So they discarded it, but accepted the idea, and then went ahead and constructed the neighborhood on the scale of their seven-year-old egocentric outlook, which is something the teacher and I should have anticipated. The school and playground were ten times larger than any other block in the neighborhood. The nearby subway station was the most dominating feature of their subway system. Their scale was based on personal significance. Disproportionate and unbalanced as it was as an overall picture, it was never-theless accurate in the remarkable detail of the selected buildings and areas that were important to the children in their daily experiences. To insist upon actual scale or upon a more objective outlook would have been meaningless at this stage of their thinking.

To help them focus on details, I encouraged the teacher to arrange a number of mini-trips around the school build-ing and yards and to the subway station one block away. The trips helped them to focus on the names of the streets, the traffic signs and signals, and the various types of stores and buildings on the block that separated the school from the subway. At one point their understanding of "uptown" and "downtown" sides of the subway seemed very vague.

This, coupled with their rather primitive attempts to build a bridge, led me to take three boys on a trip. We first went to the subway station for a careful look around. Then we took two trains to the bus terminal at the George Washington Bridge, rode back and forth over the bridge in a bus, had frankfurters and drinks at a lunch counter at the terminal, and returned to school on the subway.

Transfers, turnstiles, elevators, escalators, and the lunch counter heightened the experience. One incident in which one child tried to push all the way around in a revolving subway gate impressed the word EXIT indelibly on his mind. He had an anxious wait on the exit side, where he had trapped himself, until he could be retrieved through the entrance again.

Back at school, these experiences were recreated in elaborate labeled block structures, and in long excited narratives. One boy dictated a story about the trip, two others wrote their own. One of the latter had entered the bilingual class from an English-speaking class three months before. At that time he was a nonreader and a serious behavior problem. Extended opportunities to work with blocks not only calmed him but gave him an opportunity to become seriously involved. The block building and the chance to function in Spanish were the most salient features in his alteration.

One of the many things we have learned from the second-grade block builders is that expressive activities have no clear boundary lines. Rather, they're the bridge builders between intake and insight. Social understandings, language development, and concept formation all occur in expressive activity.

6

The box that cannot be opened

Math and science as tools and as toys

Science and math are the "hard" parts of the school curriculum. Most people take this to mean that in these areas students must knuckle down and study in order to master the textbooks and to show what they know on objective tests. Free-form "creative" activities may be all right in language arts and social studies, but here "subject matter" comes to the fore!

But where *is* the subject matter of science and math? Scientists do not study textbooks much. They are people intrigued by nature and all its ways. Of all the kinds of intellectuals, they are the ones most interested in "things," not words.

There is a beautiful exercise in science teaching that involves a black box that cannot be opened. Each student gets a box. The task is to ascertain everything you can about the contents, using whatever tests and procedures you can think of. After working for an extended period of time on the boxes, students are invited to surmise what they contain. *But the boxes are never opened.* The point of the exercise is to dramatize the position of the scientist vis-à-vis some of the phenomena he studies. There, too, hypotheses abound, techniques proliferate, theories come and go. But the box can never be opened. Knowing more and more about the ultimately unknowable can be the highest sport and the most potent tool in man's repertoire.

It can also be a menace, if it is divorced from moral sense and social conscience. We have discovered that knowledge is power. However, the technology derived from science can be used to enslave or to liberate human beings. Our students today no longer want scientific and technical studies isolated from their human implications.

Worth learning

Willy Claflin provides an example of a young
child learning science: The child digs a hole
and sees what happens.

BY WILLY CLAFLIN

Why dig a hole? Because it isn't there. This is the first and
best explanation I can think of—one I dedicate to those
who won't dig anything without first asking *why*.

Of course I believe there are lots of good, serious, respon-
sible-adult reasons why digging a hole is an especially good
project—it involves (or can involve) getting lots of exercise, learning to use tools, exploring plant root systems,
observing worms, ants, beetles, slugs and other forms of
underground life, watching the soil change color and consistency, finding rock specimens, and digging up buried
treasures (old nails, bottles and crockery, lost playthings,
even arrowheads). If you happen to have a soil testing kit,
it might be nice to test and compare various different levels.
And then there are so many uses for the hole itself—you
can fill it with water and have a wading or swimming pool,
turn it into a cellar for a small house, jump into it and
climb out of it, put wooden bridges over it to practice
balancing on, or to run toy cars over; and, when you're
finished, fill it in again.

To list these reasons, however, is to obscure what's really
going on—adventure, exploration, experimentation, research. That's what has pleased Brian (age 5) most about
the hole we've been digging together this summer: the
open, awake excitement that comes from digging to *see
what happens.*

"If we knew what we were looking for, it wouldn't be
research, would it?" Some famous scientist said that.

177

What applies to digging a hole may be applied to almost any other activity. If you get into it because you want to accomplish certain specific things, your activity is necessarily limited by the particular focus of your attention, and you run the constant risk of failure and disappointment (like if you dig for interesting rock specimens and don't find any). But if you dig the hole *for the sake of digging the hole,* you will have constant adventure, and failure will not be possible.

Here's something I just read by Suzuki, in a book called *Zen Mind, Beginner's Mind:*

"So long as you have some particular goal in your practice, that practice will not help you completely."

Holes I have known

I decided that digging a hole would be a good project for The Children's School. And then I remembered digging a hole when I was eight or nine. It was out in the back field, next to the woods near the apple trees. I wanted to find dinosaur bones. Grownups said I wouldn't find any, but this didn't affect my enthusiasm.

I loved digging my hole, watching it grow wider and deeper. I don't know how big the hole really was, but it seemed immense to me, and I had a sense of great accomplishment, great pride that *I* could have made anything so big.

I found a big bone; grownups said it was probably from a horse or a cow. I found a horse's hoof, and some rocks I liked. The only other things I remember finding were some perfectly preserved, pressed maple and birch leaves, in some claylike soil about two or three feet down. I don't remember now why I stopped digging. It may have been fall, and time for school to start.

A month ago I told Brian about my hole idea. He was

excited by it, and wanted to start digging with me right
then. So we went out with two shovels and started digging
near the garden. After digging off and on for much of the
day, I wrote down some of our adventures:

June 30—digging a hole . . . first sod, topsoil, roots.
Brian calls the clumps of sod "planets." He is amazed to
find a worm. He finds a second. worm, and says, "He
wants to play with his friend." He puts them together
on one "planet" to play. He then decides he could use
the worms for fishing, and gets a cup full of dirt to
keep them in . . .

when we have our first, outer circle of digs almost
finished, Brian notices that it looks like a big letter C.
He says, "Let's keep it this way . . . we can use the
piece of ground to walk out onto the island in the
middle." He walks out to the center circle and back
again, laughing . . .

later, we dig up the center part, and then start digging down. Brian suddenly shouts, "Ants live here,
too!" We find an old nail, a piece of glass, and a patch
of clay. We find lots and lots of other bugs and insects
. . . one slug and a very large beetle.

at one point, Brian is watching the worms in his cup
of dirt. He says, "Look, they're making furniture, out
of the dirt . . . they're making a place to live, with
furniture, out of the dirt!"

we dig down about two, or two and a half feet, sometimes standing on the big shovel and shoving down
together. I say we could fill the hole with water and
use it for an outdoor bathtub . . . Brian says, "You
know the plastic . . . the plastic to put over the windows? . . . We could tape it together and put it in the
hole and the water wouldn't leak out!"

we talk and dig a little more. I ask him if he would
like to build a little house for himself someday. He says
yes . . . "This could be my house, with the bathtub in

the middle." We decide that if we want a *hole,* we'll have to dig another hole, because this hole has turned into his *bathtub* . . .

we sharpen and drive in stakes around the outside of the hole, so nobody will fall in. Brian goes to get string, so we can tie it between the posts. But we get tired, and decide to quit for a while. Brian says, "Boy, we're doing so many experiments and thinking of ideas . . . let's get up first every morning, before anybody else, and come out and do the hole . . . my house . . . together . . ."

later, in the afternoon, we dig for a while again. I find a beautifully made Indian arrowhead. I get very excited, but Brian is more interested in the worms. He takes some in his hands and watches . . . "They can stretch!" I take the worms in my hands. It's been so long since I looked at (felt) worms . . . they tickle . . . I watch them coil and swirl and loop and contract.

coming inside, we discuss plans for Brian's house, but he has many different conflicting ideas in mind, and finally says, "I don't want to talk about it anymore." So I say we'll just go out and dig again tomorrow and see what turns up. He thinks this is a good idea . . .

Brian and I have done more digging in the hole since. Once or twice other children have come over and had a brief turn digging. The hole now measures about 5′ by 4′ in diameter (being a slightly squished ellipse), and is about 3½′ deep. Brian has given up on his plans for a house. He likes filling the hole with water. He's had a lovely time splashing in it, by himself and with friends. We notice as the hole gets bigger and bigger, it takes longer and longer for the garden hose to fill it up. One day we put two "bridges" over it—a two-by-four and a slightly narrower board. Brian walks back and forth, practicing balancing . . .

Part of my own excitement comes from a feeling of

digging back through time, as we get deeper and deeper into it. I also enjoy the constant puns dig/dig and hole/whole . . .

Digging a hole is an experiment . . . one in an infinite series of experiments. The specific activity of digging is pleasing to me, but just as pleasing to me is my approach to the activity; the feeling of adventure and exploration.

"Experiments" fascinate the children I know. To them, an experiment is any activity whose results are not known ahead of time—any time we do something to see what happens.

The way we gather most of the materials for The Children's School—by scavenging—is another experiment. We never know what we are going to find at any dump. We never know what a store may donate. And we never know what we will end up making with all the various oddments we collect.

Some final thoughts on experiments and seeing what happens

If I'm sitting at a table with some stacks of colored cubes, I'm usually tempted to try teaching the children some specific fact or principle with them. This isn't really a bad idea, as far as it goes, but it has certain obvious drawbacks: my activity is limited, the children's activity is limited, and failure is easy. But if I take the cubes and start to play, seriously, with them, something interesting and unique almost always comes up. If I *take play seriously*, I can observe and fully participate in what my hands and eyes are doing, what the blocks are doing . . . what shapes are formed, patterns evolve, sequences emerge, or fantasies materialize. And by my activity I encourage the children to do the same, either with me or on their own. It is important for me to play and take note—not take *notes,* but take *notice.* I am coming to believe that if you set out to teach, you'll never learn; and I know from my own experience that when I set out to learn, I always end up teaching. Dig well.

You can find the philosopher-scientist in the carefully balanced world of the pond and the meadow, not in the laboratory where man is all powerful. And this is where Lazar Goldberg takes his seven- and twelve-year-olds.

BY LAZAR GOLDBERG

Consider children at play inflating balloons—watch what they do and listen to what they say to each other. Some tie the inflated balloons off and hit them from below, driving the balloons almost to the ceiling. They watch as the balloons slowly descend.

"If it was the kind you get in the park, it would just stay up there and never come down."

"No, it wouldn't. I brought a park balloon home, and it got smaller and smaller, and quit."

"Must've had a leak."

Someone else is squeezing a balloon, enjoying its springy quality. Another child decides not to tie hers off, but to let it go careening through the air. The idea catches on, and a friendly competition follows to see who can get a balloon to travel the entire distance of the room. However, no balloon maintains a straight path; some even double back and go the "wrong" way. Two children try to see how large they can make their balloons. After the balloons have exceeded

182

their usual size, the children look at each other in cheerful but nervous expectation. One child rubs a balloon against the sleeve of her blouse and rests it against the wall while her neighbor announces that they always do this at her birthday parties. Everyone is startled by the noise from a "popped" balloon. When all have been suitably impressed with the volume of the sound, a lad who probably regretted that he had not been the first to break his balloon assures everyone that he can make a louder bang with a paper bag.

These are all common experiences with balloons. One may reasonably expect that children will engage in them and in others of their own invention if they are provided with balloons and time in which to try, and if no one intrudes. Left to their own devices, one or two children may pursue a puzzling feature of their experience. Perhaps someone has seen an illustration of a balloon traveling along a string and may try to repeat it. Some children may try to attract each other's balloons by rubbing them on various materials. Most children, however, will eventually tire of these activities or, more likely, break the balloons and look for something else to do.

The play must not be allowed to die of exhaustion. While only a few children may have been launched into activities of their choice, others may need a more direct challenge to come to grips with the problems that remain unrecognized. (What they do *not* need is an analysis of the nature of air.) A jar is introduced with a balloon partially inflated inside the jar, and the open end of the balloon stretched over the mouth of the jar. There is another jar with a waterfilled balloon wedged in the mouth of the jar, most of the balloon outside, and part of it inside the jar. Another inflated balloon rests inside a funnel which extends out of a length of tubing. The other end of the tubing is submerged in a pail of water. When the funnel is turned upside down, the balloon does not fall out. It requires some effort to pull it free. These are some of the puzzling things that one can do with balloons. They invite the children to try to do them, like tricks.

The play is now somewhat directed. The adult has intruded, but he has done so by turning the direction of play in order to raise the level of interest, heighten the significance, and yet leave open the reality that may be discovered. There are as many ways to do this as the adult's imagination and experience suggest.

He may show how big he can make a balloon with one expulsion of breath. It is a measure of his lung capacity. What is theirs? How is such capacity to be measured? How do the capacities of the children compare? They can measure the circumference of the inflated balloons with a tape measure or string, determine the volume however they can, and record the results in line and bar graphs: lung volume against individual children, lung volume against circumference, lung volume at rest compared with after exercise, lung volume against chest measurement, or whatever other relationships may be of interest.

The adult may play on his primitive recorder made from a drinking straw. I have never met a child who did not want to make his own. "Do you suppose it makes any difference where you place the holes?" "Will it sound different if it is shorter?" "Is there a way to make one so that the scale will be the familiar one instead of the strange one we have produced?"

If some aspiring rocketeer has brought a carbon dioxide cartridge to show how fast his model travels across the room along a wire, that is fine.

A pendulum at rest invites a push, just as the sign "wet paint" invites a touch. The pendulum may be suspended from a simple wooden frame, and a can partly filled with sand can serve as a bob. There are golf balls, softballs, marbles, and rocks for alternate bobs, and a variety of cords and thread. Available, too, are the feet of old nylon stockings to contain the bob, a simple arrangement for children not yet able to manage attaching a string to a spherical surface without assistance. There are also laths, rulers, and yardsticks. One yardstick has a nail driven through one end, and it is balanced with the nail lying across two yardsticks which rest on the backs of two chairs. It is a rod pendulum. To know what needs to be taught, and to find the teaching moment, the children are observed. Who is measuring the pendulum? How do they determine the length when the bob is regular? Irregular? Who is seeking a relation between the period and the amplitude? Between the period and the weight of the bob? Is anyone comparing the string pendulum with the rod pendulum? Is anyone using the books that were carefully selected to accompany this activity?

The play with pendulums should be made increasingly complicated, but not too quickly. After children have become absorbed by the simple pendulum, coupled and compound pendula may be introduced, raising the interest a notch or two. This is not laid down as a general thesis about going from the simple to the complex. Often children do better when confronted by confusing but interesting problems first. In this case, however, once the children are offered a compound pendulum, especially one capable of tracing the lovely curves called Lissajou figures, which are produced by the interaction of two harmonic motions at right angles, their satisfaction in generating these beautiful curves in sand and paint may dwarf the pleasures of the simple pendulum, and that would be a pity.

The strong recommendation that play serve to initiate scientific activity is not to be interpreted as a precise judgment for every child at all times. It is sometimes possible to discern distinctions in style and temperament among children in their attack upon science problems, especially once they have learned to read and to perform useful mathematics. Although eventually I should hope to interest as many children as possible in such things as gravity estimations and the powerful tool put at our disposal by sentences which relate time and the length of the pendulum, occasionally a child may not want to wait. One needs to keep a sharp eye out for the youngster who gets his pencil and pad out as soon as he observes the results of manipulating the equipment. Such children are a small but precious minority. They usually want books and to be left to their work.

The distinctions in style among children are analogous to those we find among scientists. J. B. S. Haldane, a renowned English biologist of this century, was the first man to map a human chromosome and measure the mutation rate of a human gene; he was genuinely interested in theory. Scientists so disposed seek the implications of theory and proceed to devise experiments to test their ideas. Haldane performed many remarkable experiments, even on his own body, to test the validity of theoretical propositions. C. V. Boys was temperamentally very different from Haldane. Boys generated ideas in the very process of working in the laboratory. When he was offered the services of a mechanic to assist him in the construction of apparatus, Boys refused to accept the help. It was in the very construction of apparatus that he often formulated his ideas. Children may display similar differences in the way that they prefer to work.

The outdoor laboratory
Learning about the remarkable variety of living things requires a playful, undirected opportunity to become acquainted. The scaled and clawed collared lizard resting on

the hand distinguishes himself and his kind from the toads, frogs, and salamanders. The eggs that appear in strings, masses, and spotted clusters give promise of similar yet distinguishable creatures to come. The bluffing hog-nosed snake and the aggressive milk snake soon adapt to gentle treatment. The box turtle hides completely in his shell, but the snapping turtle does not need to do so. One tree frog seems to have disappeared on the bark while another is resting comfortably on the glass of the terrarium. No models, however ingenious, are a substitute for live animals and plants. Models and pictures are useful in addition to, not instead of, the many interesting organisms that can reside among children.

The field is a source of many of the living forms in whose company children may begin to marvel at the variety, the similarities and differences, the adaptive mechanisms, and the interdependencies among plants and animals. Interest, significance, and reality abound at every hand; for the children to discover them requires only time, patience, and sympathetic but unobtrusive guidance. The decaying log and its immediate neighborhood is a little world related to other little worlds in its vicinity. Among the fungi penetrating the remaining woody tissues are springtails which are perhaps a quarter of an inch long. Later, much later, the children may put their knowledge of large numbers to work to see whether it is really possible that there may be 100 million springtails per square meter in some soils. Later also, they will fashion a Berlese funnel from a conical paper drinking cup, their soil sample inside the cup, a piece of nylon screening across the open bottom of the cup, and a 100-watt bulb hanging over it. A jar of alcohol placed underneath will catch the insects that burrow through the soil and the screening as they try to escape from the heat

187

and light of the bulb. But for now the children are observing and collecting.

There is a millipede, curled up like a watchspring, exposing the part of him that feels hard when he is picked up.
There is a sowbug, cousin to the lobster, crab, and shrimp.
The centipede runs off on his many legs. Are there really a
hundred of them? The children will have to catch one to
count them. He runs when his head is uncovered. That is
understandable. But he also runs when it seems that his
head is still hidden. That is odd. Is it true that the centipede will stop running if a vessel is provided that will allow
his body to make maximum contact with a surface? Perhaps
some tubing would be best. The snails are very ancient
citizens, having left their fossil tracks some 500 million
years ago. It may be more interesting to collect several in
order to find out whether snail mates really shoot darts at
each other in their gastropodic romance. The children need
not worry about including male and female snails because
each snail is both.

Those seemingly helpless slugs have been known to drive
birds off with a squirt gun they possess. How slimy to the
touch they are. Back in the school library is a picture W. La
Varre took of a slug gliding over the sharp edge of a blade
without harm.

Judging from the cloud of spores traveling in all directions, I should think that someone must have broken a
puffball open. How many tiny spores there must be in these
kissing cousins to the mushrooms. The children add a puffball to their collection. Perhaps some brave soul will try to
estimate the number of spores contained in the fruiting
body. Some bracket fungus is added to the collection so that
later the children may examine the lower surface with a
hand lens, see the tubes where the spores are developed,
and explore the role of this fungus in the life cycle of the
woods. Now the search is for inky-cap mushrooms—the

children will try to write with their ink—for edible mushrooms, which will not be eaten until an expert determines that it is safe, for varieties of cup fungi, and especially for morel which is good to eat. Samples of lichen, that marvelous partnership between alga and fungus, the pioneer of the plant kingdom, will be collected. Finally, after ferns, liverworts and mosses have been added, it is time to move on.

Before the children leave the school in the outdoors, they still have much to do. Last night, before bedtime, they listened to some poems. Among these was one about spiders by Robert P. Tristram Coffin from his *Collected Poems* (1929) :

> He lays his staircase as he goes
> Under his eight thoughtful toes
> And grows with the concentric flower
> Of his shadowless, thin bower.

The children want to find at least one orb-weaving spider. We have built a special frame and want to watch as it weaves its web. They also want to find at least one variety of ant before moving on to a new community—the pond. The social ants, whether food gathers, farmers, stock breeders (the hunters will be left alone), will challenge the children's understanding of mankind's unique cultural invention. In what ways are the ant communities similar to human communities? In what ways are they different? Perhaps some child will be fortunate and come upon harvesting ants among which "we find an analogue of beating swords into ploughshares; the 'soldiers' with their vast heads and powerful mandibles, crush seeds for the benefit of the whole colony." This lovely description by S. A. Barnett in *Instinct and Intelligence* (1967) stimulates the search.

The opportunities to observe and collect at the pond are

too numerous to list in any detail. The children find dragon, damsel, may, and caddis flies at various stages of development and see water striders, water boatmen, back-swimmers, whirligigs, diving and water scavenger beetles, and the ubiquitous mosquito. Growing in the water are waterweed, bladderwort, water silk, and other plants. Some of the animals and plants are collected for the aquaria at school. They also take along some of the pond water to keep the animals and plants alive and plan to examine it under the microscope. After all, the food chain in the pond may include plants and animals too small to see with the unaided eye.

The meadow presents new opportunities. What varieties of life can be found under two square feet? How plentiful are earthworms? While collecting a number of worms for their worm garden, the children try to estimate the density of worms in a given volume of soil. Their estimate is guided not only by Charles Darwin's count in *The Formation of Vegetable Mould* (1881), but by the worms' work as measured by the quantity of castings they have produced. Other children may prefer to consider the secret of the dandelion's success. There were none to be seen in the shady woods, but here in the meadow they are well established. It is interesting that people clear the land when they settle in a new place and then complain when dandelions find the disturbed land precisely what they need. If changes were to be made in this outdoor laboratory, what likely consequences could be anticipated? For example, what might happen if the pond were filled in? Or suppose that the woods were cleared to make room for more homes?

Until now everyone has been looking down most of the time. Now it is time to look up before returning to the indoor laboratory. Each of us wrapped against the night chill, we lie on our backs and gaze into a sky most of us have not seen; we wonder, dream a little, and ask a question or two, feeling subdued and awed by the darkness, the silence, and the immense sky. *Bolts of Melody, New Poems of Emily Dickinson* (1945) includes "Once a Child," a poem that expresses feelings some of us share:

> It troubled me as once I was,
> For I was once a child,
> Deciding how an atom fell
> And yet the heavens held. . . .

Ann Mele teaches math in an inner-city high school. Already her children are academic casualties. Her subject matter is specialized because the school wants it that way, and the children expect it to be that way. Though she works within these constraints, she motivates her students by awakening them not to the social realities of their world, but to the possibilities of choosing the most productive way for each individual child to learn. She involves each child in making decisions; and she finds that individualizing works best when the "programmer" is the child himself.

BY ANN MELE

Sylvester was truant. Every Friday I counted up the number of days he had been absent that week and dutifully sent a referral card to the dean. About two-thirds into the term, his guidance counselor came to see me. He told me that Sylvester was not attending my pre-Algebra class, because he could not read. It never occurred to me that a tenth grader could not read. Mr. Dallas further informed me that the only class Sylvester attended was the reading laboratory where he was just beginning to decode. I was shocked. Later, however, I made a list of vocabulary words and a short outline of the concepts I planned to cover that week and sent them to the reading teacher, along with the text, reference pages, and a listing of the daily homework assignments. Mrs. Mandel, the reading teacher, was prompt in replying: "Sylvester could not possibly cope with such advanced work." Yet this was the most basic mathematics course offered. Small wonder he is out of class so often.

Sylvester's case was not unique. There was Nathaniel, who wanted to be called Jimmy, who came to class everyday but chose to sit quietly in the back of the room, alone, either reading the newspaper or gazing out the window or sleeping. No amount of prodding or encouragement, teasing or berating moved him to participate in class. Deborah and Janella did not know the product of six times seven and surreptitiously kept multiplication tables tucked into their notebooks. Deborah, too, came to class everyday, but was so shy and afraid that she never once volunteered an answer. Calling on her surely would have shattered her completely. You could almost see her, snail-like, draw back into her shell as she slipped into her seat each day. Janella's attendance was much more sporadic, though when present she certainly made up for the days she had missed. Fidgety, constantly chattering, she tried very hard to avoid the work at hand. How could I expect them to find the median age of the students in the class?

Both Laverne and Louis dropped out of my regular algebra class. Both had similar reasons. I taught too fast. I

favored certain students and I assigned too much homework. Checking their cumulative records revealed reading
and mathematics scores several grades off level. Laverne's
parents had recently divorced and remarried. She resented
her stepfather and even refused to use his last name. She
ran away from home about the same time she disappeared
from my class. Louis had a history of being a troublemaker.
I scheduled a conference with him and his guidance counselor. At that meeting his counselor and I suggested professional help. Louis turned pale and kept repeating: "I am
not crazy. I am not crazy. Please don't tell my mother."

What relevance did factoring a quadratic equation have
for them? After listening to such speakers as John Holt,
David Hapgood, Judson Jerome, and Samuel Baskin, guest
lecturers in a course I was taking, I had become an enthusiastic advocate of the open classroom. I did not know if it
could be applied to the high school format, but I was eager
to experiment.

The result was 9PAI6P.

The students assigned to 9PAI6P were chosen because
they had a history of failure in mathematics. They were
not, as I had hoped, allowed to volunteer for this new class.
They were guinea pigs, and they knew it immediately. At
our first meeting, they looked around and dubbed themselves "the baby class." No matter how many times I tried
to explain that 9PAI6P was a special, not necessarily a
dumb, class, I could not dissuade them from this view of
themselves.

A letter was drafted and sent to each of the parents or
guardians of the chosen students. With great enthusiasm, I
spent the first few days attempting to explain how this new
class would function. Although the class was to be geared to
the needs and interests of the individual students, their
initial reaction was one of reluctance. Perhaps they were

193

frightened by the amount of freedom they would have. Sensing a restlessness to get going, I dove headlong into games and puzzles aimed at reviewing the basic skills— addition, subtraction, multiplication, and division of whole numbers. I had prepared about nineteen different activities and left them lying about the room randomly. I wanted the students to explore and choose for themselves. Everyday I introduced something new. Each student kept a folder in which he recorded his daily selections. When he had completed an exercise, he would place it in his folder for my comments.

When the novelty of this new approach had worn off and the students had more of an idea of where things were going, we held a meeting. The purpose of this second meeting was to evaluate what had gone on up to that point and to discuss ways to improve the class. Many of the students felt a lack of direction. For eleven years of their academic life, school had meant coming to class at a prescribed time, taking an assigned seat, listening to the teacher lecture, regurgitating memorized facts, taking tests every Friday. Now everything was reversed. There were no assigned seats, no textbooks, no tests. Homework was a matter of choice. It was not optional, but each pupil could choose for himself or herself from among the rexographed games, puzzles, experiments and activities scattered around the room. This matter of homework was disturbing to several of the students. They felt they were not yet ready to make decisions about assignments. A few confessed that they had deliberately chosen the easiest problems. They preferred my assigning them work each night. Some of the other students were dissatisfied with the games and puzzles. They felt they were not learning unless they had a piece of paper in front of them.

The outcome of the meeting was that I agreed to review

194

each individual folder each day and prescribe subsequent work accordingly. In addition, these pupils who wished to work exclusively with books, could do so. Copies of *Learning to Compute* were provided. In addition, a mathematics library was established. One copy of almost every textbook, workbook, pamphlet or booklet was placed in a locker in the back of the room. If a student wished to take a book home, he or she merely filled out an index card.

After this second meeting, the students themselves began to establish certain routines. They would come to class, go to the locker containing their folders, go back to a seat of their own choosing, read the "prescription" for the day, decide whether to work with a game or puzzle or in their workbooks or with one of the numerous rexographed sheets that I had prepared, then go get whatever it was they had decided upon from the cabinet and finally begin to work. Each cabinet and locker had to be secured because 9PAI6P used the room only one period per day. Unlike the reading laboratory, the mathematics laboratory was not provided with a separate room. Space was at a premium. Other classes had to use the same room. Materials could not be left lying around. Each student in 9PAI6P knew the lock combinations. Each was responsible for the materials he or she used each day. During the term only one checker was lost.

When a student was about to begin a new topic, he needed someone to help him. At first the students looked exclusively to me for explanations. However, it soon became obvious that, because of the way the classroom was structured, with each student "doing his own thing" at his own pace, I could not be with everyone at the same time. Slowly, as they gained more confidence in themselves and their abilities, they began to turn to one another for help. Peer group teaching became an integral part of 9PAI6P.

195

Not everything went as smoothly as I idealistically expected it would. Some of the students were still unable to cope with the amount of freedom, even after the routines had been established. For some, the program was not flexible enough.

Since no tests were given to the students in 9PAI6P, some other method had to be devised to evaluate their progress. This was accomplished through daily anecdotal records. A three by five index card was kept for each of the eighteen students and, each day as I reviewed the folders, I noted each individual's progress on his or her card. In addition, I would summarize the results of any conferences or incidents which had occurred that day. These cards were available to the students at any time. Without test marks, it was difficult for them to gauge where they stood in relation to the rest of the class. The fact that one could look at his or her anecdotal record and compare it with any other person's, gave the students a feeling of security. They still competed with one another rather than with themselves, but less overtly so. Of course, this was a lot of work and necessitated my staying after school everyday, but the results were certainly worth the extra time. In addition, the students were given the California Achievement Tests both at the beginning and at the end of the term. Biweekly conferences were held with the class as a whole, and individual conferences were ongoing. A two-day end-of-term workshop was held for final evaluation and feedback.

Besides attempts at peer teaching, the elimination of tests, individualized homework assignments, flexible seating and working at one's own pace, curriculum changes were also tried. The emphasis, of course, was on the fundamental skills and an introduction to algebra, but I tried other topics, such as recognition of geometric solids, calendar mathematics, modular arithmetic, tangrams, area, set theory and basic logic. I used any and all materials I could get my hands on—begged, borrowed, teacher created, commercially prepared; games, puzzles, workbooks and pamphlets. The Madison Project's postman stories created by Robert B. Davis were used in demonstrating subtraction of signed numbers. Scott Foresman's *Application in Mathematics* series was helpful for evaluating simple numerical expressions involving parentheses and order of operations. Their *Activities in Mathematics* series was invaluable for games and puzzles reviewing the basic skills.

Alphametrics are a good way of teaching number patterns. Harold Jacobs' *Mathematics: A Human Endeavor,* a delightful and charming book for people who think they do not like mathematics, contains hundreds of pertinent cartoons, pictures and diagrams and all sorts of topics such as billiard ball mathematics, mathematical mosaics, an experiment in punched card data sorting, mathematics of growth, and the arithmetic of seating arrangements. His teacher's guide spells out bright and interesting ways to introduce each new topic and includes follow up activities and fabulous bibliographies. It even contains some transparencies for the overhead projector. Material prepared for teaching modular arithmetic was lifted directly from the Board of Education's experimental curriculum guide entitled *Fundamentals of Mathematics,* which also contains excellent games for reviewing equivalent fractions patterned after Bingo. IBM sent me a game called Hexapawa, which demonstrates how a machine can be instructed to make decisions and avoid repeating past mistakes. The object of the game is to lose. Creative Playthings sent sixty dollars worth of free games and puzzles, including the Tower of Hanoi, on Sets, blank dice, attribute blocks, models of geometric solids, and Loony Loop, a topological game. Bali Buttons, Hi Jinx, and Instant Insanity were some of the other commercially prepared games used to develop logical thinking. I made cheap copies of the African stone game known as Kalah out of egg cartons and lima beans. From oaktag I created mathematical checkers. Design Lab Space-forms are an excellent way of discovering polyhedra. All the materials I used were chosen because they seemed exciting, tangible, and involving.

At our final two sessions both the students and I discussed our reactions to 9PAI6P. We talked about my original expectations and their initial reluctance to be a part of such an experiment and how both of our views had changed as the term progressed. For the most part the comments were favorable. Jimmy spoke about self-discipline. He thought that because the students themselves had established the routines, it reduced the amount of misbehavior. He felt that it had personally benefited him. Lanor decided that the amount of personal attention each student received was the most important factor in the success of 9PA16P. Janella agreed and added that she was more comfortable being able to turn to a classmate for help. It was less humiliating for her to seek out a peer than to go to the teacher and admit her ineptness. Lavern and Robert appreciated being able to work at something of their own choosing. Jimmy and I discussed his abhorrence to putting anything on paper and how such a program as this could adapt itself to each individual's differences. All agreed that the fact that each student was allowed to proceed at his or her own pace was important. I talked about how I had not expected so much emphasis to be placed on programmed learning, individual as it may have been. I had expected there to be more of an exchange and flow of information between students, initiated by students, more independent study, more willingness to use games and puzzles as learning tools. The students decided that it was a matter of readiness, that now, after a term of the open classroom, they would be much more amenable to such experiments.

Worth learning

The links between math, science, and social
studies are evident to all in the working
world. But they are rarely connected in
schools. However, just as teachers discovered
and embraced "experiential" reading
programs that give meaning and motivation
to decoding work, they are now recognizing
that math language and mathematical thinking can be taught sensibly, if they are also
taught while studying the world of "real
people." The most proper (and fascinating)
study of mankind is man. This report, from
Teachers Guide, shows how children
study themselves and their world with a stop
watch, scale, and thermometer.

It was noted, in January, in the first week of term, that
several children were absent. Why was this? Pupils suggested that the missing ones probably had colds. When do
we get colds? They thought that we catch more during
winter than summer because it is colder.

This reminded Desmond that when he was in hospital
the doctor allowed him to take his own temperature, and it
was 102° F. Angela thought hers had been "98 and 4."

Then pupils wanted to know why the doctor took a
patient's pulse, and they set up a clamor of questions and
observations:

> The doctor tells us to say ninety-nine when he puts a
> thing on our back.
> It's called a stethoscope.
> The doctor holds your wrist when he takes your pulse.
> Is everybody's pulse the same?
> Let's take our pulses.

The upshot was that they decided to find out all they could about the human body.

A group was formed to take children's pulses. The members also wanted to know if older people had the same pulse rate as they had. One boy suggested that heart beats and pulse beats were similar. Over a period of a few weeks they investigated all these points with the rest of the class and their mothers and fathers.

Members of another group investigated the pulse rates of their pet animals. Someone brought a hamster into the classroom and they found its rate of heart beat was 140 per minute.

Desmond said: "I took my dog's heart beat and it was 60. Then I played about with it and took it again. This time it was 90 and I had to take its heart beat three times before it was back to normal."

The class started to find out if their pulse rates would be faster when they moved. They experimented in the classroom, where they took their pulses before and after moving about. In each case the rate was higher afterwards. One of the boys ran round the classroom, and this greatly increased it.

"Why was this?" they asked. They did not find the answer to this question until weeks later when the class studied the human body.

In another group, Terry asked: "Is everyone's temperature the same?" These children were given a clinical thermometer, which they compared with the ordinary room thermometer. They used both to take temperatures, placing them under the arm rather than in the mouth, because "there might be germs." They eventually found the difference in the ways the thermometers worked when they discovered that the ordinary room one went down too quickly after taking body temperature and you could not easily take an accurate reading. The teacher writes:

200

There was great interest in the thermometers, and the pupils were intrigued at the way the mercury moved up. They breathed on them, held them in their hands, held them against the radiators just to see the mercury move up the glass tubing. They should have been allowed to ask and discover for themselves how a thermometer works, but I thought that a lesson on the thermometer at this point might be beneficial.

We discussed the word "thermometer." Why was it called this? No one knew, but later one boy saw that "meter" was part of the word, and the class thought of all the meters they knew, gas meter, electricity meter, taximeter, and decided that it must measure something —"heat," of course. So the other part of the word must mean heat.

The pupils realized quite easily that when the thermometer becomes warmer the mercury will move up the tube (this they had seen when they heated the thermometer, either by breathing on it or holding it in their hands). The difficulty came when an explanation of why the mercury went up when heated was given to them.

Expansion of solids was talked about and an example given of the need to leave gaps between railway lines. They had seen this, and it was obvious from looking at their faces that many could not understand—probably could not believe—that solids would become larger when heated. Some would have accepted the fact because they had been told it, but others were ready to query it. It was obvious that this lesson did not succeed.

Later, a bottle was provided and a balloon placed on the opening. The pupils did not devise this. It was made by the teacher and left on top of the radiator. The balloon began to fill up and this was noticed by some pupils, who immediately became interested and discussed it. They put the bottle into hot water and the balloon inflated, and later, when it cooled, the balloon deflated again. The pupils concluded that the air in the jar must have become bigger when heated.

The teacher constructed another piece of apparatus and left it on his desk in front of the room. At first there was very little interest, but later someone noticed that the water was moving up the tube.

"It must be the heat again," they said, so they put their hands around the jar and the level went up slightly. Later it was placed in a larger container with hot water, and the water in the tube rose rapidly. They said that this was like a real thermometer, and wondered why mercury was put in a thermometer when "water would do just as well."

They asked if they could try to make a "real" thermometer. The teacher provided glass tubing along with mercury, and a Calor gas picnic stove. Then, first heating the glass tubing, he bent it and blew a bulb at one end. The pupils showed great interest and excitement and they all wanted to try it.

The following day David brought in a piece of lead piping and asked, could he try to melt this? He said he would like to find out how many solid things could be melted in the stove flame.

Much work having been done with thermometers, it was suggested by the pupils that a check should be made to see if boiling point really was 100° C and 212° F. They had discovered these facts in books available in the classroom.

The pupils decided that a thermometer of each type should be held first in boiling water and then in crushed ice. As boiling water was used, the teacher carried out the first part of the investigation. Because of the heat and clouds of "steam," boiling point could not be established, but pupils said it was "at least 93° C." Freezing point was checked by the pupils later.

The steam seen in the first part of the experiment led to a discussion on evaporation and condensation. The pupils had not realized that water actually changed into steam. They thought this was simply given off. Together, class and teacher devised an experiment whereby a certain quantity of water would be evaporated, then condensed, to see if the same quantity of water remained at the end.

A metal teapot and two jam jars were used. A jam jar full of water was put into the teapot and boiled. The condensed water produced in the top jar dropped into the lower one. This worked well in the beginning, but it was obvious that steam was being lost out of the top jam jar and out of the lid of the teapot.

Presently, one boy suggested that the top jam jar had become too hot to do its job properly. There was, however, great excitement to see that the experiment did work, if not perfectly.

Another pupil said that his brother in secondary school had done an experiment like this to get salt from salt water. The class discussed salt in water and sea water, and the Dead Sea and how difficult it is to sink in it. Then Diane said she felt lighter in the bath even though there was no salt in it, and Desmond said his leg felt heavier when he tried to lift it up out of the water in the bath. This led a group to experiment, using stones and a spring balance, to find out if things were lighter in the water. This group later went on to study floating and sinking.

A small empty bottle with a screw top was floated in a large container. Then it was filled with increasing amounts of water until it sank. The rise in water level in the container that then occurred was measured, recognized as displacement, and discussed with the class, and the teacher suggested that the children might find out how much was displaced.

Some of them attempted this by filling a jam jar with water, plunging the bottle in, and weighing the water which spilled down the sides of the jar. They did not arrive at a definite conclusion, but thought that the weight of a sinking body was the same as that of displaced water.

Another group had been formed after the very first discussion on pulses and heart beats, to find out about blood. When the class had been discussing how to measure a pulse by placing two fingers on the wrist, one pupil said that if you held your wrist tightly, your hand would go white. "It's because you are stopping the blood," said somebody. They began to think about the color of blood. "Has everyone got the same blood?" they wondered.

DESMOND: Black people have different blood from us.

TERRY: No, everyone has red blood.

Iris said she could find out as she could write to her aunt who was a nurse in Africa. She did this and presently received a most interesting letter in return, which told her that dark people also have red blood. Meanwhile the discussion continued.

MINA: Why do your hands get wet when you are warm? (*Pause*) There are little holes in your skin.

ROBIN: Why does blood not run out of these holes?

JIM: Because your blood is in your veins.

JOHN: This can't be true, because you can see your veins and if you cut yourself even between the veins, you still bleed. (*The children later found the answer to this problem in their reading.*)

ROBIN: I was helping my sister to make the bed and I nipped my finger. Later it went black.

DESMOND: That happened to me, too, and I pierced the black part and black blood came out. (*He thought a moment, and then went on.*) When it's nipped maybe it stops the blood moving and it goes bad.

One afternoon following this discussion, John came in from the playground having fallen and cut his knee. Before he could have it bandaged, Diane asked if she could take a sample of his blood.

John had to wait while a microscope was borrowed from another classroom. A blood sample was placed on a small strip of glass and a number of pupils viewed it through the microscope. They said that the blood was "in little pieces," "like a design" and "like a stained glass window." (Later they made a "Blood Book" in which they wrote about what had happened and drew pictures of what they had seen through the microscope.)

While the children in the "blood group" were looking at the sample, they forgot about John, until they heard him say that the blood "had started to go hard on his knee." Then the questions and observations started again:

> Why does your blood not go hard inside you?
> It must be the heat of your body.
> How can you give blood to hospitals when it will go hard after leaving your body?
> Maybe it's because they take out quite a lot of blood.
> How much blood do you have?
> What happens to you when you give away some blood?
> Your heart makes more blood.
> I think food is made into blood.

As a result of this, a group of pupils turned to secondary sources of information to find out more about the human body. They enlisted the help of the whole class, brought in books, especially medical books and encyclopedias, visited public libraries, and interviewed parents and relations. They did little practical experimenting but were encouraged to continue these "finding out" activities.

The interest was widespread. The whole class became

205

involved as different members relayed each new discovery to the group, with great excitement. Notes were kept on the findings, and a book made. At the end of the week the members of the group were asked if they would like to take the class for a period, and report on all that they had found out. They received the idea with great delight, and immediately began to make notes and plans about speakers and subjects for the lesson. This was given the following week by Lorraine, Clifford, Philip, Albert, and Nigel.

They spent over an hour talking to the rest of the class, completely without shyness or hesitancy, and using the blackboard for diagrams. Each had a subject, with one talking about the parts of the body, another on the brain, another on muscles, and two on the movement of blood. The class listened attentively and asked questions during the lesson.

Lorraine labeled all the parts of the body and told about the skull, which protects the brain, and the ribs, which protect the heart. Albert talked about the brain, which, he said, received messages from various parts of the body and then passed them out again to other parts. He said that it took one-tenth of a second for a message to go from the brain to some part of the body.

At this point Harry asked if it would take longer for a message to go to the foot than to the head. Albert did not know, but an experiment was suggested to them by the teacher so that they could measure the speed of "message travel." Eight children formed a line, holding hands. The first person squeezed the hand of his neighbor, who, on feeling the pressure, squeezed the hand of his neighbor on the other side. They timed how long it took for the action to be repeated down the line and from this estimated how long one individual took to perform it. They repeated the experiment a number of times and found that they were able to do it more quickly with practice, but the fastest time from hand to brain to hand they recorded was three-tenths of a second. They also found, using a similar experiment, that a message took slightly longer to travel to the foot.

Continuing with the lesson, Nigel told about muscles and showed on the board how, when they contract, they pull the arm upwards. Philip and Clifford described how blood moved round the body. They said that it took oxygen from the lungs and gave this out on the way round, gathering up carbon dioxide which was eventually breathed out.

The class connected an experiment with these ideas later in the term. David brought in a candle, saying he had read of the experiment and wanted to try it.

He lit the candle and placed a jar over it. The candle went out. He lit it again and put it under a much larger jar, and this time it took a much longer time to go out. David said that he had read that the candle needed oxygen to burn, and this proved it because it had used up all the oxygen and then stopped burning.

He was then asked by the teacher if he could use this experiment to discover whether we breathe out oxygen or carbon dioxide. He immediately tried to breathe into a jar to see if the candle would burn under it or not. He found that he could not successfully get a jar full of breath, so his teacher showed him how to collect it by inverting a glass full of water in a vessel of water, blowing into the glass through a rubber tube until it was full of breath, sliding a glass plate beneath the rim, removing the glass from the vessel of water, and quickly inserting a lighted candle. This proved successful and he was able to show that the candle would not burn in breath. David later wanted to know why, since we are continually breathing in "good air" and breathing out "bad air," the layer of air round the earth was not used up eventually.

207

A few days after the lesson, Philip brought a sheep's heart into school. The pupils looked at a sample of the blood through a microscope, and decided that there was not much difference between that and human blood. Each pupil had a look at the heart and a number asked if they could cut it up. They found that there were four tubes leading from the top and that each led to a compartment in the heart. They concluded from their reading researches that two tubes were for taking in the blood and two were for pumping it out again. Also, David said that the shape of the heart was not like those on Valentine cards, although it did come to a point at the bottom.

A pig's heart was brought in a few days later. The pupils found this to be very similar to the sheep's. When they had finished looking at it, it was wrapped in a Polythene bag to be taken away by the teacher, but unfortunately it was forgotten over the weekend and by Monday it had begun to decompose. This started another line of inquiry as the pupils suggested many ways the heart might have been kept "fresh." They mentioned refrigerators, among other things, and Lorraine said that sometimes animals were found in the ice, dead but not having decayed, so this must be like a refrigerator. Desmond said that the ancient Egyptians put something on dead people to keep them from decaying. A number of the children showed considerable interest in the Egyptians and began to talk about the things that were buried in their tombs.

Marshall had his lunch box with him and said that this kept food fresh because it was airtight. The pupils now concluded that air must make things go bad, but it was suggested that the lunch box would not keep things fresh for as long as a refrigerator. Ann wondered how tins of peas and other things remained fresh.

Presently they decided to find out how parts of the

human body, including blood, were kept for use. They would do this by writing to half a dozen addresses, either of hospitals or blood transfusion units. Pupils who were not working on this problem asked if they could write to local industries which preserved foods. (This was essentially following up work they had begun the previous term.) The response was excellent. The hospitals sent long letters in language suitable for the pupils, while from industries came charts, photographs, samples, etc.

The following week Hilary brought a cow's heart from her father's butcher's shop. All the children were amazed at the size and wanted to weigh it. They found that it weighed three pounds. The same day a chicken's heart was brought in. This, too, was weighed and found to be ½ oz. The pupils calculated that the cow's heart was almost a hundred times the weight of the chicken's heart—Lorraine asked if a cow then was a hundred times heavier than a chicken. They asked butchers, found out the weights of various cows, talked about "live weight" and "dead weight," and worked out the relationship in weight between cows and hens.

One of the people they had written to was a sausage manufacturer, who sent, among other things, some posters advertising his products. They put these on display, and after a few days, a pupil noticed that one of them showed a vacuum pack containing bacon. They added this to their growing list of ways of preserving things.

The next day Desmond came into school with a small vacuum flask, wanting to know if this would keep things fresh. However, it was an old one and he did not know if it were working at all, and this started some of the children discussing how they could find this out. So, in fact, they completely forgot the original idea, to see if it would keep things fresh. Next day, Iris brought in another flask and compared the two, but then decided that both might not be working. After this, the children put hot water into each flask and into a big jar, to see which would stay hot longest. Other pupils brought in different types of containers, such as lemonade, milk, ink, and medicine bottles; two large dried milk tins; and jam and large sweet jars. They filled nine of these containers (leaving the lid off one of any pair of similar ones) and the two flasks with hot water, and took the temperature of the water in the eleven vessels each hour. Earlier, they had asked if they might make charts about the results—meaning block graphs, which they made last term—and they had discussed this and designed and put a block graph on each of the eleven vessels. The temperature record was on the vertical scale and time on the horizontal. The experiment worked very well and they finally decided that both flasks were working, because they kept the heat in.

The children talked again about vacuum flasks but could not decide how they worked. They looked in dictionaries and found the meaning of "vacuum." David brought in a washing-up liquid container, squeezed all the air out of it, and put the top back on. It stayed "squashed-up" and he wondered if he had created a vacuum inside.

The water was left standing in the nine containers other than the thermos flasks, and all were in the classroom. The children took the temperatures the following day and found they were all in the range 58–60° F. It was suggested by the teacher that they should take the temperature of the room, and this was found to be 60° F. After much discussion, they decided that the temperature must fall to that of the room. Diane then asked what would happen if the water were below room temperature. She brought in ice cubes and placed them in the water. Its temperature fell to 45° F, but on the following day it had risen to 58° F.

Worth learning

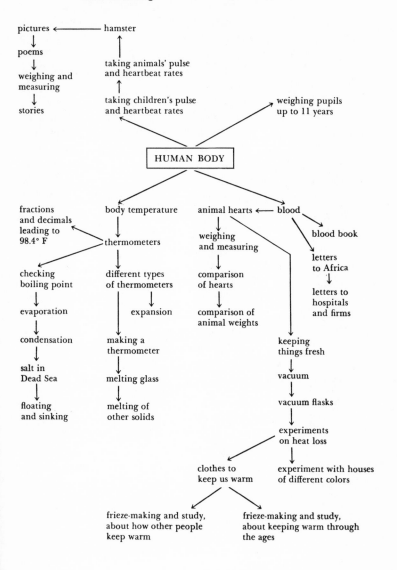

David then asked why our body temperature did not drop, since we were normally 98.4° F and the room was about 60° F. The teacher put this question to the whole class and one pupil said, "That's why we wear clothes." Another suggested that the reason why pygmies wore very few clothes must be that the temperature in their country was over 98.4° F, and another that the Eskimos had to wear so much because they lived in so very low a temperature.

This revived interest in a topic that had barely been touched on in the first week of term, when the children were talking about why we catch colds in winter: the various ways of keeping warm. As a result of this, they made two friezes in their art classes, one depicting how other peoples keep warm and the other about keeping warm through the ages.

7

The heart hears . . . and speaks

The cultivation of the senses, feelings, and imagination

Herbert Spencer used to say that if archaeologists a hundred years hence unearthed one of the schools of his day, they would probably decide from studying its curriculum and methods that it was a training institution for monks and nuns. If a comparable study is made in one of our schools, it might appear to be a place for programming computers rather than a place for nurturing the growth of children. Lately, however, teachers have been groping towards teaching that does touch the emotions, sensibility, and imagination. They are trying to provide educations for human beings.

213

Will it grow in a classroom?

Simply sharing feelings—in a relaxed,
supportive setting—can be the start of a
more human classroom and school. In fact,
it is a start which can carry a group of
children and teachers quite far into the
realms of authentic communications, as
Arlene Uslander and her colleagues found
out when they began a discussion program
on sex education (and other problems) in an
otherwise very traditional school.

BY ARLENE USLANDER

"I'm not talking today," Kenny stated flatly, as he entered
the room.

"Kenny's just angry because he had to do a paper over
again," Debby explained. "He was in trouble on the playground; he left his library book at home, and then he
didn't do his work right."

"What seems to be the matter, Kenny?" I asked.

"I hate school! It's too hard. I have to get up too early in
the morning. I don't understand the teacher. She always
yells at me. I never do anything right. I'm in the lowest
reading group; I'm in the lowest math group. I'm probably
even in the lowest lunch group."

In this angry statement, Kenny expressed not only his
own frustration, but the frustration felt by many children
struggling to reach goals that adults have set for them. At
the age of six, and only in the first grade, he was already
experiencing failure and rejection. By comparison with his
peers, he found himself lacking, and instead of being
encouraged by praise of his strengths, he was usually chas-
tised because of his weaknesses. Naturally, he was resentful.
He recognized ability grouping—no matter how subtly

disguised—for what it was, and both he and the other children felt that he would never be able to rise above the level at which he had been placed.

Greg said: "Oh, Kenny, it's not that bad. Look at me. I'm absent an awful lot because of my asthma. At first, I thought I'd never learn to read, but the teacher helped me. She gave me things to do at home, and told my mother how to help me. All you have to do is ask her."

"I ask her! I ask her! But she's always busy."

"You know something, Kenny?" Debbie said. "You ought to try harder. The teacher has a lot to do and she can't always listen to you. Sometimes you're not very polite to her. You talk back to her. I like school!"

"I'd like school, too, if we had computerized teachers," declared Steven.

"Why?" I asked.

"So we could pull out their plugs."

"That's silly," said Susan. "Besides, you have to go to school. If you don't, you won't learn to read, or anything, and then what would you do?"

"I could play all the time and watch television as long as I wanted to and be able to stay up real late," Kenny answered enthusiastically. "That would be great!"

"I think people should be born grown-up. Then they wouldn't have to go to school," Steven said defiantly. "The part of school I like best is going home."

"That would be silly," argued Debbie. "We'd miss all the fun of growing up and learning."

"What fun is that?" Kenny asked angrily. "All we ever do is work, work, work . . . Sometimes I wish I was still in kindergarten."

"What was fun about kindergarten?" asked Richard.

"All we did was play. We didn't have to work, and we didn't have to stay in school all day. I hate staying in school so long."

"What did you think school was going to be like before you came here?" I asked Kenny.

"When I first started kindergarten, I wanted to go to school," said Kenny.

Nine surprised faces, my own included, stared at him. This was certainly a reversal.

"Five years with my mother was enough!" he exclaimed, a mischievous gleam in his eye.

"Everyone kept telling me I'd learn to read and write in school," Richard said, "and I was disappointed. In kindergarten, all we did was play, and it was so short. I was bored. First grade is much more fun."

"I knew you'd say that! You probably like Sunday school, too!" accused Kenny.

"I don't go to Sunday school. But if I did, I think I'd like it," answered Richard.

"I heard a lot about school before I started," said Greg. "The older boys told me all about it. They said the teachers were mean, and you had to put your head down when they told you. They said the teacher spanked you. But my teacher hasn't spanked me yet. The kids must have been trying to scare me. School hasn't been anywhere near as bad as they said. And first grade is better than kindergarten. At least we have recess in first grade."

"I remember when we just started first grade," said Joseph. "I thought we had to know how to read already. Boy, was I scared. I felt like throwing up."

"You think that's so bad?" said Steven. "I wet my pants! I was so glad when we were finally able to go home. The whole time we were in school, I didn't think I'd ever see my mother again."

"I was lucky," bragged Sandy. "I knew all about school way before I started. My mother is a teacher, and I have a brother in college. They told me everything. I didn't even have to come to school if I didn't want to," she continued.

"I knew how to read and write and everything, but my mother told me not to tell anybody, because I would get into trouble. So I forgot it all before I started school."

Richard shook his head, a puzzled expression on his face. "How could you do that, Sandy?" he asked. The idea that someone could forget what he or she had learned seemed inconceivable to him.

"It was easy," Sandy said, casually. "I didn't really learn it so good to begin with."

"You know the first thing I made when I came to school?" asked Steven, who had turned his chair around and was now sitting astride it, as though he were riding a horse. "A mistake!"

"When I first started school, the worst thing was remembering what all the bells meant," recalled Greg. "I jumped out of my seat every time they rang, and one time I got into line for recess and it wasn't even recess time. I still forget sometimes."

As I listened to the children comparing notes on their very first recollections of school, I realized that they were beginning to view with amusement early experiences, which, at the time, had seemed very unpleasant—perhaps even traumatic. Joseph's next comment was a good example.

"Do you know what happened to me?" he laughed. "The second day of school, I went home at recess time. When I heard the bell, I thought that school was over. The principal had to call my mother to bring me back. Boy, was she mad!"

"I kept forgetting the gym teacher's name," said Greg, who had—on more than one occasion—called me "mommy." "It's hard to remember so many different names."

"It's hard to remember where you're supposed to go, too," Susan pointed out. "Yesterday, I was supposed to go to my speech class, and on the way there, I forgot where I was going, and had to go back to the room to ask the teacher. But I like going to speech. I have fun there."

"I wish I could go to speech. Then I wouldn't have to do work," interjected Kenny, who was still in a sullen mood.

"The music teacher is nice. I like it when she plays records for us," mused Joseph. "I pretend I'm a conductor leading a big orchestra and everyone has to watch me before they can do anything."

"That's sissy stuff," shouted Kenny.

"Well, I like it! We don't all have to like the same things," Joseph said, defensively.

"What do you like best about school?" I asked Laura, who had not yet expressed an opinion on this subject.

She thought about my question for a few minutes and then, instead of looking away, as she so often did, looked directly at me. Very quietly, she said: "I like to come here."

"Why?" I asked, anxious to hear what this child, who spoke up so rarely, would say.

"Because it's . . . because you're . . . you're so nice to all of us," she said, finally.

"And you're honest!" added Steven. "That's what I like. Yesterday, we were drawing winter pictures. Mine was terrible, but the teacher said it was beautiful. She didn't have to do that! I know you wouldn't."

I could see that Kenny also wanted to say something, but for once was holding back. "How do you feel about coming here, Kenny?" I asked, hoping that I wouldn't be sorry I'd questioned him.

He surprised me. "I wish we could stay here all day," he said. "You don't yell and you don't make fun of us and you never make anyone sit in the corner or stand in the hall."

"But I've asked you to leave the room several times, when you disturbed us by making noises, and falling off your chair. Or when you wouldn't give anyone else a chance to talk," I reminded him.

218

I didn't like to ask a child to leave the room, and did so only on the rare occasions when one of them—usually Kenny, unfortunately—demonstrated that he or she simply could not settle down. We had such a short time together each week that I didn't like to deprive any one of us of even a moment of it. When one of the children kept bidding for everyone else's attention in negative ways—interrupting, making fun, giggling, not giving anyone else an opportunity to speak—I would ask that child to remove his chair from the circle, telling him that he could rejoin us when he was ready to follow the one rule we had in our room—a rule which the children, themselves, had decided upon: Only one person talks at a time.

Naturally, there were moments—especially when the discussion was particularly exciting—when everyone, myself included, forgot about our rule. And it certainly was never my intention to maintain an "it's so quiet you can hear a pin drop" atmosphere. But from the very beginning, I tried to instill within each child a respect for the other person's right, desire, and need to talk. The child who denied others this right, as Kenny sometimes did, would be asked to leave the group temporarily. And if sitting outside the circle did not produce the desired effect, the offending child was asked to leave the room. I wondered whether Kenny felt that I, like some of his other teachers, treated him unfairly, or picked on him.

My question was answered when he said: "But you always said I could come back when I was ready, and I could sit in the lunch room or go back to my classroom. At least I didn't have to sit in the hall, where everyone would stare at me."

"I had to sit in the hall once," recalled Sandy, "and I kept wishing the floor would open up and I could crawl into the hole."

"I spent so much time in the hall when I was in kindergarten, I was beginning to think I lived there!" Steven admitted.

The children's comments had long since taught me that they enjoyed coming to our "corner of the world." Frequently, they said such things as: "Can't we stay longer?"; "Do we have to leave now?"; "Can't we come more than once a week?"; "Why can't the whole school be one big Study of People class?" And once, the whole group surprised me by coming into the room and sitting down after the dismissal bell had rung. "We want to study people *after* school, too!" they informed me. They always rushed eagerly into the room in their haste to start talking, and lingered as long as they possibly could when it was time to leave.

Perhaps Joseph expressed the feelings of the entire group when he said: "In this room, we can relax. In this room, we can be free."

Most of them tended to attribute their positive feelings about our class to me—to the fact that I was "nice to all of them and didn't make fun of them," that I accepted each child as an individual and listened to what each one of them had to say. But I tried to show them that they, too, were helping to create the atmosphere they so enjoyed. They, too, were beginning to accept and understand one another. They were beginning to put themselves in each other's place and—in so doing—were developing a feeling of responsibility towards one another as human beings.

When they were in third grade, I had to be absent from school on two occasions, and both times they met alone—without any discussion leader at all. From several teachers who had walked past the room during their sessions—and, of course, from the children themselves—I learned that they had carried on with their discussions just as though I had been there. They were learning how to deal with one another even without an adult's supervision. I couldn't help feeling gratified.

Worth learning

Dan Cheifetz's free theater workshop for an integrated group of neighborhood eight–elevens gave the children "the means, the encouragement and the freedom to be themselves, to learn about themselves and to express themselves." (Elizabeth Gross, age 11, selected this piece.)

BY DAN CHEIFETZ

The children straggled into the small gym by ones and twos. Some, those who had come with a friend or a sibling, eyed the singles and whispered together. One girl stood near the entrance and vigorously scratched her arms and legs and sometimes her back. A neatly dressed boy came in and went to a corner of the gym. He stood exactly where the side and back walls met, slouching and staring solemnly at his shoes. Another boy picked up a basketball that was lying around and shot a basket. His friend got the rebound and dribbled away. Two girls went up on the stage that occupied the far end of the gym and began to play house. One served tea to the other, using a battered table and bench that were there. The high-ceilinged gym was drafty and the heating system occasionally made clinking and sighing noises.

So began my workshop in dramatic play and learning. The children, ten girls and five boys, aged eight to eleven, were to meet thirteen successive Saturday mornings for an hour and a half at the Metropolitan Duane United Methodist Church in New York City. I liked the physical setup. There was room enough for the children to play and perform but not so much space that it would be difficult to round them up and concentrate them in one place when necessary.

221

I gathered them together now, asking them to sit on the floor around me. They dawdled on the way, reluctant to start, or rather, pretending elaborate coolness about the whole affair. Finally they sat, keeping careful distances between themselves and anyone they didn't know; at the same time, they stole curious glances at one another. I told them very briefly about what we were going to do in the workshop: play pretend games, act out things, pantomime, improvise (I explained that) and other activities that I hoped would be fun and also help them learn.

I asked them to stand up if they knew the game Simon Says. They all stood up. I said this would not be the usual "put your right hand on your left shoulder" kind of Simon but a Simon who would turn them into all different kinds of creatures. I would be Simon first, then give them a chance to be Simon.

"Simon says, 'Spread out and give yourself lots of room.' " They did.

"Simon says, 'Be a tightrope-walker!' "

The boy who had stood by himself in the corner before we had begun now was standing directly in front of me. He threw his arms out at right angles to his torso and planted his left foot carefully behind himself. Slowly he swung his right foot around and placed it at a slightly toed-out angle directly in front of himself, his whole body wavering and swaying in a well-imagined move-and-countermove struggle with gravity. He brought his left foot around, then the right, then more quickly the left again. He stopped, almost fell, righted himself, and got set to move forward again.

This was Brent, a ten-year-old black boy from a Chelsea tenement. He certainly did not look like the same boy who had slumped in a corner, staring at his feet. Now he stood as tall as he was, a poised and graceful figure, his eyes wide open in concentration on an inner world in which he was fifty feet off the ground while thousands held their breath beneath.

"Simon says, 'Be a snake!' "

Immediately Brent was off the swaying tightrope and onto his stomach, hissing and writhing on the floor. Another snake, a leggy, pretty, eleven-year-old white girl named Sally, hissed at him. Brent blinked at her, hesitated, then hissed back, hard. Sally smiled delightedly and hissed again. Then both stared at an entirely different creature, not a snake at all, but a person playing on a pipe and rolling her eyes. This was Margie, an imp-faced black girl of nine. Simon couldn't tell *her* what to do. She had decided not to *be* a snake but to *control* one. A sinister cobra was rising on the mysterious music of her pipe. It was Margie's friend, nine-year-old Joyce, wearing a colorful robozo, short pig-tails and a Mona Lisa smile. Her tongue-fangs flicked in and out and her head turned like a pig-tailed searchlight, look-ing for a victim to strike.

But before she could find one, Simon had said, "Be a monster!"

Cobra forgotten, Joyce rose and clumped about, neck and face rigid as a monster, but arms held out more like a scarecrow. Suddenly, a girllike squeal came from her, and she ducked away. A light-haired boy monster, ten-year-old Stan, was approaching fast. Actually, monster Stan had not been after Joyce but his friend, monster Richard (my son, a curly-haired nine-year-old). The two Frankensteins clutched each other and prepared for a squeeze-each-other-to-death match.

But, just in time, Simon had said, "Be pigs!"

And Stan and Richard were in the mud together, snuffling and oinking. Richard turned over on his back, bent his hands slightly at the wrist, held his legs stiff in the air, and

223

rolled luxuriously from side to side. For a blinding instant, boy and pig were one.

A plump, auburn-haired ten-year-old named Sandy was watching him. A while before, when we were sitting together in a circle, she had been at the edge of the group. Now she was laughing at Richard's piggish roll in the mud. Then she leaned against the gym wall and began to rub her back against it, up and down, back and forth, her eyes closed in piglike pleasure. But not for long.

"Simon says, 'Be a dog!' "

Sandy went to her hands and knees, then her haunches. She had been the one scratching herself when the other children had wandered in. Now she incorporated her nervous habit into her role: she vigorously scratched her fleas!

Near her was a frightened-looking boy dog, a towhead named Donald, who had just turned eight. Throughout the game, Donald had been copying the actions of his ten-and-a-half-year-old sister Stacey, as if we had been playing Follow the Leader instead of Simon Says. Suddenly his sister bounded away across the gym to chase a rabbit. Donald tried to follow but his way was blocked by a big mastiff with bared teeth. This was Carrie, a sullen-looking black girl of eleven. The big dog barked threateningly at the little one. The pup tried to bark back but his opponent was so big and fierce, tears came instead. Seeing his distress, his big sister left the rabbit chase and came bounding back to the rescue. But just as she arrived, the mastiff had reared up and become a light-footed vision of gentle grace who wouldn't have hurt one of Sandy's fleas. Tricky Simon had commanded: "Be a ballet dancer!"

No question about it, a game's the thing to get children involved in a new activity. Their desire to have fun playing the game overcame their social anxiety. Once they got into it, this game generated its own security and belongingness.

When they were inside the game, they were inside the group, and so could relax their fears.

And as with any game, the rules were automatically accepted. No wildness and little silliness cropped up, because playing the game by the rules is self-disciplining. The children themselves would handle any unruly player who disturbed the ritual of playing.

Playing this special kind of game also helped overcome the children's reluctance to commit themselves to this new group, because it helped define the nature of the group. It wasn't a class or a club; what was it? Simon and his magic transformations began to answer that question. He also made it fun to be part of the group, *whatever* it was. And seeing one another do interesting and funny things was a good way to satisfy their curiosity about one another.

Other things were happening too. Take Brent again. Just by looking at him gracefully defying death on that high wire, one could see how much he was involved in what he was doing. His whole body, and his inner sense of his body, were involved in an imaginative re-creation of how physical equilibrium is maintained, lost, and then found again. His memories came into play: he must have seen such an artist in an actual circus or on television. And maybe his own private dreams of glory, as well, were represented on that high wire.

Children often pretend to be someone more powerful or heroic than themselves in their private fantasies. The difference is that, perhaps for the first time, Brent had a chance to *become* his fantasy in the flesh. And he had moved his fantasy out of himself and into public view.

So often a child meets with a patronizing attitude, or even contempt, if he reveals his secret life to adults. Normally, Brent would have been afraid of being laughed at if someone "caught" him pretending to be a high-wire artist, or acting out any other cherished dream or weird story he might have told himself. If his fantasies are held in low esteem by the adults who guide him and whose love and acceptance he needs, he cannot possibly esteem them very highly himself. He will more likely feel guilty about them. He will wall off his acceptable "real life" from his secret, made-up one.

But on that imagined high wire, Brent's fantasy life and real life become one. By encouraging him to play out his fantasy, and by praising his public expression of it, we can begin to break down the psychic wall between his "real life" and his secret one. In this way, his secret fantasies become more available to him as a source of creative power in his everyday life, rather than a part of himself to feel guilty about and reject.

Children are often made uneasy by adult questions like: "What are you going to be when you grow up?" Or: "What do you like to do the most?" Though they are natural role-players and experimenters, such questions and the attitude they represent may make children feel they would be more acceptable and loved if they could more clearly define themselves: as an aspiring fireman or nurse, or someone who likes only to play marbles or draw pictures. It may persuade them to find safety and definition in a single role, or in a very limited number of roles, and discourage them from trying new ones. Experience in role-playing, such as our game of Simon Says, helps counteract this pressure to specialize too early and validates the child's natural inclination to experiment. Another benefit is that by trying on different roles— like hats, to see if they fit—a child may discover elements in himself he did not know were there.

A boy like Brent, who sits himself in a corner to wait for someone's instruction before he moves, probably never thought of himself as poised or graceful or brave. But he could not be so skillful playing a high-wire artist unless he too had some of these gifts. This role is a way for him to discover new qualities in himself that his everyday life might never have given him the opportunity to sense.

Simon changed Brent and the other children into snakes and dogs and monsters, as well as heroic tightrope-walkers. To portray each role, the child had to identify, however imperfectly, with a creature completely different from himself. He had to seek in his own imagination and experience for some inner connection, some understanding, of such a creature. Since he has identified with it, he may thereby be motivated to find out more about it. Certainly he has stretched his general capacity to identify and imagine.

"I am not sure that I ever had a happier impulse," says Frederick Buechner about his experience of simply and silently enjoying a sunset with his students.

BY FREDERICK BUECHNER

Late one winter afternoon as I was walking to a class that I had to teach, I noticed the beginnings of what promised to be one of the great local sunsets. There was just the right kind of clouds and the sky was starting to burn and the bare trees were black as soot against it. When I got to the classroom, the lights were all on, of course, and the students were chattering, and I was just about to start things off when I thought of the sunset going on out there in the winter dusk, and on impulse, without warning, I snapped off the classroom lights. I am not sure that I ever had a happier impulse. The room faced west so as soon as it went dark, everything disappeared except what we could see through the windows, and there it was—the entire sky on fire by then, like the end of the world or the beginning of the world. You might think that somebody would have said something. Teachers do not usually plunge their students into that kind of darkness, and you might have expected a wisecrack or two or at least the creaking of chairs as people turned around to see if the old bird had finally lost his mind. But the astonishing thing was that the silence was as complete as you can get it in a room full of people, and we all sat there unmoving for as long as it took the extraordinary spectacle to fade slowly away.

For over twenty minutes nobody spoke a word. Nobody *did* anything. We just sat there in the near-dark and watched one day of our lives come to an end, and it is no immodesty to say that it was a great class because my only contribution was to snap off the lights and then hold my tongue. And I am not being sentimental about sunsets when I say that it was a great class because in a way the sunset was the least of it. What was great was the unbusyness of it. It was taking unlabeled, unallotted time just to look with maybe more than our eyes at what was wonderfully there to be looked at without any obligation to think any constructive thoughts about it or turn it to any useful purpose later, without any weapon at hand in the dark to kill the time it took. It was the sense too that we were not just ourselves individually looking out at the winter sky but that we were in some way also each other looking out at it. We were bound together there simply by the fact of our being human, by our splendid insignificance in face of what was going on out there through the window, and by our curious significance in face of what was going on in there in that classroom. The way this world works, people are very apt to use the words they speak not so much as a way of revealing but, rather, as a way of concealing who they really are and what they really think, and that is why more than a few moments of silence with people we do not know well are apt to make us so tense and uneasy. Stripped of our verbal camouflage, we feel unarmed against the world and vulnerable, so we start babbling about anything just to keep the silence at bay. But if we can bear to let it be, silence, of course, can be communion at a very deep level indeed, and that half hour of silence was precisely that, and perhaps that was the greatest part of it all.

Wanda Gray's reflections on how she "generates creation" in her classroom of ten- and thirteen-year-olds reads like it works: beautifully.

BY WANDA GRAY

I find myself singing the same song over and over today as I get ready for my first class.

> The wind is coming down the road,
> The sun is shining and the sky is blue.
> The wind is coming down the road,
> The sky clouds up and there starts
> a weeping snow.

There's another verse, but I can't remember it, so I sing the same one again. It only became a song yesterday. Before that it was a poem, written by nine-year-old Tom on a piece of blue paper.

A volunteer teacher comes in with his guitar, and we start the song again. As the children come in, they sing, too. Then we sing some other songs they've written.

Blue is bright.
Blue is light.
Blue is a color, like no other.
Blue is the mountains,
Blue is the sea,
Blue is the sky we look upon.
Blue is you and me.

That's 11-year-old Lisa's. Words a little trite, maybe, but the music is beautiful, and we sing it twice, appreciating the universality at the end. "Let's sing Neils'," somebody says. We do, and Neils sings loudest, beaming.

I like cloudy days,
They're so nice and cool.
And on sunny days,
I feel like jumping in a pool.
Or shussing through the powder,
La la la lala la-a-a!
I like almost all days.

"Let's sing a different one . . . Ann's."

I walk in the woods,
Where the shade is deep,
But the sun shines, softly,
On the pine and the aspen trees.

Hers is long and we only know one verse, so she rolls out a long piece of newsprint and starts to copy the words for us.

After Ann's, we sing the many verses of 10-year-old Saga's, belting out the chorus:

Oh, I want to be a grownup,
Over twenty-one.
I want to be a grownup,
They have all the fun!

"I'm going to write one," somebody says. Another child, leaving with the guitar teacher to finish his composition,

230

leans back in the door to call, "I need a flute and a drum," and two others go with them. Our class is rolling.

Saga has written a myth about how the world came to have colors, and now she is directing it as a TV play to be videotaped. She and her actors start to practice the play on one side of the room where two girls are already lettering the credits and scene changes. "Let's decorate the signs," one says, and they begin drawing pictures around the words.

At the opposite end of the room, four kids are making a sound and light show, using colors with sound and music to create various emotional effects.

"This is angry red."

"No, I think it's war. Blood and war. Let's use part of *Dr. Zhivago,* that thundering part."

"OK, then we'll flash to light blue and some birds singing."

"I think green is more like peace. You know, that yellow-green when the leaves first come out in Spring."

They are using solid colored slides in a slide projector and taping bits of music from a stack of records. The arguing and negotiating is constant as they work.

One boy is looking at a book of art reproductions, a girl is rummaging through the prop box selecting costumes for the play, and another boy is reading *Moby Dick* in a corner.

A well-dressed lady visitor comes in. "What do you do in this class?" She chooses the boy who is reading, perhaps because he is doing something "normal." He looks up, "Well, right now we're playing around with color," he says, and starts to read again. I hear another boy's half-growl, "Shoulda said we're making a color bomb." He has picked up the apprehension in her voice, and he and I exchange smiles as the lady wanders around the room, observing and being observed, then leaves.

If she thinks we are playing around with color, she is

right. By now, someone may be making a color bomb, too, I think to myself, for we never know quite where we'll go from our beginning. The beginning that led to today's class took place about a week ago.

What I mean, here, by beginning is a planned experience, shared by a whole class, that provokes response, reaction and questions to stimulate the kind of self-motivated creating and exploring described above.

Many teachers decide to stop being dispensers of knowledge and become resources to kids. It's an important change. If made effectively, it can give kids much experience in thinking creatively and using resources. But often, in changing their practice, teachers become frustrated and discouraged. Some common complaints are: "They do so little, they don't need a resource!" "If I let them do what they want to, they don't do anything. Maybe they don't *have* any strong interests." "Their behavior has gotten awful, and they *still* don't express their feelings." "They just run from one thing to another and destroy things as they go. It's chaos."

These teachers, in effect, are saying, "I want to change, but the kids won't let me." They are waiting for the students to somehow spontaneously involve themselves so the teacher can be a non-directive resource. I have yet to see that happen.

Although the responsibility for learning belongs with the kids, the teacher is still responsible for the way he teaches. That is his art. He must still design and structure.

My approach is to first generate purposeful activity by designing and leading beginning experiences. When the children become caught up in exploring, questioning, and creating, I no longer need to direct and I can become a useful resource. Whatever was created or discovered during our beginning experience is used for further exploration and learning.

Worth learning

The rewards for the children come through creating and using the creations, in being stimulated by one another's feelings and ideas, and in seeing their own ideas and creations stimulate other people. I do not grade the children's work; I acknowledge and appreciate it. Mistakes are challenges for further work, not "black marks."

Let me describe the beginning that led, over the course of a week, to the class described above.

In preparation, I gathered pieces of paper in all the colors and textures I could find. In class, I said, "Everybody sit in a circle on the floor and close your eyes." They sat quiet, eyes closed, and I said softly and slowly, "Listen. You hear a color. Hear it? It is close to you. You are becoming that color. Breathe it in. It is going to your toes, up to your knees, up your legs, all through your body to the tips of your fingers and the top of your head. You breathe it in . . . and you breathe it out. You are that color, and nobody else knows what the color is. But you know and you feel the color, because you are the color. Softly, open your eyes. Colors are raining from the sky." Pieces of paper I had dropped were floating to the floor. "Find your color, or one you like, and write anything you want on it."

Everybody wrote (including me), then we read what we wrote aloud and passed the colored papers around and read and commented on each other's. Two of the songs quoted above were written, as well as many other descriptions and comments. We laughed and talked and admired each other's work, and considered the questions and ideas that came up: "What if there were no colors; everything was black and white. I'll bet it'd hurt your eyes if you saw colors!" This was Saga and later she explored her idea in the play she wrote.

"I wonder if you could make people mad if everything they saw was red." This and similar comments inspired the light and sound show experiment.

233

"I was scared when I was blue. I was this icy, icy blue and when people saw me their blood ran cold. My blood was cold, too, and all my hair stood up." We talked about being scared.

"I am deep, soft purple. I wrap around and hold things, and love them. When light hits me I shine, and I like it when I am in a play or on the costumes of kings and famous people. Sometimes other colors are jealous of me, but I can just melt and cover them all, so I don't mind." We talked about loving and feeling jealous, and then about colors that are usually associated with jealousy and love and of other color symbolism. I told them about *The Scarlet Letter* and *Moby Dick* and one of the boys told about reading *Invisible Man*.

"Yellow is my kitten. She bounces and rolls and sometimes scratches when she plays. Like yellow." We talked about animals and other things that make us think of colors.

"I am dark, mean red. I creep up on things and squeeze them till they are mean and red like me." We talked about feeling mean and whether or not we feel "squeezed up" inside when we feel mean.

The writing is full of personal feelings. We question and talk about them, but we don't analyze or make judgments.

We looked at the pictures around the room, some our own and some reproductions. Looking at a Gauguin print, Gail said, "I like that picture because it has a red dog. I mean, if the dog was brown, it would just be plain, not any good at all." Turning to a Lautrec poster, she continued. "I don't like those green and yellow faces. The people look sick or something. Why did he make those . . . ghouls . . . instead of the way people really look?"

"I know this woman who has pink lights in her house because she says it makes people look pretty!"

234

This conversation went on until suddenly Tom announced that he'd written a poem but it would make a
better song. Humming, he went off to find the guitar
teacher to help him compose the music, leaving all of us re-
reading what we'd written to see if, perhaps, ours were
songs, too.

That was a beginning. I call such experiences beginnings
because reaction and response begin. Whatever follows
cannot be planned by the teacher. It is the child's own, with
no right answers. The teacher can, and should, provide
media through which the responses can be expressed and he
can acknowledge and accept responses, but it is the child's
questions and reactions that determine the action and
creation. For example, I did not foresee, when the children
sat on the floor and became colors, that poems, songs, plays,
a book, a sound and light show, and dozens of other things
would come from the experience, and I did not assign any
of those projects. But they didn't "just happen."

They happened because everybody was interested in the
experience, and each had a chance to communicate what he
thought and felt about being a color. Nobody was cut off or
ridiculed, every contribution was accepted as worthwhile by
the entire group. Every question and comment was regarded as a possibility for further exploration. For example,
when Robert said, "I wonder if you could make people mad
if everything they saw was red?" I said, "I don't know. How
could you make everything red?" Comments came from
around the table.

"If you had a big red light, everything would look red,"
someone suggested.

"We don't have a red light," another said.

"Use a projector, and put a red cloth over the light," the
first responded.

"Yeah," said Robert, who had asked the initial question,

"I'll bet we could. Let's try it . . . wanna help me?" turning to a friend. Three kids wanted to help, and in the course of "trying it," they figured out how to make slides using colored gel and decided to use many colors, not just red, to see what would happen.

Every project evolved in a similar way, with no assignments from me. My job, and that of the entire group, was to respond, probe, make suggestions, provide materials, and to be ready to go in any direction.

During the next three weeks, we continued to talk and explore as we painted and drew, colored with felt-tip markers and crayons, and branched off into separate projects. We became aware that it's difficult to look at colors in isolation and, on one child's suggestion, went downtown and looked at the color schemes of different places. We tried to figure out such things as why the library had a soft brown carpet and warm walnut furniture and an elegant French restaurant had red carpets, gilt furnishings and white tablecloths. Someone asked why most schools have drab halls and white classrooms, and we made some changes in our own school. We read the color poems from *Hailstones and Halibut Bones*.

We also had several other group experiences to reinforce the beginning one. One morning, full of crazy energy, we all danced to music, becoming vari-colored autumn leaves, floating wildly through wind and storms and finally resting in a heap on the floor, waiting for the winter snow. Another morning, feeling quieter, we blocked white paper into four equal parts with masking tape and, while soft music played, we each painted our color impression of ourself and three other people in the room. After that, we tried to guess who each picture was, and talked about why we had used the colors we did for each person. Then we took the masking tape off and tacked the pictures to the wall as a reminder of how we see ourselves and how others see us, in relation to color. Each experience helped us to feel and see color in a different way. Meanwhile, individual projects were going on and generating other work.

Finally, we capped our exploration of color. We finished the play and videotaped it, using some of the color songs as part of the soundtrack. We finished the sound and light show and gave it in a school meeting. Some of the poems appeared in the school newspaper; some decorated our walls. The songs were used in a movie about the school. The color myth inspired several other myths and plays, not about color, which we dittoed and made into an illustrated book. The book was a present to a class of younger children, and some of our group went every day for a week to read it to the little kids. We had felt and explored color, used our creations, and were ready for new adventures.

Demonstrating the usual progression, our work with color had unfurled through a three part process. (1) The beginning experience itself, shared by the entire group. (2) Communicating, exploring, and creating from the experience, done together and individually. (3) Using the creations.

In planning beginnings, the idea is to use objects and concepts that are already familiar, but to see these and our feelings about them in a close and different way. We magnify, take apart, and play with the experience and our responses. The experience should be physical and sensory: we have to use both our bodies and minds in order to experience it. It should be dramatic and stimulating enough to provoke sensations and questions, but not so threatening as to inhibit the expression of whatever was felt or experienced. It should be open-ended, so that we can see it from many points of view and take it in many directions: there is no one right answer. A sense of daring to go into the unknown, of adventure and expectation should be heightened by the experience.

Ideas for beginnings abound, and I collect them wherever I can—in reading, in watching and hearing other teachers, in creativity tests—and when the time seems right, I modify them to fit the children I'm teaching. Here are a few beginnings designed to heighten sensory awareness, particularly vision, hearing, and touch, and to increase the ability to communicate quick, unusual, and apt analogies, which many researchers see as the most accurate determiner of creative ability. (I use other beginnings for problem-solving and body movement and have, with some modifications, planned beginnings to explore math, science, and social studies in useful and creative ways.)

Blindfolding is a dramatic way to focus on sight, or the lack of it, and it brings to the surface quick, strong feelings. An exciting beginning is to explore the school while blindfolded: the classroom, the halls, and outside, the yard. All the familiar places suddenly become strange, maybe dangerous, full of surprises, and a little scary.

When we do this, I call out instructions and warnings as we go, my voice the only link with the familiar world of authority. All else relies on the hands, feet, and body of each child. Their feet clutch the ground, their hands and arms become antennae. After we've tried the swing and the slide, explored the fort, lost our way, bumped into strange things, recognized familiar ones, and listened and felt until our bodies strain, we feel our way back inside, rip off the blindfolds, and write.

This beginning goes in and out of our conversations, writing, drawing, and reading for the entire year and we experiment with it in many ways. Some kids do it again, with other friends. Two kids come to class blindfolded every day for a week, keeping a diary about losing their vision. We all blindfold ourselves to see if we can identify each other, or we try to identify objects that we pass around. Once we went to a Braille Nature Trail blindfolded and tried to identify the plants and objects along the trail and to read the Braille messages with our fingers. Again, we had a "taste test," trying to identify a dozen or so tastes while blindfolded and holding our noses.

Sometimes we close our eyes and listen intently to music or the random sounds around us.

Almost the opposite of being blindfolded, or removing sight, is to focus vision closely on one object. We have a beginning the children call Trying to See What You Didn't. This consists simply of collecting interesting objects, taking them one at a time and seeing them every way we can. For instance, I place a rock in the middle of the table and say, "What do you see?" Everybody looks. Somebody turns the rock over so that it looks like a shelter and says, "A bug house." Another says, "A giant jewel," and holds the rock archly to one ear. A boy giggles, "A birdbath for hummingbirds," turning the rock again to show an indented spot. Responses are lightning fast: "A weapon . . . solidified sand . . . a petrified cloud." By this time everybody has held the rock, it has been listened to ("Earplug for a giant with insensitive ears"), felt ("Paperweight or doorstop"), and even tasted ("Tongue-sharpener, or sharpener for birds' beaks"). I continue to give objects as long as there are requests for more.

Sometimes I offer a situation with the object. "You are alone in this room and it is empty. Your job is to decorate it and all you have is three million of these." I produce a large silver safety pin. Laughs, groans, they pick it up and hand it around. "I would hook some of them together into chains and hang them at the windows and doors like those beaded curtains." "I would put a big stack in the corner

and we could slide down it." "Melt some for a sculpture."
"Yeah. A chair sculpture and a table sculpture." "Use them
for toothpicks when you have guests." At some point during
these suggestions, one will catch our fancy and we pause for
a conversation, and our ideas flow into action.

We explore objects further by using pantomime, which is
an excellent medium for heightening vision and awareness,
for in it the mime has to be aware of how he looks to others.
Here, an object is passed around our circle as we sit on the
floor, and each person, in turn, pantomimes a different
function of the object. A hat may become a steering wheel,
a frisbee, a wash basin, a mirror, a mixing bowl, a treasure
hugged and hidden from the rest of us, or a container with
a strange and magic essence inside.

Sometimes, instead of having a real object, the first person will pantomime an action with an imaginary object.
When it is recognized by the next person, it is passed to
him. He continues the action until he can transform the
object. For example, the first person starts pantomiming
using a yoyo. The second transforms it into a bouncing
ball. The third bounces the ball a few times and pops it
into his mouth: it has become a ball of rubbery gum. The
next person takes it, chews awhile, then pulls out a long
strand, which he starts to play with a bow, like a one-
stringed violin. This play with objects is a physical way of
making comparisons and analogies, and almost immediately
similes and metaphors related to the experiences begin to
appear in children's writing.

Briefly, a few other beginnings:

Collect commanding-looking faces from magazine pictures, take them to class and "read people." Become the
character for a dramatic improvisation.

Use a Polaroid camera to make pictures of just hands,
feet, or backs of heads of people in the class. How can you
tell who they are?

Make your own musical instruments and try to "talk" to each other with just the instruments.

Pair off and give instructions for doing something using only gestures and gibberish. How much do you rely on hearing to communicate? How much on sight?

Sit, facing one another, and express with just your face such words as "hungry," "hate," "angry," "love," "happy," "cold," "revenge." Try it again, standing and using the whole body.

Tape short, representative excerpts from eight or ten different musical genres: electronic music, Bach, Mozart, rock, Dixieland, jazz, a country instrumental, a popular song. Play them and ask one "unanswerable" question with each: What is this place? What is happening here? What kind of girl is this? What kind of day? Jot down responses, then tell why you heard as you did.

Intentionally, the ideas I have suggested for beginnings are sketchy. Fleshing them into dramatic, stimulating experiences appropriate to specific children is a design job for each individual teacher.

As you start to design beginnings, look at your idea to see if it can become a dramatic, physical, sensory experience. Then ask: Is the experience open-ended? Stimulating? Safe enough? A little daring? Can my students relate to it . . . does it fit them . . . is it already part of their lives?

If you answer yes to these questions, you have a good beginning. If you can also insure open, respectful communication, can encourage questions and ideas, and are willing to venture with kids into strange places, you are likely to generate truly exciting exploration and creation. In the process, you may find yourself less often handing down static information and beginning to serve, instead, as an instigator of experience and a useful resource to the creative work of children.

Will it grow in a classroom?

Fights in the classroom, hurt feelings, and
even deaths are openings for dramatic plays
or discussions that explore children's feelings
and help them deal with anxiety. Here, the
death of Martin Luther King, Jr., caused grief
and tension. Miriam Wasserman saw and
responded to it. She allows the children to
"mourn" through a homemade drama. The
subject is social studies (as a response to
history in the making). The technique is
improvisational dramatics. And the message
is: teachers do not need a "confluent-arts"
program to teach to the heart!

BY MIRIAM WASSERMAN

It was in I.S. 201, just then the center of the whole city's
fury, and it was the day after the M. L. King funeral. A
group of girls in a domestic science class started a play,
being ladies talking about King, the funeral, peace, nonviolence, etc. They acceded to my request that I be an
audience, even starting again from the beginning after they
had seated me. The play quickly became a discussion in
which they revealed the fears and anxieties aroused in them
by the murder, the subsequent rioting in Harlem, and
violence in general, I suspect, including the violence and
general disorder of the school. They kept referring to King
as a man of peace, trying to make peace all over the whole
world, "even in Africa." In order to point out the resistance
rather than simply the nonviolent element in King's philosophy, I asked permission to be in the play "for just one
question." They gave it. Other kids started to gather around
and wanted to contribute. At first the original cast wouldn't
let in outsiders, saying they couldn't talk because they

242

weren't "in the play." I asked if they couldn't be in the play, and they said, "No, 'cause she was running around." Eventually you could earn entrance into the play by sitting around quietly and listening for a bit. By the end of the hour the entire class was either "in the play," or listening.

What we had then was an organic group, not a coerced one created by the teacher. It grew out of a common pressing concern, whose consideration was initiated by one or two natural leaders and which took a form which, when the anxieties became too great, could mask the participant's personal involvement. (They were using a bowl of artificial flowers as pretend grown-ups' refreshment, although of course some of them had M&M's, etc., in their pocketbooks and pockets, and from time to time as feelings would begin to rise precipitously, the "hostess" would jump up and pass the artificial flowers around with little simpering ladylike murmurs and smiles.) At the end of the hour there was a kind of relaxation in the room which suggested that some gratifying catharsis had occurred.

I don't know that I contributed much to the process. Possibly the following: (1) I didn't try to take over the class, so at least I didn't prevent it from happening. (2) I perhaps gave the proceedings legitimacy by attending them myself. (3) I may have helped the nucleus grow by asking if other people couldn't be in the play. But I'm not sure this wouldn't have happened anyway. On the other hand, I am pretty sure that if I had ordered that everybody be let in it, I would have smothered the whole thing. (4) Maybe somebody got the political message that King was murdered not for his nonviolence but for his resistance.

I think with more experience, I could have developed the technique of helping a concerned nucleus grow and then leading the students to new insights. I would of course like to see some other teachers try it. I'm beginning to believe that that's one of the most important legitimate functions a teacher can perform, maybe the only one.

Ron would like to add a few words about love:

If you have thought much about education, you probably have an ideal image of teaching and learning. For instance, Plato's ideal was mature men discoursing, seriously but joyfully, over ample food and drink. Comenius' was an enlightened schoolmaster opening unformed young minds to the light of revelation and science. For Montessori it was a community of children in an environment responsive to their awakening powers, under the benign guidance of sensitive young women.

I've always been attracted by Pestalozzi's simple image: Gertrude slicing pieces of bread for her children. As each child comes up to the table Gertrude slices just the right amount, because she knows how much each child likes this kind of bread, how big an appetite each has, how well they ate at the last meal. Here is the poetical inspiration, the gravid myth, which underlies much of our

244

recent school experimentation with "individualization," where this means adjusting the curriculum, the matter to be "covered" or mastered, to the capacities and interests of each student.

Translated from physical to temporal terms, it becomes "going at your own best pace" through the curriculum. Translated from quantitative into qualitative terms, it becomes permitting different students to master the same basic material according to their different learning styles and predilections: rote drill, physical manipulation, didactic instruction, multi-media presentation, collaborative learning.

Still, it's the same loaf being sliced, though our knives have now become sharp enough to slice time as well as matter, and to slice even according to the eater's personality and tastes, as well as his appetite.

But suddenly, today, at an ice-skating rink, I was struck hard by another image—as hard as Pestalozzi's had struck me when I first read it. A woman was being taught to skate by a man who swept her over the ice with his arm around her waist. In love, they glided around together, she carried along—by him, by their speed, by the fearlessness of being held expertly, and, I suppose, by the fact that

learning to skate didn't *really* matter,
compared to the joy of being with him, so
close.

Because they were going so fast, she really
couldn't stumble, and by moving just as he
did, she learned—through a kind of combined
empathy, imitation, contagion, and love. The
erotic blended with the didactic, of course
—the skating was continuous with their
love-making.

She did fall, once. He stopped, they
laughed a lot, he helped her up, brushed her
off, kissed her, they kissed again, laughed,
then clumsily got back attached and started
skating again. Nothing had been lost by
the mistake, it was just as pleasurable as the
successful skating. If anything, it was an
added delight, because it put them,
momentarily, in a slightly altered relationship,
always a pleasure for lovers: she looked
slightly different, sitting on the ice, so he saw
another little aspect of her face, her figure,
her spirit. And they had a chance to laugh,
kiss, brush off.

Gertrude's eye was keen, her mind clear,
her heart open, and her knife sharp. But if we
need all the love we can get, and hunger,
too, always for growth in our lives, then we
had better make our learning a part of our
loving.

Toward teaching—and beyond

8 Other ways

No teacher can escape asking
these questions: *Can* schools be reformed?
Are there alternatives?

At this point a myriad of new ways of
teaching have been explored. But a few
teachers, together with students and parents,
are beginning to go beyond innovations in
classrooms and schools. They seek other ways
than schools to learn and to grow.

Schools without walls, voucher systems, the
"deschooling" proposals of radical critics
like Ivan Illich and Paul Goodman—all of
these raise some basic questions that every
teacher, no matter how committed to working
within the existing framework, must now face.
Does the teacher, no matter how dedicated,
run the risk of doing more harm than good?
Are there feasible alternative ways to learn?

Will it grow in a classroom?

John Holt wrote the following letter in response
to an invitation from the National Association
of Elementary School Principals requesting
that he participate in a symposium on
educational alternatives. Holt expresses his
doubts about entering into such a discussion
and states his reasons for feeling as he does.
(If you are interested in whether or not Holt's
apprehensions were justified by what happened
at the symposium, the transcript appears in the
April 1973 issue of the Association's *Journal*.
We were two of the participants, and in our
opinion, Holt was right about what would
happen!)

BY JOHN HOLT

Thank you so much for your letter of 16 November. I have
some doubts about attending your meeting, and I think the
best thing for me to do is to try to explain as concretely as
possible what they are.

What troubles me about the present discussion on educational alternatives is that people seem to me to be trying to
find alternative ways of doing what the schools are now
supposed to do, but are obviously not doing very well—that
is, getting large numbers of people to learn what other
people have decided will be good for them. It is this fundamental notion hidden in the word "education" that I now
have to reject.

My position is a good deal more radical than merely
saying that the state should not have the right to compel
people to go to school. I don't believe that it is the proper
business of the state, at least one that calls itself democratic
or free, to tell anyone what he *should* know or learn. I fear
that this discussion may start from the premise that schools

are not doing a very good job of teaching everybody the things that they *should* know in order, as the popular saying goes, "to function in a technological society," and that we must therefore find other ways. I altogether reject this notion of the proper function of *any* kind of educational resource. The only educational resource that I will recognize as legitimate is one that helps people learn whatever it is that they may happen to want to find out.

So I'm very much concerned and distressed with anything that limits access to what is already known, or to people who can do things. In the case of medicine, medical knowledge, and medical tools, Illich has put it very well when he says that we must learn to take the syringe out of the hands of the doctor. In the case of children learning to read, I do not know why we cannot put a lot of the kinds of information now only available in classrooms on the sidewalks and walls and windows of our streets and buildings and public spaces. It is not just poor children but poor people of every age who do not have access to reading material. In a poverty stricken area of a large city, there are practically none of what my neighborhood is full of—branch libraries, drugstores with a big supply of magazines, bookstores, and so on. I am interested in the idea of mini-libraries in storefronts or in converted trucks or school buses, using mostly newspapers, periodicals and magazines.

Beyond that, I am even more interested in the idea of a free press. We are so used to thinking in abstractions that we think "freedom of the press" means the right of people who own newspapers to publish whatever they want in them. But it initially meant something much more concrete than that: free access to printing presses, the right to print *yourself* whatever it was you wanted to say. Modern technology now makes this fairly easy. For very much less than what it costs to build a classroom—indeed for a small fraction of that cost—we can put into each neighborhood a multilith press and associated equipment that would make it possible for the people right in that neighborhood to produce their own neighborhood newsletter (what in older times used to be called broadsides) about whatever interests them, or to prepare texts on many subjects for all the people in the neighborhood, including children and students in schools. I read all the time that schools in poor neighborhoods are in a bind because they don't have enough materials, because they cannot afford to buy the expensive materials commercially produced. Why not give them the power to print and distribute their own materials to their own communities? This is the sort of thing that interests me and that I would like to talk about.

Herb Kohl has written eloquently about the social and educational function of graffiti, but in our cities there is a big outcry about it. Great campaigns are waged against graffiti; all kinds of threats of fines and so on are made. This seems to me to be a step in exactly the *wrong* direction. It is easy for people with money to get access to ways of making their ideas widely known. Why should it be so hard for people without money? Why shouldn't there be a great deal more than there is in the way of public bulletin boards, or spaces deliberately prepared for graffiti writers? The kind of thing that Herb Kohl had when he was running the Other Ways School.

Some of the things I have suggested are the kinds of things that people in a community, a community as small as a single block, might be able to do if every family in that block had the $500 or $600 or $1000 that the schools spend, and exceedingly badly, on each of their children. A multilith offset printing press does not cost very much; a mimeograph machine or spirit duplicator costs even less. For a small part of what we spend and misspend on schooling children, and more and more on providing guards and police protection, we could make available—quite literally

252

to every block—tape recorders, photographic equipment, language tapes and texts, various kinds of laboratory equipment, and so on. But people might not choose to spend their money this way. They might prefer to spend it on travel, music or musical instruments, or I don't know what. In short, I would like to expand enormously our definition of what we understand by educational resources, and not just limit them to those items that would help people learn out of school the kinds of things now being taught in school. I've done an immense amount of self-educating since I left school twenty-nine years ago, and none of it has been in classes or with school textbooks. Thus a textbook is almost by definition a book that nobody would read unless he were compelled to.

Why not, as people have suggested, provide libraries of toys, games, puzzles—the kinds of things that rich kids get for Christmas, use for a week or two, and then put away in a closet somewhere?

Paul Goodman wrote more than once that there was probably nothing that could be done that would be of more educational value to people growing up and living in New York City than to ban cars, trucks, and buses from most of the streets. We hear people say all the time that if the children weren't in school they would be on the streets. The streets of a good city, or of a healthy community in a good city, are one of the most exciting and fertile educational environments that men have ever invented, which is why people left the farms and the small towns to go to the cities: There was such a greater variety of people there and things to see and things to do.

If in fact we have made our streets unlivable, unusable, and dangerous, and not just for young people, then this is the problem we must remedy. If the streets of a community are so dull and boring and so unsafe and crime-ridden that the schools are truly better places to be, then the children of that community are not going to learn much even in their schools. The schools, whether public, independent, parochial, alternative, storefront, or whatever, can at best only add to and enrich what a person learns in the community and streets he lives in; they cannot make up for it or undo it or reverse it.

In this connection, I would like to urge with all possible force—and indeed I think I would make it a condition of my taking part in such a symposium—that all participants read and ponder what Jane Jacobs has written in her book, *The Death and Life of Great American Cities.* She talks eloquently and hardheadedly about what the streets can do and can be and how they can once again be made safe and interesting.

And we might talk, too, about how the whole city can be made more available to people as a resource. I'm not talking here about things like the Parkway Project, which is just fine for the 700 students who are able to attend it—out of the 10,000 or so who applied and the I-don't-know-how-many hundred thousand students in Philadelphia. I am talking about making much better directories of the city and what is in it and making them much more widely available; about systems of street signs and transportation signs that will make it much harder for people to get lost; about reducing (or eliminating) the cost of public transportation so that people, and particularly poor people and young people, can make full use of it. There is an awful lot going on in most cities, a hundred times more than could ever be put within the walls of a school building, even in pictures or slides. We need to think of a community, and a community of communities, in which it will be much easier for people to share what they know, or to get their questions asked and their curiosity satisfied.

I have probably already written more than I would be

254

able to say in the entire length of a symposium, which makes me wonder whether such get-togethers, with all their expense and inconvenience, are really the most efficient way to generate ideas and get them spread around. Still, if you hadn't asked me I wouldn't have written this letter. Anyway, this gives you an idea of where my thoughts are and the kind of things I want to talk about. So if there is some substantial overlap between my current concerns and those of other people you are thinking of inviting, we can certainly pursue this matter further. Some of the people you are inviting are good friends of mine, and it would be nice to see them. There is always the possibility that we might strike sparks off each other and together think of things that none of us have thought about singly. So my mind is still open.

Voices from the oppressed sometimes echo
Holt's despair with schooling. Fred Gonzales
writes from New York's Lower East Side.

BY FRED GONZALES

I am pro education but I am anti school. School is a heartless gamble with young people's lives. Our young people are looking for a new way of life and finding only a way to survive.

My name is Fred Gonzales. For many years I have lived on the Lower East Side with my brothers and sisters. I've been in school for 11 years and only have begun to read and write at the age of 16. There are many reasons for this and I will try to explain. One is that my parents didn't have sufficient education to teach us and it was up to the school to do it. In all this time all they've taught me is "Freddie you're stupid and you're never going to learn anything." They said "you're illiterate, you're never going to amount to anything, you're wasting our time, quit." For a long time I believed it. But then I took a good hard look at what was really there, and realized you're only recognized by your 90's and 80's. Anything below that and you are an outcast to the school system. Many times I have found that teachers become psychiatrists and if you don't react and just sit in your corner you get a pat on the head and told "he's a nice boy, I wish all my students were this way." But if you're loud and rowdy you'll find in your records that this child is a "disciplinary problem" who probably will end up dropping out of school and going to the streets. I know, I was that cat and I had to face the reality that in order for me to survive I had to read and write. And during that year that I was out of school and in the streets I learned more than I ever had in my whole school life. Many other young people may never get the same opportunity.

If educators don't start re-educating themselves and take a new look at what science has to offer in reading machines and new ways of educating they will continue to cripple the people instead of serving them.

Education to me means a door to open and if you want to walk any further you can—it's your choice—it should never have ratings or averages. But you should have some way of measuring what you've learned. It shouldn't be a race you're forced to join if you don't want to join. It shouldn't be something pounded into you—it should be free and most of all it should be a choice.

They should make it a family type environment and not a competition. Then we would have one thing in common—to explore learning. We're not going to hold back because we're ashamed. There should be a lot of sharing—like "what did you get out of that book." If I could share my experience with one other person, teach him what I'd learned, it'd be outta sight.

Education is a process of not living. Schools don't allow new reading machines. They don't use anything that will make learning faster. They want some to go to the top but they want some to stay on the bottom. I tried to rap to some of the guys about school about what they are doing and trying to tell them that their only road is school.

In order to fuck the system you have to join it. Education is the true revolutionary gun to free our oppressed people. They can stop you and shoot you for throwing bombs but if you stop and think about it your greatest weapon is that pen and piece of paper and all the knowledge you can get.

Jim Aufderheide expresses the confusion that so many teachers feel today. These teachers are brave enough to know that none of the old answers will work, but they are unsure of what comes next.

BY JIM AUFDERHEIDE

We've got a problem, and we're not alone.

Last year, as a first year teacher, I taught in a very traditional, very conservative school. I was amazed at the apparent apathy of the student body toward education. Nothing "turned them on." Mistakenly, as I now perceive, I blamed it on the traditional type system, and the people in it. We tried many of the traditional methods, some new innovations—a little bit of everything. Nothing got those kids moving.

I moved to Apollo School because I had heard it was one of the newest, best, and most innovative in Minnesota, and I think it is. They try here. Each department continually tries new methods and approaches. The curriculum is examined quarterly. Scheduling is examined yearly. Emphasis is on the student: What does he need, or want? How can we fill his needs, or wants? What can we do to make education more meaningful, more worthwhile?

The building itself houses perhaps one of the best facilities in the Midwest. We have the equipment, supplies, books, and supportive personnel. Everything was tested for its practicality, durability, and educational need. The most practical and relevant, and we're trained to use the stuff.

Each faculty member has his own office, and free time to spend helping students, just being with students. Stress is on helping them to learn on an individual basis.

But something is missing.

There is even educational apathy here—towards school, towards education, towards learning, towards success in anything. It's the same I've found in the "best of both educational worlds." And from discussions with educators in other areas, and other fields, it's a common situation that is spreading.

We've spent many hours trying to find the problem. Are teachers to blame? Aren't teachers capable of reaching students? Are we doing something "wrong"? Is it the school? Was our beautiful facility misplanned? Curriculum? Scheduling? Environment?

But it's none of these, or all of them. Society, the world,

has changed under our noses. Values have changed, and the means to attain the changed goals have changed. Education does not seem to be, to these kids, the way to achieve those things important to them. Success, as we see it, is no longer important, is no longer success. Achievement is so commonplace it is no longer a goal. We're used to it. The world has achieved the moon, the sun, artificial organs, and artificial life in these kids' lives—plastic, changing people in a plastic, changing world. Toffler's "storm" of change is upon us in all its fury, and it's touching everyone, and everything.

To a world that has been desensitized to achievement, other things have moved into the needed place of importance. Peace, a clean world, personal, inner happiness, a self concept, a quiet place in the midst of the storm—these have moved into the limelight now. The kids want life. Students feel they have the skills to survive; perhaps they do. As adults they learn what they want and need to know, as the need arises. Too many college graduates are jobless. Too many high school graduates are without jobs. Perhaps their reasons for not wanting or needing the type of education we are offering are valid.

Priorities have changed, and the type of institution we are using no longer fills the bill. Perhaps the type of education we are offering is no longer relevant.

We haven't found a solution. We've been shocked by the realization that we, and our system, might be obsolete. We've had a difficult time convincing ourselves that the things we've been teaching, and enjoying, might not be necessary. Perhaps we're wrong. We're searching for alternatives. I wonder if anyone, anywhere really knows . . .

259

Will it grow in a classroom?

Hal Lenke found one answer that is suited to his own needs and those of his community. He calls his answer "teaching less." It is a model mainly because it suggests that we, too, must similarly seek personal answers that are suited to our personal situations. "The way of the masters was to find their own way."

BY HAL LENKE

For two years I have been a teacher-at-large—at large in the sense that criminals or wounded or rogue animals are spoken of as being at large. For the two years before that, I was a teacher positioned, located, a classroom teacher, a teacher-at-small.

I was a teacher, in a classroom, in a school. My first year on the job, I yearned to be one of my students. I was confused in my role, seditious in my loyalties. It was confusing to my students, too. All they knew of me was that I, like all the other teachers they shuttled among, had a big desk and was paid to blare into their privacy, to tinker with their impulses, and to teach them. I, of course, didn't want to see myself that way. I wanted them to know I was with them—but it was not until I accepted my position as a faculty member that I gained any strength, first for myself as a person with them, and then for myself as a teacher who could be their advocate and justify what I was doing. My first year's lesson was: accept the power you have, and use it.

But I found other lessons equally informative. One of the operational root assumptions behind public education is that it is a collective, public, democratic enterprise, and everyone is involved in a common benevolence toward the

260

well-being of the individual children. So-called anecdotal report forms, guidance counselors, testing, evaluations, which call upon a teacher to express his (intimate) feelings and sense about a child with whom he shares a class are predicated upon the central thesis that all who avail themselves of such materials do so in an enlightened way and will apply them to the best interests of the child. But this is a deceit and an invidious seduction. For to pour out what you really know about a child, far from adding to a sum of material which will be applied in such a benign way, often merely consigns the child to an inescapable label. To make such material available to the file folder, the dossier, the computer, the machines of continuity charged with the tracking of the child, is irresponsible and destructive, and yet it is at the crux of what is required of teachers. How many teachers characterize their students this way, fill in the forms, and violate the indescribable status of a personal relationship? So the child is treated as a game, ephemera, without meaning to you—for to the extent that the person had meaning you would be unable to fill in those blanks.

Such obvious things as that dawned on me in flashes through the year. My revelations were mundane, vulgar, yet they nourished me.

So much recent school reform forgets that school is part of the society, and that each person who comes to it every morning is a multi-faceted carrier of that society, its culture, its latent deviance. School is itself, ipso facto, a society without culture, an aggregate population without correlations. It's a short-circuited organism, a disordered molecule.

I was interested in questions other than those promulgated by the administration. For instance, do the kids behave differently in the classroom when I am out of the room? How are the combined irritations, daydreams, enthusiasms of thirty people manifest in a classroom period?

261

How do my own patience and moods, my own generalizations, get reflected to the students? To what extent can/should a classroom period transcend the constraints of being in school? To what degree is it doing a disservice to high school kids to be so different from their other teachers? How can I be a learning specialist?

What is there to be learned in a classroom? First of all, there are the concomitant lives of thirty other people. That is the shared-time-and-space reality. There is the head-knowledge, the abstractions, information, theories, and ideas. There is body-knowledge, the fact that all of us have a difficult time training ourselves to be docile, passive, pliable for seven hours a day. (Though television has eased that burden: they wanted me to entertain them, polished productions, clever commercials, and all.)

Then there was the woman teaching a Problems of Democracy course: the first thing she told her class was that there would be no discussion.

Eventually, I lost my job. That is, I left the classroom.

Jonathan Kozol: "The school that flies the flag is . . . accountable to that flag and to the power and to the values which it represents."

So what of the teacher who defines himself in the terms of that school, which is defined in the terms of that flag, which is defined in the terms of that power and those values?

If all you are is a teacher, in those terms, you can't be doing any good. The professionalization of the function denatures it. All true teachers—gurus, maestros, masters—have been adepts, practitioners, disciplined embodiments of some facility. They have been exemplars with the expertise of experience. But if you do not permit yourself experience growing toward proficiency, fluency, outside the pronouncements and postures of pedagogy, your teaching is vacant; it lacks authority because it profoundly lacks authenticity—

262

the authenticity of one who can tell the tale because he came back from the adventure. Only such a one can replicate the experience for his cohorts. He has scanned the experience for its sources, its intent, its implications, its consequences, its modification, its applications, and he can lay it out for examination and analysis.

That is part of the lecture I gave myself periodically.

Professional teachers are often accused of being ineffective because they have not been able to make concrete what they have "internalized," so they convey their own conclusions and ask their students to accept them as premises, without knowing whence they derive nor where they tend. A learned thesis is personally defensible because of its apprehended closeness. The professional teacher too often keeps the tenets at a distance, dimly accessible to students who are forced into formalizing their exterior guises. Thus, they are never learned, and never truly at the service of the student. The classroom is less distended if the teacher's presence is a connection that could be made any number of ways, and finding themselves in this room now is a happy accident for which students and teacher have both prepared.

A teacher gives himself, gives himself out, expends himself, becomes expendable. If there is no chance of a teacher being excelled by his students, he is holding out on them and should be deposed. It is easy to fix on the teacher: the teacher is the student of his students, attentive to each. His authority comes from realizing that knowledge cannot be withheld. His teaching is a style of learning. A teacher gives other people back to themselves, he returns them, turns them around, turns them on, turns them out finally to face their changes. The teacher restores wholeness, unifies fragments, enabling energy to go beyond its former limits. The teacher is a practitioner of his own wholeness.

So I am striving to be a teacher-at-large, which is something other than being an unemployed teacher at loose ends. While he is in the classroom—most classrooms, perhaps not all; most of the time, perhaps not always—the teacher is an extract of a person. The new teacher acknowledges his limitations, to himself and to his audience. The new teacher disavows any educative imperative: it is all right, he assures us with his whole manner, he will not be out of a job if you don't want to study this now, if you disagree, if you have a different style. The new teacher encourages diversity, uniqueness, interplay. The new teacher doesn't have all the answers.

The new teacher has his own inklings, intimations, hints. He may reveal them, he may teach in parables. The teacher's teaching will be accounted in how he handles himself, and in what comes of it. We have no way to measure such teaching now. An effort to codify and instrumentalize it may not be a step forward. But we might try to describe features of it.

One function of the teacher is to reveal, to exhibit. The teacher is an exhibitionist: he does a thing, he performs an operation, he displays, uncovers, disrobes, decodes, unhampers, and by this process he makes something accessible that wasn't before.

"A man isn't what he seems but what he desires," wrote Adrienne Rich in a recent poem.

There is so little one person says directly to another. It seems to me that we should be showing people how to learn without us, but that makes us crucially important while we're with them.

Are teachers learning specialists? Not the ones I've known and worked with. They've thought remarkably little about learning, remarkably little about what is "best" for either their students or themselves.

In our clumsy reckoning, the most advanced sovereignties institutionalize and internalize their violence with little regard to the submerged traumatic effects. The societies we think of as more backward and underdeveloped acknowledge their violences with far more openness. Thus, the civilizing process is one of masking fundamental traits. Its dissemblings are maintained by a sophisticated despotism.

So with individuals, nations, classrooms. Instead of presiding over a vicarious world, a teacher might become part of an actual community. I am living in a rural West Virginia county. With 2500 students in the schools; about 25 percent of the high school graduates go to college, mostly state colleges. In some recent attempts to affect local practices, I realized that I was turning for assistance to the parents of that 25 percent, when in fact there was nothing more than amenities that they could desire from the system. It was the other 75 percent that I wanted to assist.

Is it the missionary impulse, this being an ombudsman-on-call, a "learning resource," a teacher at large? Is it what Jacques Ellul calls "The Political Illusion"—that these machinations of mine will ameliorate matters? There is a modern careerist dichotomy, dividing us as recklessly as the mind/body dilemma split schools of philosophy. Is a teacher a moral/spiritual force, or is he a political organizer? Or something else, a cross between a "child advocate" and a "technician of the sacred"—some rare mutation out of the ordinary dust?

A teacher must be intelligible, must acquire a native approachability. That has occupied my time for the past year. The teacher at large that I would like to be depends in part upon hard thinking and strategy and in part upon happy coincidence. To be of use to people, they must first see me as usable to them. That's a very different mandate from the one imposed upon the classroom relations.

265

The teacher-at-large that I am groping for is a teacher of and to his community. His motto is to rise to the occasion. As a financial proposition, he might either open up shop the way a doctor or lawyer does, advertise for clients, and charge them, or work in exchange for services or goods. Or, he might be paid from a community fund. It is important that he not be exclusively dependent on any factional payroll. He might incorporate an agency, with a board of community people who would provide suggestions and guidance on priorities.

Specifically, such a teacher would do research for people and bodies of the community, from town government to a bank to the Chamber of Commerce to the school board to a farmer to a woman on welfare. He would obtain information, or show others how to find out what they want to know.

Things I have done include writing interviews with the school board candidates for the county newspaper, the first time anything like that had been done. I was invited by the superintendent of schools to talk to the county principals about ways of using non-school people to help students. I have proposed ways to use the library as a community resource, reading to children on Saturdays, getting volunteers together to tutor children there, eventually showing films. I have been asked by the local retired people's group to talk to them. I am interested in challenging the license renewals of local radio stations whose programming doesn't contribute anything to the population. I am talking with people about establishing a learning resources exchange such as exists in a number of places around the country, to provide instructional companions in a variety of areas. I am working on developing an apprenticeship program with local craftsmen and women. I am in touch with people who are interested in marketing co-ops, in child care centers, and in youth centers—none of which we have now.

266

It is slow. I have just been called for the first time to do substitute teaching, and that opens up all the old sores. I have substituted in second and third grades, the first time I've taught in an elementary classroom. I am beginning to talk with some of the thirty teachers in the county who are teaching for the first time this year, to implement in a more concrete way my ideas of a Teacher Support Center.

I am talking with the local doctors about people's nutritional problems, and with lawyers about the problems they see, and with ministers, mothers, old people, mechanics, grocers, and with people who defy classification. That's a large part of it.

I am not talking about some deified teacher. I am really still mired in old Movement terms—talking about being a "change agent," a provocateur, a catalyst, a facilitator, and so on, words that were romantic but never meant much to me. If I call being occupied this way a teacher-at-large perhaps it is just an excusable extravagance of my saturation with the vocabulary of schooling. Here I am, amidst what Sylvia Ashton-Warner in *Spearpoint* calls "the agitation of the race itself," and, as she says, we have no words for it.

Other people are doing the same thing in other ways, certainly. That is what some of them mean by "open classrooms"—although I think no classroom can be open enough to circumnavigate the constriction of its setting. It is what some mean by "free schools"—though there is something of a contradiction in the phrase.

All those things we were told about being a teacher that beguiled us, all those epiphanies about affecting eternity, all the fantasies about "helping" little children, have brought us up against our own bedrock capacities. Finally, we see where we have been evasive with ourselves. Finally comes the test of what we have learned—survival and love must not be irreconcilable. We have finally undertaken to teach ourselves all that our education darkened. That is what we shall be occupied with for the foreseeable future, inspired by each other, sharing what we can, eager in our work, filled with life.

Some parents who have the time and credentials are opting to "grow their own" —return to the traditional mode of educating children at home instead of sending them to school. Art Harris is one of these enterprising and articulate parents. He describes how he and his family undertook "one small step toward de-schooling society." One of the two children is unusually gifted academically, the other is more social, but Art feels the experiment has been successful for both.

BY ARTHUR S. HARRIS, JR.

Elsewhere, in magazines like *Outside the Net* and even in the Sunday supplements, I've chronicled how Phyllis and I, both one-time teachers, became so disillusioned with public schools that we just *had* to withdraw our two boys at the end of their fourth and sixth grade years and oversee their education ourselves. Rather than go over all that ground again, I'd like to move on to how we're doing.

First, who does the teaching? Frankly, we don't have much teaching. We believe that children learn best what they want to learn when they want to learn it. Too often adults actually get in the way of learning. Taken to its infinite end, one could wonder whether schools with all those instructional hours don't sometimes hinder learning.

Both Phyllis and I are ex-teachers. In fact, Phyllis was a part-time public school "art teacher" as recently as last year. I put "art teacher" in quotes because Phyllis brought up all manner of subjects in her disadvantaged schools. Auditing art supervisors and principals loved it. So what if she showed slides of our trip to Japan or arranged to bus a class to see maple syrup being collected? The children were interested, weren't they? My own full-time teaching, in college and prep school, ended some years ago. But both of us began to question increasingly the structured establishment in which we taught. Were people being "taught" or did they "learn" in spite of us?

So we sit back and let our older son Kevin read. For six months he read almost nothing but books and articles about astronomy. For awhile he got hooked on the American Revolution after seeing the play *1776*; then he got back into the A's again with astrology, architecture, and archaeology. They're not subjects ordinarily offered in grade school, but who are we to dictate a child's interests? Our youngest child, Clifford, who is no reader, is always taking engines apart or building something or fixing a leaking radiator in my car. Is this learning? Why not? Since he has more "personality" than almost anyone you'll meet, we recently were gratified to learn from the Christopher Jencks study that personality (along with luck and graded performance) had much to do with success in life.

Our own children seem to learn without that omnipresent teacher. Probably Professor Louis Agassiz demonstrated this in the way he taught his student, Nathaniel Shaler; he had poor Shaler spend over a hundred hours examining a fish without telling him anything about the fish. He wanted Shaler to learn *for himself*. In the same way, we feel the most important thing is for a child to learn

269

how to learn. The trouble with school is that too much is "taught." Too often a teacher is positioned between a child and the material, blocking natural access to that material.

Curriculum: The word is anathema to us. If we laid out a course of study for our sons, they'd surely feel they were back in school again with those narrow subject areas of history, English, geography, and math. Sometimes I get the idea that the mere defining of a subject is the first step toward robbing it of its mystique. When Kevin is reading about some archaeological discovery in Mexico, he isn't consciously thinking, "Now this is archaeology." In the truest sense, subjects all fuse with one another. Once Kevin became absorbed in Transcendental Meditation (and took a college credit course in it at Queens University in Kingston, Ontario), he began to delve into psychology, religions other than Christianity, the culture of India, mysticism, even elementary Sanskrit—all sorts of things, almost none of them offered in school. Who are we to fence in his learning with narrow subject areas of math, history, English, and civics? All right, so far as American history goes, he knows nothing whatever about corruption in the Harding administration, probably doesn't even know a man named Harding was ever President. But I'll bet he knows more about the American Revolution than anyone on our block. Is this bad?

And if you tell me he isn't becoming well-rounded, I will show you most of his school contemporaries (I probably should slip into jargon and call them his "peer group") who know *nothing* of architecture, archaeology, astronomy, or astrology (just to take the A's), to say nothing of zen, penology, psychology—well-rounded *indeed!*

Social Life: It's the same as before: Kevin, our introspective reader, is still a loner without friends as he was throughout the first six grades. Clifford, our gregarious one, has dozens of friends *of all ages* just as *he* always did. We don't try to change either one and admire Kevin's self-sufficiency. In general we feel American schools are too obsessed with "interpersonal relationships" and thus give the "loner" a complex. By the way, either boy may return to school anytime he wants. So far, no takers.

Physical Education: They exercise as they used to—i.e., one boy is very athletic, the other somewhat sedentary. Both have ten-speed bicycles and do a lot of cycling. Our so-called non-athletic one has lately been entering 18-mile bicycle races and spends time "training." Both take swimming lessons to perfect their crawl strokes. Clifford is an ardent bowler. Both ski. By the way, not *one* of these sports was offered in school where the concentration was on sports requiring large groups.

Compromises: Kevin does take a course in guitar and an adult education course in touch typing.

Classrooms: Who needs a room with thirty desks facing north and one desk facing south? Take away all that glass and brick and learning is likely to take place anywhere. Since our boys left school, we spent six months in Mexico. I'm not going to make big claims our children learned sociology and geography out in the field, but I do hereby solemnly attest that Clifford picked up elementary but fluent Spanish, and nobody set out to teach him a single word of the language. Incidentally, he was the only one among us who could understand rapid Spanish spoken to us, and often translated before the rest of us could say *despacio, por favor.*

Diplomas, Certificates, Regent Exams, Report Cards, College Boards: We have successfully weaned our children away from all these tons of paper. When we feel they've "finished high school," we'll get our friend Kari, an artist, to make them up diplomas with more scrolls, ribbons, and

271

fancy printing than anything the high school offers. A college admission director has already told us (at a cocktail party, not in his office) that a home-educated applicant would be most appealing—what a challenge to track him along all those traditional high schoolers with their grade-point averages! This admissions director told us Kevin's application would undoubtedly stand out among many others as rather intriguing—it would be hard to turn down flat.

Legally: Although we both feel that our state's compulsory school laws are unconstitutional and were once prepared to stand on these grounds as long as the money held out, we reached an accommodation four years ago with the city school system. Our attorney found a provision of the state's education laws pertaining to the education of a child at home. Granted the provision was undoubtedly drafted for the infirm who couldn't make it daily to a classroom, but still this section of the law happened to be marvelously applicable to our situation, for it allowed at-home education provided that the instruction offered was substantially parallel and equivalent to that provided in the schools.

Once we'd dug this provision out and shown it to the school authorities, they began to be more reasonable. Also I spent a weekend writing for them in term-paper length our philosophy of education and how we'd expect to proceed once our children were weaned from those brick school buildings. In good term-paper fashion, we listed the writers who had influenced us—Holt, Kozol, Leonard, et al. Finally the school "authorities" mellowed and eventually agreed to let us try to provide this "alternate and equivalent education" ourselves rather than continue with their legal harassment which had already caused them to give us an enroll-or-else-go-to-court ultimatum.

At first, regarding our venture as a sort of experiment,

they appointed a go-between, a school system staffer with a doctorate in education. He was charged with getting us off to a good start. Fortunately he seemed surprisingly sympathetic to our ideas and immediately understood when he handed over to us a bunch of dull textbooks that we really weren't going to use them; he seemed to sense that we felt schools emphasized the printed word too much and that traditional textbook-learning was something we wanted to get away from. In the four years since we had this first meeting with our "go-between," we have left each other alone. Once he hinted that we really ought to keep some kind of record or documentation of what we were doing— "just in case," but neither he nor the system has bothered us. In turn, we have borrowed through him such things as a microscope, but have had no long dialogues. In a word, I guess he has confidence in us and feels we are making it all right.

Sometimes we feel we got off so easily because the brand-new Superintendent of Schools on his first really big job in our city didn't need our curious dispute breaking out in the newspapers and wanted the whole case swept under the rug. Then again, perhaps the fact we'd both been teachers was decisive. Perhaps more ex-teachers should consider our approach.

Questions Often Asked: Q. But what about science? A. If Thomas Edison could drop out of grade school and never return, why should we worry? Is science only something taught in Science 1-A? Our family friend, Charlie Fox, a geology freak and professionally a geologist for the State of Vermont, has been pointing out rock formations to our children for half a dozen years. Is this science? Kevin has built an enormous telescope. Two years ago he attended a rocket convention alone in Pittsburgh.

Q. But aren't they missing the fundamentals? A. What

fundamentals? If you mean reading, we have always felt that Kevin originally taught himself to read, just as both of them taught themselves how to talk. Kevin only recently became interested in algebra when he realized it would help him with his telescope and his interest in astronomy. (Notice that I said *his interest in astronomy* rather than *his study of astronomy*.)

Q. Aren't they missing a social life? A. Our house, filled with animals, records, tapes, work benches, photographic equipment, plants, and so on is envied by every kid in the neighborhood and is a magnet for them all. Sometimes we wish there were fewer children around on winter afternoons after 2:30 P.M.!

Q. Why not a free school? A. We see "free" or "open" schools as an improvement on traditional schools, but wonder whether more people might not be encouraged to try No School. We have friends in a Vermont commune; none of their children go to school, yet they are obviously learning so much—especially nutrition, crafts, silk screening, photography, farming, music, art. Who is to say that Latin is more important than nutrition, or ancient history more significant than ceramics?

Q. All well and good for you two; you were both teachers and can teach your children, but what about the rest of us who've never been teachers? A. Our five-pronged answer to that would make a long essay in itself. Basically we feel that our teacher experience has helped us most of all to realize how bad schools can be, how little is actually "taught" in so much time. As I said, we really don't look upon ourselves as teachers of our children or their tutors. They teach themselves. Since we got Kevin out of school before his love for reading had been completely killed, he spends more time in the library than any twenty children put together. Not long ago I noticed he was reading the *Autobiography of a Yogi*.

Shortly after that, on his own, he became a vegetarian, questioning the whole concept of eating meat, the ecology of meat-processing plants, the idea of getting protein secondhand from animals, etc. Lately he's been reading about nutrition.

But I'm now rambling when all I wanted to say was that deschooling could take place in a lot more homes than anyone imagines. True, I've been a little cozy about what city we live in for fear the publicity might hurt our truce with the city schools, but for what it's worth we live in the State of New York. Since each state has different education laws, I hope someday to compile a list of various state provisions providing for at-home education under some sort of guidance. Yet all this compliance with those insidious compulsory school laws bothers us, and we hope the day comes when state by state these laws are declared unconstitutional. Perhaps then more parents will feel comfortable with their children learning at home.

A "deschooled society" means that no one would be legally compelled to attend a public school or have his fate hang on possession of a school diploma or credential. More positively, deschooling means breaking the public school's monopolistic grasp on the vast resources we allot for education. "A deschooled society," Holt writes, "would be a society in which everyone shall have the widest and freest possible choice to learn whatever he wants to learn, whether in school or in some altogether different way . . . people would have many more chances to learn things and many more ways of learning them than they have today. It would be a society in which there were many paths to learning and advancement, instead of the one school path as we have now."

The question of deschooling is one that must command attention from every teacher. As for ourselves, we do not see deschooling coming to America the way the deschoolers would like. Rather, we envisage a various, halting, impulsive, sometimes troubled groping toward more diverse options, finer possibilities. Our hope is that through the gradual erosion of those constraints of place, time, age, and mode of learning that now define schooling, it will gradually become impossible to tell where school begins and life stops—a more feasible goal that would reinstate, under more benign conditions, the preindustrial unity of learning and living.

Already there are schools without walls, free universities, human potential growth centers, the *Whole Earth Catalog*, and a myriad of other initiatives, inside and outside the formal education system, for enabling

what we call "free learning" to commence.
Many educators seem reconciled to the fact
that the present generation of ten- to
twenty-year-olds is just about the last one
that will voluntarily trudge through the
lockstep from kindergarten to college.
Something has got to be done—or many,
many things.

We have seen too many good classrooms
such as those described in this book, to say
that nothing can be done in the schools—
which is, after all, where the vast majority
of kids are and will remain. Particularly
heartening is the emergence of a new spirit
among some groups of teachers, joining
together through what Joseph Featherstone
calls "a common conviction of what it means
to do a good job." Once teachers, students,
and parents come together and begin to take
themselves seriously, to ask what they are
really doing in school, why they are doing it,
and what they could and should do, we think
we will see some extraordinary changes.

9 Starting over

Each of us can do *something*—
but only together can we change the schools

"The school movement is over," wrote James
Herndon elegiacally toward the end of 1972.
"The spokesmen for the movement and their
list of brilliant books, among the best written
in America during the last 10 or 12 years,
hadn't done it, no one had listened (or having
listened, shrugged). . . . Now that there is
no movement . . . we start all over. We
start over from the beginning with what we
really know, with the relationship between
children and adults in a situation called
school."

This book is our contribution to that fresh
start. It deals in "what we really know"—our
own experiences with children and with
learning. It raises the question:

278

What do teachers need to make a fresh start, to renew themselves and their schools?

We need a completely new approach to the process of becoming better teachers. The present system is stupid and corrupt. Teachers are forced to take courses they do not want or need, in order to "earn" credits and certificates required to maintain their status or win salary increments. We have seen hundreds of teachers, and teachers of teachers, walking through their parts in this sad charade. It is a demeaning experience for both. Credits are being sold for tuition, and professors of education are assured of captive audiences for their ministrations. Credit accumulation is the criterion for advancement as a teacher, not increased competence. This is a notoriously ineffective way to encourage teachers to improve, and it is a cruel hoax on children and the public. The system is a corrupt paper palace that needs a strong gust of common sense to blow it over.

What teachers really need is the power, the resources, the time, and the help to take command of their own growth and development.

Will it grow in a classroom?

The resurgence of teachers' confidence in
their capacity to survive within the system
and make it work for themselves and for
kids inspires Charles Suhor to wonder if
". . . maybe the bogey man in your system
doesn't exist. . . . Or maybe he exists but
is, behind his mask, more afraid of you than
you are of him."

BY CHARLES SUHOR

Every school system has its bogey man, and some systems
have dozens of them. The bogey man is the reactionary
force that clings to outmoded structures and methods,
threatens the jobs and saps the energies of creative teachers,
and in general keeps the lid on progress in a system by
discouraging or forbidding experimentation.

The bogey man dislikes long hair, short skirts, rock and
roll, *Media and Methods,* most twentieth century literature,
all black literature, the AFT, SDS, and, if he has heard of it,
the MMI. The bogey man takes many forms. He might be an
individual like a principal, department chairman, supervisor, or superintendent; or he might be an abstraction like
"policy," "the Establishment," "the administration," or
"the power structure."

I would like to propose a disturbing idea: maybe the
bogey man in your system doesn't exist. Or maybe he once
existed but is gone and is being kept alive to explain why
teachers don't seem to be getting anywhere with their
problems. Maybe he exists but is, behind his mask, more
afraid of you than you are of him. Maybe you have over-
estimated his strength and his resolution so that you can
say, "if it weren't for _____ _____, we could get something done around here." Maybe the bogey man's real
name is Rationalization.

280

In many school systems—especially big-city systems—the anonymity of the teacher protects him from the encroachments of the administrator-bogey man. How often, for example, does your chairman, principal, or supervisor visit your classroom? Does anyone from the central office really know you well enough to remember your name if he were to meet you on the street? Have you, in fact, done combat with the bogey men in your system, or is your knowledge of them based on teachers' lounge chatter? Can you or can you not close the door and teach in your school?

If you have been personally attacked by the bogey man, he will be real enough to you. At the same time, it is reasonable to ask whether you might be giving the devil a little more than his due. Everyone has known teachers who do things that are absurd and infuriating, and any individual should be willing to apply some simple rule-of-thumb test for determining whether he has been the victim of an administration that is characteristically repressive or whether he has created a bogey man out of resentment, frustration and wounded pride.

Simple Rule-of-Thumb Test: Look down the hall. If someone is departing from traditional content or methodology and is getting no administrative flak about scope and sequence or official policy, you have some reason to re-examine the causes of your conflict with the administration. If the creative teaching is going on in your subject matter area, you might even entertain the thought that you are more sinner than sinned against. If officialdom has recognized and supported the more adventurous teachers in your midst, forget about bogey men and apply for in-service training immediately.

Second Simple Rule-of-Thumb Test: Pinpoint the exact source of your conflict with the administration. You might very well be fighting the community and your own lack of tact. A principal or supervisor who gets frequent calls from parents complaining about a particular teacher can't help wondering about that teacher's relationship to his students and his subject matter. Let us face the fact that innumerable teachers work with controversial materials year after year without incident, while others cannot assign *Nurse Jane Gets Her Diploma* without mounting a soapbox, or at least appearing to do so, thereby releasing a flood of community reaction.

There are, of course, instances of ultra-conservative communities demanding comfortable, traditional, irrelevant curricula, communities where moderate and liberal voices are either non-existent or insufficiently organized to exert an influence. But this is a situation of a different order, far more complex, far more severe, and far sicker than an oppressive school administration. In large cities the radical right and radical left tend to devour each other, leaving a broad, habitable middle ground where teachers can carry out issue-oriented programs.

The profession is in urgent need of a massive Search-and-Destroy mission for its bogey men—carried out, however, by individuals rather than organizations that build up their own bureaucracies and their own unbending points of view. We can no longer afford to hurl clichés and generalized accusations at the Establishment. The real bogey men must be separated from the apparent ones, and each concerned individual must take action that will expose, embarrass, and harass the real oppressors in his system.

Search

Assume that the bogey man doesn't exist, even if everyone else swears that he is bugging every classroom and preparing a dossier of your transgressions. Plan your program with your students in mind, carry it out with aplomb but without fanfare, then look around for frowns and arched eyebrows. You might be surprised to find that the earth does not tremble and the heavens do not roar. There are schools where an open policy exists in particular teachers' classrooms or in the journalism department while the rest of the faculty cringes under the rule of a principal who is reputed to be a goose-stepping martinet.

Seek out administrators who are actually hip. There probably aren't many of them, but one might be enough, especially if he has the broad confidence of the teachers and officialdom as well. Enlist his support for your ideas; ask him about better materials; have him talk to the obstructionists about getting your projects into gear. Expect him maximally to produce tangible and intangible things for your system and your classroom. If he can't produce these things, expect him minimally to leave you alone.

Destroy

If you are in a repressive school situation, transfer out. If the entire district or system is no go, apply in a neighboring system. Commuting is a nuisance, but participating in the miseducation of hundreds of students under degrading conditions is positively immoral. Any teacher who stays more than three years in such an environment has lost his right to complain. He deserves all the punishment he is getting plus permanent bus duty, hallway patrol, and responsibility for collection of cookie sale money.

If you have latched on to a bona fide bogey man, don't assume that he is invincible. Many administrator-bogey men will retreat at the first sign of reasoned resistance or pressure. Couch the rationale for your new program or your request for supplementary materials in his favorite terminology and drop some of his favorite names to give the impression that, after all, you are partners, however unequal, in the educational enterprise and you are both privy to the esoterica and gris-gris of the profession.

If he is politely negative, confess that you are in a state of

283

confusion about means and ends in the educative process, and you feel that a joint conference with someone from the central office would be stimulating and beneficial. This can be the time to call in a member of the hip hierarchy; but even if no such person exists, the suggestion of a conference will frequently cause the security-minded administrator to shift uneasily in his chair and "rethink" your proposal.

"Rethinking" is one of the many clichés that the administrator-bogey man has on hand for deliverance from the ultimate evil of getting into trouble downtown. He can "experimentally" approve your proposal on a "pilot" basis in the interest of "democratic administration" until it proves "viable," thus demonstrating his "flexibility" and "openness to new ideas."

Give him every chance to utilize these face-saving devices. You are not (presumably) interested in literally wiping him out but in swiping the cork from his obstructionist popgun. When the assault on the bogey man becomes a bitter personal duel, the teacher can lose sight of the real object of the struggle—providing a better program for the students— and get bogged down in the exhausting logistics of a sustained ego-clash.

Keep it simple. When embarking on a minor project that you suspect the administration would question, don't ask for permission. Few teachers have ever received an enthusiastic response when they asked someone whether they could teach *Catcher in the Rye* or *Malcolm X Speaks*. Such questions frighten the hell out of the administrator. He has not read the book, probably, and reasons that something must be wrong if the teacher is uncertain. On the other hand, an isolated parental complaint about a book that a teacher has made bold to place on a reading list is not likely to become a major issue. You might ultimately lose the book, but you won't invite censorship, and you will have taken responsibility for your own program instead of leaning upon a less knowledgeable source than yourself.

The name of the game is creative subterfuge. Listen to policy statements attentively, ask occasional questions, make copious notes, say *yes* to everything, and then teach the program that your students need and want.

But be sure it's a damned good one. Once you have escaped from, overpowered, or hoodwinked the bogey man, you are not necessarily done with the powers of darkness. You might, in fact, have only murdered your rationalizations, leaving you with the dark brown taste of yourself, the heart of dullness that was there all the time while you raged and shook your fist at the bogey men *out there*.

E. E. CUMMINGS: *At the end of the bloody battle I tore the mask from my enemy, and it was me.*

POGO: *We have met the enemy, and he is us.*

The following is part of a fine and lengthy journal by Beatrice Altman, an eighth-grade teacher. It demonstrates what affective and effective teacher-training is like. No credit points were given at this open-education workshop in Greenwich, Connecticut, in the summer of 1972. The seventeen-day experience was at the teachers' own expense. How were the teachers rewarded? Beatrice sums it up in her journal: "We have listened, observed, shared, and learned ourselves into openness. Indeed, the goal we set before us has been achieved. We have been enabled

Will it grow in a classroom?

> to enable. Are you with me? Child, we have
> walked your paths and felt your uncertainties,
> your hungry gropings, your fast, opening self.
> Yes. We are with you, because we have
> learned to be *with* ourselves."

BY BEATRICE ALTMAN

July 7

At 1:00 we assembled in the Drama, Dance, and Movement
Room. I felt rather blue and intellectually spent and was
uncertain what to expect.

Richard spoke to us of the value of coming to know
oneself and others through these media, to first enjoy ourselves, and then to take with us what we wanted as teachers.

He first asked us to spread far apart in the large room,
leaving space for ourselves between others. Here there were
thirty-five or so school teachers ranging from ages twenty to
fifty, many geographical locations, and many levels of interest and skill. Perhaps few of us knew each other at all
before this gathering. But here we were ready to go!

First we were asked to lean over waist down and flop like
ragdolls in our little area of space. Flop, flop. Let go, let go.
Is that my body, my arms, lolling aimless circles above the
floor? Then, "Now, focus your eyes on a spot across the
room and move very slowly to it. Now find another spot
and move to it quickly. Now move within various movements: jumping, skipping, hopping, etc. My horizons were
expanding. The room seemed to grow between focus points,
and space was filled to and fro by my spontaneous movements. I felt myself hop, skip, snake dance, and wiggle. I was
losing myself as I experienced myself. How long it had been
since I hopped, skipped, and leaped, and early childhood
movements of Leap Frog, Rolly-Polly, and Hopscotch came
back to me in fleeting memories.

286

"Now, hurry, hurry from one spot to another." We were bumping into each other, laughing; space was diminishing, encounter was growing.

"Now, form a group of five and in five minutes prepare a Nursery Rhyme script without words." Whom would I join? Could I think that fast? What *are* some Nursery Rhymes? Somehow five of us came together and we were a group of individuals. Quickly our ideas flew together. "How about Old McDonald?" "How about Hickory Dickory Dock?" Then we were into "There was a Crooked Man." In seconds we were acting out each stanza forming a crooked stile, a crooked cat and mouse, following the crooked man. Each person contributed, and it somehow felt together. My body contorted in strange bends, and I was the crooked cat scooting lopsidedly after the furtive, crooked cat. A production in five minutes! Ragged, but total, and full of just plain fun.

Each group presented their skits, and they were great. The old troll roared at the billy goat, the munching mouse scurried up a human clock hand stretched out on the floor, and a yellow submarine shuffled across the floor.

"Now find a partner." Who will I choose? I don't know anyone. But there was young, bespectacled, and freckled Kathy eagerly looking at me. We squatted yoga fashion on the floor facing each other.

"Now partner one must tell partner two about the story of a dwarf who couldn't grow a beard."

Judy asks Richard, "Do you mean each pair is number one or two, or each person in the pair is one or two?" I thought of kids trying to follow instructions.

So Kathy told me the story of the little dwarf, making it up as she quickly went along. She was enchanting and I listened eagerly: there was a dwarf, a woebegone dwarf, who couldn't grow a beard, but who had hair all over his feet. Now stop! Now partner two must tell the story of a

Coca-Cola can who didn't feel he was this little Coca-Cola can that no one would accept as a Coca-Cola. He grew up in an orphanage of 7-Up, Rootbeer, Orange, Grape, and Pepsi drinks. None of them knew who they were. So they opened their own lids and poured themselves into a huge vat and became all mixed and bubbly and delicious. Well, their Oversoul remained in the cans and the cans jumped in and filled themselves and jumped out again. Then they rolled in catsup and mustard and dried themselves and had yellow and red covers. They decided they were now the Auto-Drinks because they autonomously decided what they were.

"And were they happy?" asked Kathy. "Oh, yes, because they had decided what they were from the inside, not the outside, and—"

"Stop. Now partner one must tell his dwarf story to partner two while partner two tells his Coke story to partner one. Begin."

It was wild. Kathy spoke to me about the sad dwarf, while I tried to tell about the rejected Coke. Words all mixed, facial expressions and hand gestures.

Beard, 7-Up, hair on feet, vat or Rootbeer, elf, Orange, autonomous, old elf. "Stop."

We laughed in relief. I was struck by how I closed out Kathy to keep my own thoughts going, and that this is much of what we do when we converse. Each talking, neither listening. Richard got various responses from different people. Some interchanged stories unwittingly; some got lost; others were able to listen and speak. Everyone was intrigued.

"Now. Each partner pretend that you have met in a foreign country; you do not speak each other's language, and you are to . . ." I lost the instructions in a low buzz of voices, and Kathy started talking jabberwocky with great

288

confidence and facial expressions of complete understanding. I was much slower on the pickup and felt lost. I made sounds, but not fluently, as Kathy did. She looked like Raggedy Ann jabbering doll language to a rock wall. We were also to keep our hands behind us.

"O.K. Now you can use your hands." Then I gestured, dipped and reached, and Kathy said, "But you've stopped talking!" I had. I was relying completely on bodily gestures, abandoning vocal expression in my oral inhibition. She was so quick to pick up observations.

"Stop!" Then we exchanged responses. How much we rely on language. Nothing was communicated between Kathy and me except her youthful exuberance. What a good way to show children our need for shared language, our enjoyment of it.

"Now! Half of the room be an orchestra of city sounds, half of you be an orchestra of country sounds, and each side present a concert to the other side." We were the City, and we were now a new larger group. About seventeen of us were talking at the same time making various sounds: car horns, sirens, pigeons, cops, babies, etc. How to get together? Several people emerged as leaders, suggesting various ways to structure. We could be early morning sounds, noon sounds, and night sounds. A young boy of thirteen was chosen to be conductor, and then many of us were suggesting to him ways to conduct. "Direct separate sounds, now quiet, now loud, now together." Slowly, an older girl became leader and pointed at various sounds. It just happened, and I think the young boy was glad to get out of the squabble. Sound in flexible unity emerged: early morning. A soft purr of a pigeon. Coo-Coo. "Henry, wake up!" Car horns. "Lady, let me see your license." "Get a horse." Sirens. "Help, help." All together. Louder, louder, Cut. Presented. A minor, quick miracle of various backgrounds, aptitudes, natures, and gregarity in one orchestral sound of laughter and mimicry. People were working and playing together, forming a unity of spontaneity. Socialization in its most vital intercourse—a shared task—had taken place.

At this point in our interaction we were reaching the point of wanting to perfect, to achieve unity of effect and sense of art. The two separate groups began to interact to form a finale. Perhaps the excellence of the Country group presenting in concert the pastoral sense of chickens, cows, roosters, sheep, crickets, frogs, and hogs created in us this groping for artistic form.

Somehow in all this I realized that I'd lost all my tension, and I felt young and joyous. I knew what Richard meant by "getting to know yourself and others." As I moved, I felt my own body; I experienced myself and muscles and motions that had long been dormant—not just physically, but emotionally, socially, and even spiritually. As I worked with others I felt their importance and uniqueness, and the solidity of a group. I noticed that whenever group work came up, the same five of us found each other again. I wanted kids at school to be having this much fun, this much self-exploration and other person discovery—to be continually opened up in activity and inquiry.

"Now! Get in groups again and this time act out a family scene using only singing." Five minutes. Richard was a voice somewhere in the background that started us and stopped us, guided us, and kept us moving. It was like floating on a raft with the water moving me. I was safe on the raft and moved with it, yet the buoyancy of the water touched me personally and the response was my own. Just a soft voice which gave unity and continuity but sometimes became gently irritated by how long it took us to settle down for new instructions. I knew that feeling well!

So, with thrown around ideas, we quickly became a

family of Father, Mother, teen-ager, and little kids planning a trip together around the kitchen table. How revealing. I became my nineteen-year-old daughter who refused to go along and leave her friends. Father roared and I sang back in improvisation: "I can't tell you what I think, or you will think you are a fink." Laughter. I knew where that came from. Then refrains of "We're going to go away, and not come back til another day." Father would cry "Peace." and then the little ones would cry "Peas." Having to use every word, every syllable of which was spontaneous, was no easy task. Spoken language, taken for granted usually, was now wished for in its naturalness. There were four really clever skits, with some people feeling more comfortable than others with song, some more comfortable in hamming it up. Each sociodrama was not without psychological depth. I was amazed to find myself really in there, agile, comfortable, and even sometimes dominant.

"Now! In your own space again, focus on a point and move to it with forceful, jerking movements—not undulations, or circles—but harsh, sharp strong movements. Change them. Get stronger, stronger. Use force. Faster, Faster." The spaces filled again and we touched in passing agitation. I was a machine, a robot of power. Lost in space; lost in motion.

"Now! Someone volunteer to go in the middle and be a machine. Then, each of you, one by one, join his movements and motions and add on to him, and on and on until you are all one working machine." I felt conspicuous again, and thought it would be hard to join on.

But the machine grew quickly and I saw just where I could extend the robot's motion. I quickly stretched out with one leg jutting back and forth from the side hip position, and thus the moving machine of human steel grew and grew. My leg ached and I felt every muscle. My breath-

291

ing was fast and hard; but, at last, the machine was whole. What a feeling! Such centering! Isolated jerks, stretched out arms like toy soldiers, bent heads on chests, necks twisted, all somehow in rhythm and symmetry.

"Now. Three or four of you form a machine of your own." I stood there swaying back and forth from waist to floor forming large circles with an "irk" squeak and some-one dipped into my left arm circle at timed intervals with an angular motion. Someone intercepted into her rhythm, and a fourth person jerked into my right arm circle and out again with hands extended, crying, "Tickets, please." It was just great. Four separate brains that formed a unity of action again. We watched each group and they were mar-velously co-ordinated, timed, complementary, and creative as hell.

Then we ended our two and one half hours of fellowship with a laughing machine. Someone volunteered to lie on his back in the middle of the floor and laugh. It wasn't hard feeling like a happy idiot, I'm sure. Richard put his hand on the young man's flattened, quivering stomach, and his hand moved by the vibrations, which caused further laughter. Think of actually *touching* laughter. He asked for two people to come lie on their backs, head on the volun-teer's stomach, facing opposite directions, heads touching, and so on. There were soon thirty-five of us touching heads, stomachs, and hearts in riotous laughter in a pattern of outstretched bodies in community on a classroom floor. Just the physical oneness was a terrific feeling. We were one undignified whoop of laughter. I looked up somewhere in all this, and there was a large black and white retriever dog with his front paws resting on the window sill absolutely staring at us in wide-eyed wonder. Need I say more?

We sat up, and Richard said: "You see, movement, drama, and dance are not to be simply an addition to the curri-

292

culum. There is a great correspondence between self-discovery, joy, physical well-being, social ease and academic prowess. A happy, healthy person can learn much more readily than a stiff, isolated person." Now I agreed. I was determined to break academic moments with such activities as these, to explore with my students not just knowledge of material, but self-knowledge, social knowledge. I wanted most of all to share with them the opening knowledge that life is a delight, a joy, an astounding discovery just in the living. "Life, as it is lived, suffices."

Saturday night I read further in Charity James' book, *Young Lives At Stake,* and I found the term, "social self-realization." I knew now exactly what she meant. She said that the values that are learned in school "should include caring, tenderness, optimism for self and others, trust of circumstances instead of wariness, collaboration instead of competition, 'social self-realization' as the basis for our well-being rather than anti-social self-realization as the source of egotistic advantage." Amen. I was there Friday afternoon.

We wanted to meet together as a group again. We named ourselves "The Town and Country Players." No longer strangers, we had played ourselves into learning, and once unfamiliar faces will always be remembered sounds, movements, laughter—each unique, each belonging. Drama, Movement, Dance: interdisciplinary, intercreation.

I look forward to Monday. I feel that I have some small grasp now of Open Education just from the few pages in Charity James' book and Mr. Smith's lecture. I realize that many of us are so teaching even in our cells and bells. As I try to write this, I realize how truly expansive and open-ended this kind of education is. I can't begin to cover all the activities of all the people, not even all my experiences. There is Math, Science, Art, Music, Crafts, Drama, Curriculum, Methods, and in multiple combinations just springing

293

up like dandelions. If we were all doing the same thing every day, reading the same books and listening to the same people, one person could at least cover the surface. But this way the learning going on, the experiences encountered, are as manifold as the persons present. As I once read about religion, "there should be as many religions as there are people." So be it with education.

A MODEST PROPOSAL

"Teachers will take reform seriously," insists Stephen Baily, leading member of the New York State Board of Regents, "only when they are responsible for defining their own educational problems, delineating their own needs and receiving help on their own turf."

The initiative, the moving force for this new style of professional continuing education is *you*. If it is to come, and if it is to work, it is you —you and other teachers as individual professionals—who must begin to think through what you really need to learn, what you want to learn, why and how and where and when you best learn it. These are not the sorts of things that most of us come by naturally, despite the fact that we all graduated from schools, which claimed that their foremost aspiration was to teach us "how to learn." But

if that is what we really do want to teach our
students, then it is the first thing we must learn
ourselves.

How to begin? Here is one modest two-part
proposal: First, plug yourself in. Do not rely
on secondhand reports or reviews. Teaching is
your profession—you cannot rely on hearsay
about its critical problems. For twenty dollars
you can purchase a mini-library of the works of
Holt, Kozol, Kohl, Goodman, Dennison,
Herndon, McLuhan, Ashton-Warner, Postman
and Weingartner, Leonard et al. There are
also periodicals that regularly express the
views of serious critics, and there are other
periodicals that provide a wealth of ideas for
your classroom program. You will find a list
of magazines in the index of this book, along
with lists of other useful resources.

Second, get together with other teachers
who have a serious commitment to the profession—serious enough to have moved beyond
defending the status quo and toward working
for change in themselves, their schools, and
other teachers. Form a study group with them,
as formal or informal as your own style suggests, to read some of these writings and
discuss them. Occasionally, invite a local person
working in a so-called free school or who is
teaching school reform at a nearby college
or university. They will usually welcome the

opportunity to meet with other teachers. If some funds become available, films and resource people from farther away may be utilized.

After you have heard the critics out, you will probably find that you agree with some of their points, but not with others. You will also probably find that your perceptions of what goes on in schools and classrooms, what is really happening to children and teachers, are much sharpened. And to that degree, you are on the way to becoming your own radical critic!

Now it is time to really test out what the critics are saying. Attempt to translate their findings and recommendations into action. It has been said that you cannot know the taste of a pear without biting into the pear.

The best kind of professional inservice-work teachers can do is to undertake a self-conceived, self-designed, self-executed, and self-evaluated project to improve their own teaching.

As Charles Silberman says, "Almost any teacher will testify that his education—his real education for teaching—began the day he took over his first class. The education that counts is the informal education that goes on in the classroom every Monday through Friday from nine to three. This 'inservice education' is far more powerful and effective than anything teachers receive in college, in schools of education, or in the traditional inservice teachers' workshop or course. The tragedy is that it is education to the wrong ends and to the wrong means."

What we propose is a scheme to redeem this in-classroom education, or at least a significant part of it, by consciously harnessing it to constructive ends and by providing the necessary means to help teachers. Here's how it might work in your own case, if you are a practicing teacher.

Identify a problem—perhaps one illuminated by your study of the radical critics or the practicing teachers in this book. Explore alternative ways of solving the problem. Devise an experimental way to solve the problem, and construct a means to measure the results. Throughout, keep a special running record of what happens, including your reactions to the whole process.

Of course, consultation from an experienced, knowledgeable, understanding colleague is essential. But it should be just that: individual help in assisting you to achieve your own aspirations for better teaching.

A great advantage of this scheme—which has been called Action in the Classroom as Training (ACT)—is that it puts teachers back in a real learning situation. The teachers take command of their own learning in a major way, sometimes for the first time in their entire educational careers. Instead of being told when and where to go, and what rote tasks will satisfy the requirements for a course, they are on their own. They are in full charge; however, there is help at their disposal if they require it. As Dorothy Canfield Fisher wisely pointed out forty years ago, those who teach others for a living are not notable for being continual learners themselves. And thus they lose touch with the excitement and the frustration of the learning process. This program reveals to teachers many of the aspects of the learning process they may have never known before or long forgotten. It turns teachers back into learners.

If you want to read about how some other teachers followed just this process, a list is provided at the end of this book, of writings by teachers for teachers about teaching.

If you want to get a little help from your friends or want to share what you have got to offer as you begin learning and changing, why not start a *Teachers' Yellow Pages?*

Going Ma Bell one better, young people around the country have invented this tool. We teachers can use it to learn and grow. Rather than listing products and things you can buy, this Yellow Pages offers things you can get free, services being offered on a voluntary basis, resources you can develop yourself. In New York, Boston, and San Francisco, it is called the *People's Yellow Pages;* in Washington, D.C., the *Red Pages;* in Boulder, *Do It.*

A typical edition of the New York *People's Yellow Pages* has sections ranging from Alcoholism and Animal Care to Housing, Food Coops, and Legal Help, to Media Workshops, Printing, Theater, and Crisis Switchboards. (If your community has not yet generated such a publication, and you would like to see how one looks, send $1.00 to *People's Yellow Pages,* Emmaus House, 241 E. 116th St., N.Y.C. 10029. Or you can get the *Source Catalog,* published by Allen Swallow, Publishers, and distributed nationally. It is a monster listing of over 500 grass-roots groups at work in various aspects of communications, together with reviews of books, films, tapes, and so on, on the subject.)

As teachers, we need comparable "tools" to help us work collaboratively much more than we do now, "a little help from our friends." We need to get our hands on inexpensive services and materials in ways that cut through bureaucratic red tape.

You can start your own *Teachers' Yellow Pages* in your school. Just circulate blank sheets, and let your colleagues fill in answers to the following questions:

299

Teachers' Yellow Pages

A Guide to Some Colleagues, Friends, Mentors, Experts, Tools, Materials, Places, and Other Resources

Yes! I'm interested in getting together to discuss common problems and possibilities.

I know of, and can share the following resources, which might be useful to others:

I have, or know someone who has, the following expertise that could be made available to us free or on an at-cost basis:

My current interests, concerns, enthusiasms, obsessions are:

Name:

Address:

Phone:

Class:

Put the sheets together in a loose-leaf book near the mailboxes, and, presto, you have got a *Teachers' Yellow Pages* for your school. To add a "switchboard," put up next to the book a blackboard or corkboard on which teachers can post requests for help, offers of help, along with other information and items of interest. Of course, most teachers' rooms have this, but it is usually dominated by junkmail announcements. It is time for teachers to take over and *use* these resources!

If it proves useful in your school, it is easy to spread the idea. Have someone in each of the nearby schools create a comparable book for his school, then exchange the books for a week. If this, in turn, proves potent, consider going big time: At the next large conference or inservice convocation, distribute sheets to everybody. Have the system zap them, and send a book to each school.

When such sheets were distributed to the participants in a recent Open Education conference the following skills, ideas, helps, and resources were offered from the teachers at this one gathering: mill-rejected drawing paper; free workshop in haiku; how to use attribute blocks for social studies; portable videotape equipment and free instruction in

301

how to use it; postal chess; access to a printing shop; instruction in slide rule and free slide rules for every child; participation in an experimental project to measure children's values; free magazines only two-months-old; auditing privileges at sixteen different courses at local colleges and universities; art movies on the weekend at a local home; demonstration of microfiche production and use; consultation on how to equip a class cheaply for macramé, plus how to provide cheap instruction.

Teachers' Yellow Pages—for a school, group of schools, or district-wide basis—will dramatically reveal how many resources for mutual help exist within your community of teachers. And it will provide the model for extending the directory with input from other teachers. Moreover, the directory itself and the act of initiating it are significant educational acts in themselves. You are saying: We teachers are the most authentic sources of our own growth; let us get ourselves together, see what we have got to work with and begin to share and help each other to grow.

The last day
BY GLORIA CHANNON

The children revert
to childhood.

Our fantasied trolls
who tormented us
all year—vanished;
cast out, the devils
who clamored at our souls
taunting us with obscene pleas
to be let in.
Freed from our prison
for a day,
they are transformed
by laughter.
The tough man-child
came and planted a soft kiss
on my Judas cheek—
I who have so often betrayed him.

Prayer for a teacher
BY RONALD GROSS

May your foot not slip
on bureaucratic dogshit.

May furious red tape
never callous over
your spry groping hands.

May your eyes wrinkle
always at the corners,
and your back stay supple
bending down to where
the kids bloom forever
just out of reach.

May your heart bulge
at such things as
a dog at school,

a child bedeviled by Euclid,
or the pride of first-time lovers.

May your curriculum comprise
white-water wildness,
an emerald grasshopper from Tiffany's,
the curve of Venus' orbit,
fear of failure-to-be-great
in our only time,
a single gleaming paper clip,
delicious Puerto Rican Spanish,
the duty of doctors to heal,
and diesel grease's splendid smell.

May your methods, like lilies,
curl beautifully as they die,
and your goals
like my battered Datsun's
broken windshield
splatter into fake diamonds.

Above all, I ask for you,
only and always and, perhaps,
at least once,
that you feel the walls fall away,
the ceiling stretch into the sky,
the floor fail,
and something deeper come
even than understanding:
an occasional victory
over the teacher in you—
that moment (a gift
from God-knows-where)
of simply learning again
how to be human.

Stay beautiful, now.

304

Books by teachers for teachers about teaching

ASHTON-WARNER, SYLVIA. *Teacher*. New York: Simon and Schuster, 1963; New York: Bantam (paper), 1969.

CHANNON, GLORIA. *Homework*. New York: Outerbridge and Dienstfrey, 1970.

CHEIFETZ, DAN. *Theater in My Head*. Boston: Little, Brown, 1971.

CONROY, PAT. *The Water Is Wide*. Boston: Houghton Mifflin, 1972; New York: Dell (paper), 1973.

CRAIG, ELEANOR. *P. S. Your Not Listening*. New York: Baron, 1972.

DANIELS, STEVEN. *How 2 Gerbils, 20 Goldfish, 200 Games, 2,000 Books and I Taught Them How to Read*. Philadelphia: Westminster (paper), 1972.

DECKER, SUNNY. *An Empty Spoon*. New York: Harper and Row, 1969.

DENKER, JOEL, and BHAERMAN, STEVE. *No Particular Place to Go: The Making of a Free High School*. New York: Simon and Schuster, 1970.

DENNISON, GEORGE. *The Lives of Children.* New York: Random House, 1969; Vintage (paper), 1970.

FADER, DANIEL, and MCNEIL, ELTON. *Hooked on Books.* New York: Medallion (paper), 1970.

FADER, DANIEL. *The Naked Children.* New York: Macmillan, 1971; New York: Bantam (paper), 1972.

FUCHS, ESTELLE. *Teachers Talk.* New York: Doubleday (paper), 1969.

GAINES, RICHARD. *The Best Education Money Can Buy.* New York: Simon and Schuster, 1972.

GINANDES, SHEPARD. *The School We Have.* New York: Delacorte Press, 1973.

GOLDBERG, LAZAR. *Children and Science.* New York: Charles Scribner's Sons (paper), 1970.

HASKINS, JIM. *Diary of a Harlem Schoolteacher.* New York: Grove Press (paper), 1969.

HAWKINS, FRANCES. *The Logic of Action: From a Teacher's Notebook.* Elementary Science Advisory Center, University of Colorado, no date.

HERNDON, JAMES. *How to Survive in Your Native Land.* New York: Simon and Schuster, 1971; New York: Bantam (paper), 1972.

————. *The Way It Spozed to Be.* New York: Simon and Schuster, 1968; (paper), 1970.

HOLT, JOHN. *How Children Fail.* New York: Dell (paper), 1965.

————. *How Children Learn.* New York: Dell (paper), 1972.

————. *The Underachieving School.* New York: Dell (paper), 1970.

————. *What Do I Do Monday?* New York: Dell (paper), 1972.

KOCH, KENNETH. *Wishes, Lies, and Dreams.* New York: Chelsea House, 1970; New York: Vintage (paper), 1971.

Books by teachers

KOHL, HERBERT. *The Open Classroom.* New York: Vintage (paper) , 1969.

————. *36 Children.* New York: New American Library (paper) , 1967.

————. *Reading, How to.* New York: Dutton (1973) .

KOZOL, JONATHAN. *Free Schools.* Boston: Houghton Mifflin (paper) , 1973.

————. *Death at an Early Age.* Boston: Houghton Mifflin, 1971; New York: Bantam (paper) , 1972.

MARSHALL, KIM. *Law and Order in Grade 6-E: The Story of Chaos and Innovation in a Ghetto School.* Boston: Little, Brown, 1972.

MIRTHES, CAROLINE. *Can't You Hear Me Talking to You?* New York: Bantam (paper) , 1971.

O'GORMAN, NED. *The Storefront.* New York: Harper and Row (paper) , 1970.

————. *The Wilderness and the Laurel Tree.* New York: Harper and Row (paper) , 1973.

RICHARDSON, ELWYN S. *In the Early World.* New York: Pantheon, 1964.

RYAN, KEVIN (ed.) . *Don't Smile Until Christmas: Accounts of the First Year of Teaching.* Chicago: University of Chicago Press, 1970.

SMITH, CAM. *What It Is, What It Ain't: The Teacher's Report.* Published by the author, P.O. Box 17632, Los Angeles, California 90017 (paper) , 1972.

STERLING, PHILIP. *The Real Teachers.* New York: Random House, 1973.

USLANDER, ARLENE et al. *Their Universe: A Look Into Children's Hearts and Minds.* New York: Delacorte Press, 1973.

WILLIAMS, SYLVIA BERRY. *Hassling: Two Years in a Suburban High School.* Boston: Little, Brown, 1970.

Teachers'
resource guides

One or more of the following paperback books should be readily available and will place at your fingertips an excellent guide to materials, publications, people, and organizations. All have proved their usefulness to innovative teachers.

Ascheim, Skip (ed.). *Materials for Open Education*. New York: Delacorte, 1973.

A caring selection of materials, techniques, and resources.

Greer, Mary, and Rubinstein, Bonnie (eds.). *Will the Real Teacher Please Stand Up?*. Pacific Palisades, California: Goodyear Publishing, 1972.

This "primer in humanistic education" is a lovely lively collection of dynamite articles, games, graphics, and commentary. The appendix contains lists of people, places, and things.

Teachers' resource guides

Kozol, Jonathan. *Free Schools.* Boston: Houghton Mifflin, 1972.

The most incisive critique of the Free School Movement contains an appendix of contacts, leads, readings, clearing-houses, and assorted favorites of the brilliant author.

Nyquist, Ewald B., and Hawes, Gene R. (eds.). *Open Education: A Sourcebook for Parents and Teachers.* New York: Bantam, 1972.

This nice fat, inexpensive anthology contains an annotated bibliography and source listing, including: publications on equipment and materials for elementary open education; recent books, pamphlets, papers, and articles; bibliographies; films; a listing by states of schools with open education programs; and a list of consultants and authorities.

Postman, Neil, and Weingartner, Charles. *Teaching as a Subversive Activity.* New York: Delacorte/Delta, 1971.
_____. *The Soft Revolution.* New York: Delacorte/Delta, 1973.
_____. *The School Book.* New York: Delacorte/Delta, 1973.

All contain splendid, if idiosyncratic, lists of swell stuff.

Yanes, Samuel and Holdorf, Cia (eds.). *Big Rock Candy Mountain: Resources for Our Education.* New York: Delacorte, 1973.

Very uneven and sloppily edited, but it is still the best graphic display-counter of groovy therapy, dome-building, dance, videotaping, puppetry, Zen hitch-hiking, and things to make, read, do, hear, see, taste, touch, love.

Teachers'
underground press

There is a plethora of magazines and journals in education, serving virtually every specialization and special interest. The National Education Association, American Federation of Teachers, and U.S. Office of Education each have their own glossy magazines or newspapers. Teachers at every level and in every subject specialty have their own journals, ranging from the *Grade School Teacher* to the *Phi Delta Kappan,* for the "elite" among teacher-administrators. And there are the "slick" commercial enterprises, like the *Saturday Review/World* Education section, and Learning, which are usually livelier and better-written than the "professional" magazines.

310

Teachers' underground press

The following list is different. It consists of lesser-well-known, grass-roots, "alternative"-oriented, low-budget, high-energy, creative, authentic, useful publications. Some are merely newsletters on local developments. But these can be fascinating for the insight they give to what is possible on the grass-roots level ("if *they're* doing that, why can't we?"). Send for a sample copy of each, and decide for yourself which are most useful and stimulating for you. (Of course, you'll best meet your own needs, and those of your colleagues, which you know most about, when you start your own.)

Alternatives for Education, Box 1028, San Pedro, California 90733. (Monthly, $5.00/year.)

Big Rock Candy Mountain, Portola Institute, Inc., 1115 Merrill St., Menlo Park, California 94025. (No longer publishing, but great back issues still available.)

Centerpeace, 57 Hayes St., Cambridge, Massachusetts 02139. (Occasionally, $3.00/year.)

Ed Centric, 2115 S. St., NW, Washington, D.C. 20008. (Address for subscriptions, $5.00/year for 8 issues.) Address for submitting articles is Box 1802, Eugene, Oregon 97401.

Education Exploration Center Newsletter, 3104 16th Ave. S., Minneapolis, Minnesota 55407. (Monthly, $3.00/year) and **EEC Journal** (Bimonthly, $5.00–$10.00/year or reasonable contribution.)

311

FPS, High School News Service (Triweekly, $5.00/year) and **CHIPS, Cooperative High School Independent Press,** both from Youth Liberation, 2007 Washtenaw Ave., Ann Arbor, Michigan 48104.

Inequality in Education, Harvard Center for Law and Education, 38 Kirkland St., Cambridge, Massachusetts 02138. (Monthly, free.)

Innovative Education Coalition Newsletter, 1130 N. Rampart St., New Orleans, Louisiana 70116. (Free to folks in New Orleans, $2.00 donation requested of others.)

Media and Methods, 134 N. 13th St., Philadelphia, Pennsylvania 19107. (9 issues, September through May, $7.00/year.)

National Froebel Foundation, Manchester Square, London, England.

New School News, c/o American Friends Service Committee, 407 S. Dearborn, Chicago, Illinois 60605. (Bimonthly, $5.00/year to libraries and institutions, no fee to individuals.)

New Schools Exchange Newsletter, P.O. Box 820, St. Paris, Ohio 43072. (The unofficial newsletter of the Free School Movement— and a continuing listing of good things, upcoming get-togethers, schools and teachers seeking one another.)

New Schools Network, 3039 Deakin, Berkeley, California 94705. (Bimonthly, $2.00/year.)

New Ways in Education, 1778 S. Holt Ave., Los Angeles, California 90035. (Monthly, $5.00/year.) Also Gladys Falken broadcasts "Alternatives" on KMET/FM (94.7) at 9:30 a.m. Sundays.

No More Teacher's Dirty Looks, Bay Area Radical Teachers Organizing Committee (BARTOC), Box 40143, San Francisco, California 94140. (Quarterly, $3.00/year.)

Northeaster, Unschool, Educational Services Corp., Box 753, New Haven, Connecticut 06503. (Occasional newsletter about alternatives in the Northeast.)

312

Notes from Workshop Center for Open Education, Workshop Center, Room 6, Shepard Hall, City College, Convent Avenue at 140th St., New York, N.Y. 10031.

OCEAN Newsletter, Ohio Coalition for Educational Alternatives Newsletter, 87 E. 12th Ave., Columbus, Ohio 43201. ($5.00 donation for occasional newsletters, legal paper, directory of Ohio alternative schools.)

Oregon New Schools Catalog, 2127 NE 10th, Portland, Oregon 97212. (People from 4 of Oregon's alternative schools who intend to make information on Oregon schools continually available. A very nice catalog.)

Outside the Net, Box 184, Lansing, Michigan 48901. (Occasionally, $3.00/6 issues.)

The Red Pencil, 131 Magazine Street, Cambridge, Massachusetts 02139. (Newspaper, $3.00/year, including a monthly bulletin.)

Return to Learning, Folk School, Box 681, Fort Wayne, Indiana 46801. ($3.00/year, single issues $.75.)

Switchboard, 613 Winans Way, Baltimore, Maryland 21229. ($4.00/year for 10 issues dealing with educational alternatives in the greater Baltimore area.)

Teacher Drop Out Center Mailouts, Box 520, Amherst, Massachusetts 01002.

The Teacher Paper, 2221 NE 23rd, Portland, Oregon 97212. (Quarterly, $3.00/year.)

"Teacher Works in a Box," from *Teacher Works,* 2136 NE 20th Ave., Portland, Oregon 97212. ($10.00/year membership.)

This Magazine, 56 Esplanade East, #408, Toronto 215, Ontario, Canada. (Quarterly, $4.50/year.)

Work Force, Vocations for Social Change, Box 3, Canyon, California 94516. (Bimonthly, $5.00/year.)

313

Will it grow in a classroom?

Worksheet, Committee of Community Schools, 760 West End Ave., New York, NY 10025. (Free, mimeographed more or less monthly from September through June.)

Zephyros, 1201 Stanyan St., San Francisco, California 94117. ($10.00/year for 2 big Z-Boxes, a materials exchange.)

An invitation to join the conversation

We hope this book stimulates teachers to share experiences. We invite you to communicate directly with any of the contributors, by addressing them care of us at Delacorte Press, 245 E. 47th Street, New York, N.Y. 10017. Of course, we, the authors, would welcome hearing from you about your own experiences, as well as about any reactions you have to the materials in this book, or about your efforts to increase teacher-to-teacher communications in your school and community.

Index of contributors